Studies in Political Theory

edited by

Prof. Dr. Rainer Schmalz-Bruns (Leibniz University Hannover)
Prof. Dr. Hubertus Buchstein (University of Greifswald)

Volume 4

Enrico Zoffoli

Beyond Consensus

Public Reason and the Role of Convergence

Nomos

Die Deutsche Nationalbibliothek lists this publication in the Deutsche Nationalbibliografie; detailed bibliographic data is available in the Internet at http://dnb.d-nb.de.

a.t.: Darmstadt, Techn. Univ., Diss., 2013

ISBN 978-3-8487-0506-1

D17

1. Edition 2013

Preface

The dissertation on which this book is based is part of the research project "Politische Normativität", funded by the Cluster of Excellence "Die Herausbildung normativer Ordnungen" and conducted at the University of Darmstadt under the supervision of Prof. Peter Niesen. I owe special thanks to the following people for their precious help and guidance:

Peter Niesen: for his thorough, extensive and penetrating comments throughout every stage of the drafting of my dissertation; for his extraordinary patience in helping me develop a consistent research project; for prompting me to combine analytic and continental philosophy; for arranging numerous meetings, colloquia and seminars, from which I learned a tremendous amount; for much needed, priceless encouragement.

Gerald Gaus: for having me as a visiting scholar at the University of Arizona; for addressing over and over my questions and arguments (often over a couple of delicious IPAs); for writing *Justificatory Liberalism* and *The Order of Public Reason*: my dissertation would have been completely different if weren't for those great books.

Kevin Vallier: for some incredibly helpful and inspiring conversations at a crucial stage of the development of my dissertation; for regularly commenting on my papers; for helping me find my way in the heat of the Arizona desert.

Rainer Forst and Emanuela Ceva: for kindly accepting to serve as "Gutachter" on my thesis committee. To Rainer Forst I am also grateful for letting me participate in his seminar on political theory, from which I greatly benefited.

Rainer Schmalz-Bruns and Nomos Verlag: for accepting my dissertation for publication in their prestigious book series.

Leonardo Ceppa: for giving me the opportunity to translate some major works in contemporary political philosophy and theory of law, which helped me both gain a better insight into those works and improve my translation skills.

I had the opportunity to present many sections of this work at several meetings, such as the Darmstadt Clusterkolloquium, the 9th Pavia Graduate Conference, the 56th annual conference of the Florida Philosophical Association, the SLU Graduate Conference and ECPR workshops and conferences. Many comments, suggestions and criticisms from those audiences have found their way into the final version of this book, especially those of David Owen, Kevin Vallier, Maria Paola Ferretti, Jens Steffek and Gerald Gaus.

Finally, I want to thank the following colleagues from Darmstadt for their support and companionship: Friedrich Arndt, Carlos Becker, Andreas Corcaci, Sabrina Engelmann, Dorothea Gädeke, Niels Genzel, Gesa Heinbach, Leonie Holthaus, Kim Joohyung, Jörg Kemmerzell, Markus Patberg, Kahraman Solmaz, Andreas von Staden, Linda Wallbot, Gabriel Wollner, Lisbeth Zimmerman and especially Angela Marciniak.

Darmstadt, April 2013 Enrico Zoffoli

Table of contents

Introduction

I. Public reason as a theory of liberalism

I.a Varieties of liberalism

If anything is distinctive about liberalism, it is the idea that freedom should be given pride of place. In one way or another, liberals have typically rehearsed Locke's famous claim that humans are naturally in "a *State of perfect Freedom* to order their Actions…as they think fit…without asking leave, or depending on the Will of any other Man".[1] Liberals thus insist that, as general rule, a just society should be built around principles that safeguard an extensive scheme of equal liberties. However, as soon as one examines it more in detail, liberalism fractures into a variety of competing political theories, which often share little with each other.

According to John Gray, liberalism must be understood as a *modus vivendi*.[2] On this first view, liberalism serves first and foremost a pragmatic purpose, in that it guarantees a peaceful coexistence among different groups, especially religious ones. Historically, the birth of proto-liberal orders in early modern societies is largely attributable to this pragmatic urge. As Habermas notes, the middle ages were characterized by "the branching into sacred and secular law, whereby, within the horizon of one of the few great world religions, sacred law was closely tied to the order of the cosmos and to sacred history".[3] But with the advent of modernity "religious worldviews gave way to a pluralism of privatized gods and demons, and common-law traditions were more and more penetrated", leading to an increasingly "disenchanted" vision of the world.[4] Especially with the religious wars of the 16th and 17th centuries, Europeans came to the painful realization that some degree of mutual toleration was necessary to safeguard social stability. It was necessary, in other words, to converge on a social order which most religious groups could see as a reasonable compromise or *modus vivendi*. This is, in a nutshell, the idea behind Gray's conception of liberalism: given the fact that different parties have conflicting interests, and the fact that neither has the power to repress or root out the other parties, it is rational for them to agree to a compromise that secures a mutually acceptable scheme of liberties.

1 J. Locke 1960 [1689]: 287.
2 See J. Gray 2000.
3 J. Habermas1988: 261.
4 Ibid.: p. 262.

A second liberal view, which has been extensively defended by Isaiah Berlin, suggests a different route from pervasive disagreement to liberalism. Berlin's conception, which we could dub "pluralistic liberalism", does not regard pluralism as a bare social phenomenon which calls for a pragmatic solution, but rather as a metaphysical claim about the incommensurability of ultimate values. If we explore the range of values people affirm and cherish, according to Berlin, we cannot but conclude that "there are many objective ends, ultimate values, some incompatible with others, pursued … by different groups in the same society … and any one of which may find itself subject to conflicting claims of uncombinable, yet equally ultimate and objective, ends".[5] Although Berlin's argument for liberalism is quite obscure, in numerous places he suggests that accepting value pluralism involves placing "an immense value upon the freedom to choose".[6] Berlin is adamant that, given value pluralism, a just social order cannot lapse into a form of legal paternalism concerned with furthering some specific values to the detriment of others: unless citizens are allowed to freely pursue ends and life plans in different ways, there is "no possibility of remaining human as we understand the word".[7]

A third liberal view, which we could label as "perfectionist", holds that pluralistic liberalism gets things almost exactly wrong. On the one hand, the perfectionist liberal concurs with the pluralistic liberal that allowing citizens to choose from a wide range of ends and values should be a primary concern. The ruling perfectionist thesis is in fact that, in order to flourish, moral person should be able to choose, revise and pursue their life plans as they see fit, without being interfered with by others. On the other hand, though, the perfectionist liberal firmly resists the relativistic metaphysics underpinning pluralistic liberalism. Rather, perfectionist liberalism starts from the opposite metaphysical assumption: some values, life plans and conceptions of the good life are objectively superior to other values. Hence, the liberal state should in some way alter the set of options from which citizens can choose, encouraging them to favor good life plans over bad ones. As Raz stresses, "autonomy [understood as freedom to choose ends and develop life plans] is valuable only if it is directed at the good, [thus] it supplies no reason to provide, nor any reason to protect, worthless let alone bad options".[8] Perfectionist liberalism thus drifts dangerously toward the kind of paternalism against which pluralist liberals *à la* Berlin warn: liberalism, on this third

5 I. Berlin 1990: 79-80. For an overview of contemporary theories of value pluralism see G. Newey 1998.

6 I. Berlin 1968: 168.

7 Ibid.

8 Ibid.: 411. For a similar statement see Ibid.: 381. For other perfectionist views of liberalism see W. Galston 1990, T. Hurka 1991 and S. Wall 1998.

view, is nothing but an effective means for enabling citizens to pursue worthwhile life projects.

There are, of course, many other forms of liberalism. However, the three conceptions I have canvassed are interesting because they differ in many crucial respects from the theory of liberalism I shall deal with in this book. This alternative view is normally referred to as *public reason liberalism* or *justificatory liberalism.* Public reason liberalism is a sophisticated and attractive conception, which in the last two decades has gained tremendous currency among theorists of liberalism. These include, among many others, "political" liberals such as John Rawls, Stephen Macedo, Samuel Freeman, Joshua Cohen and Charles Larmore. However, "political" liberalism is not the same as justificatory liberalism, but rather a specific version of it (see §II.c below and especially chapter 3, §3.3). In fact, justificatory liberalism also comprises "non-political" conceptions, such as Joel Feinberg's, Stanley Benn's and Gerald Gaus's. Furthermore, deliberative democrats such as Rainer Forst, Amy Gutmann, Dennis Thompson and Jürgen Habermas have developed accounts of political deliberation that are in many ways consistent with justificatory liberalism's core commitment: *the need to justify coercion through public reasoning.* By comparing and contrasting justificatory liberalism with the three conceptions of liberalism I have sketched, we can cast light upon the fundamental commitment to publicly justify and its intimate connection with liberal thought.

I.b Justificatory liberalism

Justificatory liberalism resists the view that liberalism should be understood as a *modus vivendi.* Some justificatory liberals have stressed that a *modus vivendi* fares ill with respect to the desideratum of social stability, in that it hangs on a contingent equilibrium of power, which each party tacitly aims to overturn in its favor.[9] As I see it, though, the core element that sets apart justificatory liberalism from a liberal *modus vivendi* is the fact that the latter does not require that citizens be reasonable. As Rawls explains, reasonable persons have two features. First, they view society as fair system of social cooperation over time between free and equal people, and so are willing to propose and abide by fair terms provided that others are as well. Second, they accept the "burdens of judgment" and the consequent fact of reasonable pluralism, thereby refraining from imposing their views on others.[10]

9 See, for instance, J. Rawls 1993: 144-50.
10 J. Rawls 1993: 54-8.

Insofar as they are reasonable in the first sense indicated by Rawls, citizens view adherence to fair principles of justice as the norm, while they regard deflection and non-compliance as unwelcome exceptions, which are permissible only in the case a large number of other people free ride or refuse to cooperate. The parties to a *modus vivendi* view things in exactly the opposite way. Since they tacitly aim to exercise their power to the detriment of others, they accept fair principles as a temporary compromise. From their perspective, compliance with fair principles is not the norm, but a strategic exception. By the same token, the parties to a *modus vivendi* lack the second feature of the reasonable, for their ultimate aim is to model their society after principles of justice which would be unacceptable to many under conditions of reasonable pluralism.

Let me fill in behind this point a bit. In the previous paragraph, I have described a liberal society as being governed by (fair) rules of social cooperation, which reasonable citizens are expected to obey. However, insofar as they are laid out in the form of legally sanctioned and coercively enforceable laws, principles of cooperation place restrictions on citizens' freedom. They dictate some courses of actions and bar others. This does not mean, of course, that coercive laws modeled after fair principles of cooperation are illiberal – to say this would be to confuse liberalism with some radical form of libertarianism. Still, the term "fair principle" is an honorific one on a justificatory approach. To say that a principle is fair is to say that it is a *publicly justified* rule of social cooperation, to wit, a rule of cooperation that all reasonable citizens *have reason* to endorse. This is the key idea rallying behind justificatory liberalism: principles and rules of social cooperation, being coercive, are legitimate only if they are publicly justifiable to all their addressees.

But of course, public justification must come to terms with the fact of reasonable pluralism. That is, it must be a justification that all reasonable citizens can be expected to endorse, despite their pervasive disagreements over ethical, religious and philosophical issues. The idea, then, is that the use of political power is legitimate only if it is acceptable to all reasonable people without them having to give up the religious or philosophical doctrines they reasonably espouse. In this respect, justificatory liberalism sees the two features of the reasonable described by Rawls as two sides of the same coin. On the one hand, to defend a coercive principle as fair simply *is* to claim that it is publicly justifiable to others. On the other hand, to accept reasonable pluralism is to recognize that principles based exclusively on sectarian considerations are unfair. Insofar as we side with justificatory liberals in regarding the commitment to publicly and reasonably justify as fundamental, we have strong reason to resist interpreting liberalism as a *modus vivendi*.

Perfectionist liberalism is also at odds with justificatory liberalism, though for different reasons. On the one hand, perfectionist liberalism rightly stresses that the tenets of a liberal order cannot rest on the shaky grounds of a contingent *modus vivendi.* On the other hand, though, perfectionist liberalism deeply misconceives the normative role of freedom within liberal thought. For the perfectionist liberal, freedom is mainly a necessary means to foster and promote human flourishing. For the justificatory liberal, instead, liberty has a deontic value. Coercive laws, on a justificatory view, call for public justification not because they put obstacles in the path of human flourishing, but simply because they are coercive. To use Joel Feinberg's terminology, public reason liberalism sees liberty as a basic deontological "norm", in the sense that coercion and legal interference must present themselves as publicly justified exceptions to liberty.[11] This fundamental intuition, shared by liberals such as John Stuart Mill, Alan Gewirth, Stanley Benn, Gerald Gaus and John Rawls, is normally referred to as the "presumption in favor of liberty".[12] Liberty is the normative baseline or default position. Those who advocate a legal interference must provide an adequate case, not those who wish to remain free. The idea behind this liberal assumption is nicely captured by Stanley Benn's example of the pebble-splitter:

> Imagine Alan sitting on a public beach, a pebble in each hand, splitting one pebble by striking it with another. Betty, a casual observer, asks him what he is doing. She can see, of course, that he is splitting pebbles; what she is asking him to do is to explain it, to redescribe it as an activity with an intelligible point, something he could have a reason for doing. There is nothing untoward about her question, but Alan is not bound to answer it unless he likes. Suppose, however, that Betty had asked Alan to justify what he was doing or to give an excuse for doing it. Unlike explanations, justifications and excuses presume at least prima facie fault, a charge to be rebutted, and what can be wrong with splitting pebbles on a public beach? … Suppose Betty were to prevent Alan from splitting pebbles ... Alan could now quite properly demand a justification from Betty, and a tu quoque reply from her that he, on his side, had not offered her a justification for splitting pebbles, would not meet the case, for Alan's pebble splitting had done nothing to interfere with Betty's actions.[13]

While Alan is under no standing requirement to justify his pebble splitting to Betty, she is required to justify to Alan her stopping him from what he is doing. Whereas the would-be interferer has a case to answer, the person interfered with is not required to justify her liberty. To be sure, Benn is concerned with interference in general, while theorists of public reason focus primarily on legal interfer-

11 J. Feinberg 1984: 9.
12 See chapter 1, §1.2.1-1.2.2.
13 S. Benn 1988: 87.

ence cast in the form of legally binding coercive laws. But of course, the core idea is the same: liberty has a deontic value in the sense that it constitutes the default position. This places a special burden of proof on those advocating legal interference, for they wish to deviate from the default.

By shrinking the deontic character of liberty, perfectionist liberalism also ends up unduly restricting the range of state actions for which citizens can legitimately require a public justification. Perfectionist liberals typically claim that to the extent that the state prevents citizens from pursuing bad life plans, its coercive authority does not stand in need of justification, for liberty loses its instrumental value when it is used to choose bad options. Justificatory liberals reject this view. While they do not rule out perfectionist policies as such, they insist that, like any other forms of coercive interference, perfectionist measures call for public justification.[14] As Gaus stresses, for justificatory liberals "[a]ll use of force or coercion by the state against the persons of its citizens requires justification".[15] Unless they meet the justificatory burden set by the presumption in favor of liberty, perfectionist policies are inherently illiberal, and illegitimate for that reason.

But what about pluralistic liberalism? On the face of it, pluralistic conceptions *à la* Berlin seem more in tune with the justificatory model I have been canvassing so far, for they reject both the pragmatic rationale of *modus vivendi* liberalism and potentially illiberal forms of perfectionism. Now although there is some truth to this view, justificatory liberalism differs from Berlin's model in at least two crucial respects. First, public reason liberalism neither affirms nor rejects Berlin's claim about the incommensurability of ultimate values, for metaphysical views of this kind are themselves the object of reasonable and justified disagreement.[16] Justificatory liberals thus do not deny that some people may be justified in rejecting Berlin's relativistic doctrine. Rather, they maintain that such people should refrain from advocating legal interference on grounds that other citizens might have reason to reject. Second, and much more important, Berlin's pluralistic conception places too much weight on *negative* liberty. Berlin pits negative and positive conceptions of liberty against each other along the following lines. On a "negative view",

> [p]olitical liberty … is simply the area within which a man can do what he wants. If I am prevented by other persons from doing what I want I am to that degree unfree; and if the area

14 This is not quite right, for some justificatory liberals admit of publicly unjustified perfectionist policies if these do not infringe fundamental rights. I shall take up this point in chapter 1, §1.2.3-1.2-4.

15 G. Gaus 2010a: 238.

16 I say more about this in chapter 2 (§2.3.1), in which I distinguish between "metaphysical" and "epistemic" conceptions of pluralism.

within which I can do what I want is contracted by other men beyond a certain minimum, I can be described as being coerced, or, it may be, enslaved ... The 'positive' sense of the word 'liberty' derives from the wish on the part of the individual to be his own master. I wish ... to be moved by reasons, by conscious purposes which are my own, not by causes which affect me, as it were, outside.[17]

Liberals, Berlin argues, are naturally committed to a negative conception liberty. Apparently, this seems uncontroversial. If we understand political liberty in this negative fashion, restricting liberty means implementing legal interference. And public reason liberals' fundamental claim is precisely that whenever the state upholds coercive proposals, public officials are under a duty to publicly justify them to the public at large.

In the remainder of his famous essay, however, Berlin does not simply defend negative liberty as a truly liberal view. Rather, he takes a step further and attacks positive liberty on the grounds that it runs the danger of giving way to despotism. If we accept a positive conception of liberty, Berlin argues, we are driven toward a form of perfectionist liberalism understood as a way to promote other people's "fuller" freedom. In effect, advocates of perfectionist liberalism typically avail themselves of this sort of strategy. Perfectionism liberalism involves advocating the use of legal sanctions to force someone to do things for his own good, insisting that this will enable him to become a better person, or to free him from irrational cravings. But this is precisely the kind of interference which liberalism prohibits, according to Berlin. To be sure, Berlin does not dismiss positive liberty altogether. Rather, he claims that positive liberty is a value among many others, upon which different people will inevitably assign various degrees of importance, depending on the conceptions of the good life they affirm.

For justificatory liberals, however, positive liberty plays a much more relevant and specific role. Indeed, a positive conception of liberty is necessary for the project of public justification to get off the ground in the first place. The importance of positive liberty lies in the fact that public reason liberals typically conceive of citizens as *free* and *equal.* On a purely negative understanding of freedom, though, citizens are obviously not free, at least not entirely, for they are subjected to coercive laws which restrict their negative freedom to act as they see fit. Nor are they equal, at least not entirely, for judges, congressmen and public officials in general are legally entitled to lay down coercive laws, and hence to claim political authority over citizens. So how can the use of political power be made consistent with the conception of the person as free and equal?

17 I. Berlin 1969: 125-30.

Public reason liberalism's response to this pressing question harks back to the social contract tradition. Social contract theorists sought to test the legitimacy of political arrangements by conceiving of an original lawless state, in which free and equal individuals were not bound by any antecedently given principles of justice. Contractualists thus reversed the relationship between individuals and political orders, for the latter were no longer seen as natural facts existing independently of the will of individuals, but rather as artificial bodies, created by the individuals in their own image to promote the satisfaction of their own interests.[18] Some 150 years later, Immanuel Kant and Jean Jaques Rousseau turned this intuition into the powerful idea that those *subjected* to the law must be seen as the *authors* of the law – they must be seen, that is, as *autonomous* agents. On this reading, the ideals of freedom and equality require that political orders be justified in a certain way. On the one hand, freedom implies that acting in accordance with the law must be in some way consistent with reason. In other words, one is free to comply with the law when one has reason to accept it as a general norm. On the other hand, equality demands that members of the public be symmetrically placed, while nobody has a natural duty to defer to the reasoning of others. When it comes to justifying political norms, then, each is to be given an equal right to verify whether or not he or she has reason to accept them as binding prescriptions. As Charles Larmore says, "the distinctive feature of persons is that they are beings capable of thinking and acting on the basis of rea-

18 In its most basic form, the contractualist argument hinges upon some interrelated claims, which Norberto Bobbio has summarized as follows: "1) The state of nature, which is a non-political and anti-political condition, is the starting point for the analysis of the origin and the foundation of the state; 2) The state of nature and civil society are opposed to one another, since civil society arises in antithesis to the state of nature, in order to correct or eliminate the shortcomings of the latter; 3) The constitutive elements of the state of nature are primarily and fundamentally individuals, who do not live in society but are sociable; […] 4) The constitutive elements of the state of nature […] are free and equal. […]; 5) The passage from the state of nature to civil society does not occur by necessity, because of the nature of things. It rather takes place through one or more conventions. These are voluntary and deliberate acts […]. Consequently, civil society is conceived as an "artificial" being. […]; 6) The principle of legitimation of political society is consent. […]" (N. Bobbio 1993: 2). Of course, as Bobbio notes, this core idea has been couched in different ways in the natural law tradition. Variations on the basic contractualist line of reasoning concerned for instance the status of the state of nature (either historical or fictitious), the form and scope of social covenants, the form of political power (either absolute or limited) arising from such covenants, and so forth. The basic claim contractualists made, however, is clear enough. According to the model of contractualist justification, civil society should be understood as a political and artificial state (1 - 2), which free and equal individuals (3 – 4) would voluntarily and deliberately set up (5 – 6).

sons. If we try to bring about conformity to a political principle simply by threat, we will be treating people solely as means, as objects of coercion".[19]

Admittedly, this interpretation of the ideals of freedom and equality rests on a *positive* conception of freedom, according to which being free means acting in accordance with reason. While Hobbes understood the idea of "freedom" in a "negative" fashion, to wit, as the mere absence of external barriers preventing an agent from moving or acting, Rousseau thought that "the mere impulse of appetite is slavery, while obedience to the law which we prescribe to ourselves is liberty".[20] In a similar vein, Kant labeled as "heteronomous" and "arbitrary" a will which does not conform to reason. Kant and Rousseau thus maintained that only those actions that reflect one's rational commitments can properly count as free. In the eyes of the justificatory liberal, the political upshot of this view is that although a negative conception of freedom plays a fundamental role in determining *what* stands in need of public justification, a positive conception of freedom is needed to make sense of the idea that, though coerced, citizens can still be seen as *free and equal* viz. *autonomous* moral persons.

Of course, none of this necessarily rescues justificatory liberalism from the charge of falling back into the kind of autonomy presupposed by perfectionist liberals such as Raz and attacked by pluralistic liberals such as Berlin. Indeed, Berlin's main point is precisely that it is very difficult to draw a clear line between "genuine" commitments to public justification and paternalistic (though of course sincere) impositions purporting to do justice to some controversial ideal of positive liberty. This is a real challenge for justificatory liberals. If a theory of public justification is ill-formed or assigns undue weight to certain kinds of reasons, it will indeed yield results that some citizens could legitimately regard as paternalistic impositions. In order to live up to its fundamental commitment to publicly justify coercion, justificatory liberalism must pay heed to Berlin's warning, thus presenting itself as a clear alternative to perfectionist liberalism. In short, an adequate theory of public justification should distinguish in a convincing and thorough way between "good" justificatory reasons and "bad" considerations in disguise. The fundamental question which justificatory liberals need to address, then, is simple but pressing: *what is a good reason*? The purpose of this book is to answer this fundamental question from a peculiar and hitherto rather unexplored perspective.

19 C. Larmore 2008: 137.
20 J. J. Rousseau 1973 : 178.

II. Questioning the dominant view of public reason

II.a Consensus and convergence

Thus far, I have stressed that justificatory liberalism has a number of distinctive and interrelated features. First, justificatory liberalism views citizens as reasonable, in a twofold sense. They are willing to propose and abide by fair (i.e. publicly justified) terms of cooperation, provided others are as well, and they recognize that reasonable pluralism is an inescapable feature of liberal societies, without however necessarily embracing value pluralism. Second, justificatory liberalism sees liberty as the default position, thus placing on the would-be coercer a special justificatory burden. Third, justificatory liberalism rests on a conception of the person as free and equal, emphasizing both the negative and the positive aspect of liberty. Justificatory liberalism seeks to bring these elements into accord through the construction of a sophisticated and ambitious architecture – the doctrine of public reason. Ultimately, the doctrine of public reason holds that legitimate laws must be backed by good reasons, but, again, this opens up a crucial question: What is a good reason?

On the face of it, there seems to be a simple and attractive answer to this question. Since justification is addressed to the public, it must draw on reasons that are themselves public. A good reason, then, must be a public reason. And typically, the qualification "public" is thought to apply only to those reasons that can be seen by all reasonable citizens as good reasons for accepting or rejecting the law. As Gerald J. Postema points out, a "public reason R* is shared in the robust sense that it is a reason for *each* in virtue of its being a reason *for all*".[21] *Public* reasons thus differ from *private* reasons in the sense that the latter, though acceptable to some citizens in the light of their "comprehensive doctrines", can be reasonably rejected by other citizens. This seems to provide a promising answer to the fundamental question I have sketched: only shareable or public reasons count as good reason at the political level.

In effect, the overwhelming majority of justificatory liberals subscribe to this general view. For instance, Charles Larmore argues that once collectively binding principles of justice have been publicly justified, "the conception of justice by which we live is … a conception we endorse, not for the different reasons we may each discover … but instead for reasons that count for us because we can affirm them together".[22] Similarly, Samuel Freeman claims that the ideal of public justification requires "limiting arguments to shared reasons in political con-

21 G. J. Postema 1995a: 70.
22 C. Larmore 2003: 368.

texts"[23], while S. Macedo insists that "citizens owe each other reasons that they can share".[24] Micah Schwartzman (2011), Jonathan Quong (2011), Thomas Scanlon (2003), Gerald J. Postema (1995a; 1995b), Christine Korsgaard (1996a; 1996b), Rainer Forst (2012) and many others concur.

The idea that reasoning publicly must in some way come down to reasoning on the basis of public viz. shareable reasons is even more dominant among deliberative democrats. Generally speaking, and despite the diversity of their views, deliberative democrats share two fundamental views. First, they think that disagreement can be overcome, at least with respect to certain crucial issues, by means of a free exchange of reasons and relevant information. As Joshua Cohen puts it, "deliberation is *reasoned* in that the parties to it ... give reasons with the expectation that those reasons (and not, for example, their power), will settle the fate of their proposal".[25] The parties thus engage in deliberation with the expectation that a discussion among open-minded and well-informed citizens will yield *reasoned agreements*. Second, and most importantly, deliberative democrats believe that such reasoned agreements should be backed by *shareable reasons*, to wit, by reasons that all participants in deliberation could reasonably accept.

Cohen rightly emphasizes that according to a deliberative conception of democracy, ideal deliberation should be driven solely by what Habermas famously called the "force of the better argument".[26] The idea, then, is that agents of deliberation should not simply *agree* on some given policy. Rather, they should do so by appealing to what they take to be the *better argument(s)*, which, as such, should be *unanimously acceptable*. To use another Habermasian term, deliberation aims at "rationally motivated consensus" (*Einverständnis*), whereby participants agree on the basis of reasons that can be intersubjectively and unanimously recognized as justificatory.[27] Rainer Forst endorses a view of this kind: "To the extent that they claim to be valid for *all*, ought sentences must be justified to all with the same reasons".[28] Gutmann and Thompson agree, arguing that justificatory reasons should be "acceptable to anyone who is similarly situated in morally relevant respects".[29]

As Fred D'Agostino rightly points out, however, there is an interesting alternative to this widespread view. In particular, D'Agostino distinguishes between

23 S. Freeman 2007: 382.
24 S. Macedo 2000: 35.
25 J. Cohen 1997a: 74.
26 J. Habermas 1994: 31.
27 See, for instance, J. Habermas 1996: chapter 4.
28 R. Forst 2002: 194.
29 A. Gutmann / D. F. Thompson 1996: 52.

two families of justificatory conceptions, which he groups under the headings of "consensus" and "convergence":

> If both A and B share a reason R that makes a regime reasonable for them, then the justification of the regime is grounded in their *consensus* with respect to R. If A has a reason R_A that makes the regime reasonable for him, *and B* has a reason R_B that makes the regime reasonable for her, then the justification of the regime is based on *convergence* on it from separate points of view. [30]

Like Habermas, D'Agostino uses the term "consensus" to refer to a unanimous agreement backed by shareable reasons. Consensus conceptions thus reflect the dominant view, in that they hold that, at least as a general rule, a theory of public reason should in principle eschew any appeal to *private* reasons, which, albeit reasonable in the eyes of those who reasonably hold them, cannot be reasonably shared by all. Convergence conceptions, by contrast, employ a much weaker standard of justifiability, in that they hold that reasonable individuals can accept laws and political proposals for their individual or private reasons, which may happen to converge or overlap in support of them. A good reason, on a convergence view, need not be public, though of course convergence models do not imply that public reasons are bad reasons. Note that convergence is a superset of consensus, just as private reasons are a superset of public reasons. Hence, the idea behind convergence conceptions is that being shareable or public is not a necessary condition for being a good reason, although it is a sufficient one.

Relatively few justificatory liberals deviate from the prevailing consensus view. A first timid suggestion in favor of convergence comes from Bruce Ackerman, who thinks that "liberalism's ultimate justification is to be found … in a web of talk that converges upon it from every direction".[31] P. F. Strawson is also sympathetic to diverse reasoning.[32] He argues that in order to justify a collectively binding system of social morality "[w]e need not, perhaps, insist upon just the same answer for all; but, if we take the question seriously, we must insist

30 F. D'Agostino 1996: 30.

31 B. Ackerman 1980: 361. However, Ackerman's convergence model borders on a modus vivendi conception, as it primarily seeks to show that liberalism ensures a viable coexistence among different and potentially conflicting conceptions of the good. The same could perhaps be said of N. Rescher's view (1993), which D'Agostino describes as a convergence view.

32 By "diverse reasoning" I mean ways of reasoning based on different assumptions and rules of inference and leading to different conclusions. To take diverse reasoning seriously, then, is to recognize that citizens can, and often will, rely on different non-shareable reasons and considerations.

on *some* answer for all".[33] David Gauthier defends convergence much more explicitly, although we will see that his conception is quite peculiar.[34] Another declared advocate of convergence is Jeffrey Stout, who claims that while "one should try to argue from universally justifiable premises, whenever this seems wise and possible", one should also feel free to "pursue other argumentative strategies when they seem wise".[35]

The most insightful and explicit defense of convergence, however, has appeared in Gaus's recent works. According to Gaus, the idea that public reason should be in some way constrained by a Shareability Requirement, as implied by the dominant consensus views, is simply an error:

> It is almost universally supposed that public justification requires that for every justified law there is at least one justificatory reason that all citizens accept — upon which there is consensus. This is an error. Respect for each as free and equal requires that for a law to be justified every citizen must have some conclusive reason to accept it: they need not all have the same reason.[36]

Indeed, Gaus maintains that it is "immensely important" that citizens can affirm the laws they are subjected to on their own terms and for their own private reasons.[37] The idea behind Gaus's convergence model is, of course, Rawls's intuition that the political conception affirmed in a given society is not fully legitimate unless it gains an "overlapping consensus" of comprehensive doctrines. However, although the "overlapping consensus" is a clear example of convergent justification, Rawls is notoriously unclear about its normative role.[38] Gaus, instead, is explicit that the search for convergence points (i.e. agreements based on different non-shareable reasons) is what public justification is ultimately all about.

II.b Overview of the argument

Apart from Gaus and few others, justificatory liberals are skeptical about diverse reasoning; in fact, until very recently convergence has received little if any attention in the literature on public reason. Surely one explanation is that some find

33 P. F. Strawson 1961: 7.
34 See chapter 3, §3.5.2.
35 J. Stout 2004: 75.
36 G. Gaus / K. Vallier: 2009: 51.
37 G. Gaus 2011b: 336.
38 See chapter 1 (§1.4.2).

the convergence view of public reason somewhat contradictory. How can we achieve *public* justification if we do not focus exclusively on *public reasons*? It seems obvious that if we embrace the fundamental commitment to reason publicly, we thereby commit ourselves to reasoning in shareable or public terms. Others simply deny that there are such things as "private reasons", insisting that reasons are by definition essentially public and sharable. Finally, some critics think that consensus fares much better than convergence with respect to some important desiderata connected with the ideal of public reason, such as sincerity, stability, publicity etc.

The fundamental thesis of this book is that this widespread allegiance to the consensus model is ultimately unwarranted. In fact, we will see that convergence is not only an enticing conception of public reason, but also truer than consensus to the ideal of public reason. I shall argue that although Gaus's own view should be weakened in one important respect, an adequate conception of public reason should strongly tilt toward the convergence model suggested by Gaus. This book is divided into three chapters.

Chapter 1 serves as a threefold prelude for my substantive argument. Firstly, it offers a comprehensive analytic overview of the general concept of public justification. Secondly, it defines consensus and convergence models as two competing interpretations or conceptions of that general concept. Thirdly, it argues that convergence is prima facie preferable to consensus. Specifically, in chapter 1 we will see that there are two major considerations that render convergence prima facie preferable to the standard consensus view.

First, convergence seems better able than consensus to do justice to the ideal of public reason. The problem is that in liberal societies people will hold different "conceptions of the good", systems of values and evaluative standards. In short, many reasons and considerations that citizens may find salient or even overriding in *their* view will not be reasonably shared by all. The question, then, is how we should proceed in the face of such disagreement. Consensus and convergence models address this question in two completely different ways. The latter take pluralism and disagreement as source of justification: to achieve public justification, on the convergence view, requires showing that all reasonable doctrines and views that thrive under liberal institutions can converge on some common principles of social cooperation, each from its own perspective and for its own non-shareable reasons. Consensus models, instead, suggest bracketing disagreement and pretending, as it were, that all reasonable citizens reason in the same way; in order to achieve public justification, on a consensus view, we need to abstract from citizens' system of values and evaluative standards and take account only of the few reasons they can share. But to simply "assume away" disagreement and the consequent fact of diverse reasoning is to ignore the problem, not to solve it. As Rawls himself seems to admit, shared reasoning can only usher in "pro tanto" justified principles. Hence, "pro tanto" justification must be supplemented with a further twofold justificatory stage ("full justification" and "public justification by political society").[39] Public justification is successful only "when all the reasonable members of political society carry out a justification of the shared political conception by embedding it in their several reasonable comprehensive views".[40] Gaus's great insight is that this "convergence stage" is crucial to public justification. By restricting the set of reasons relevant to public justification, consensus theorists lose the ideal of justification to the reason of the individual, which is only in part "public". Insofar as it ignores some of the reasons citizens have, consensus runs the danger of upholding proposals that are unjustified to some citizens, thereby undermining the very ideal of public reason.

But consensus also incurs a second, deeper problem, which even advocates of the convergence view have thus far overlooked. Both defenders and critics of convergence seem in fact to rely on a misguided assumption, which in my view unduly weakens Gaus's case against consensus. This misguided assumption is that public reasons are "freestanding" considerations that can be identified in isolation from private reasons, to wit, by bracketing citizens' comprehensive doctrines. I shall call this general assumption the Freestandingness Thesis: *R* is a public or shareable reason if, and only if, every reasonable citizen, putting their comprehensive doctrine into account, would share *R*. Now critics of consensus such as Gaus, K. Vallier and J. Stout do not reject this view. What they claim is rather that private reasons should be taken into account in a separate justificatory stage, whereby the strength of the "freestanding" argument is assessed in the light of citizens' comprehensive doctrines in order to ensure that coercive laws are fully justified to their addressees.

As we will see, however, the Freestandingness Thesis seems false. It seems false, because in order to consistently claim that *R* is a shareable reason, one must show that *R* is not defeated (in a sense that will become clear in chapter 1) by other citizens' private objections. If some reasonable citizen has private defeaters for *R*, I shall argue, *R* is not a public reason. But once the Freestandingness Thesis is rejected, the consensus view turns out to be paradoxical and self-defeating: to rely on public reasons, as consensus models demand, already requires bringing private reasons into the picture, for these are necessary to determine what counts as a public reason in the first place. Therefore, consensus should be resisted not simply because citizens' private reasons might defeat or

39 J. Rawls 1995: 143.
40 Ibid.

"override" shared reasons, as Rawls and Gaus contend, but rather because defeated reasons are *not actually shareable*.

All this seems to suggest that there is a strong, twofold presumption in favor of convergence. First, "pro tanto" justification might be defeated by private reasons, thereby failing to justify coercive laws to all members of the public. Second, it is questionable whether the freestanding reasons on which "pro tanto" justification relies are shareable in the first place. The fact that such a twofold presumption is in place shifts the justificatory burden onto consensus theorists. For this reason, this book is devoted to analyzing arguments for consensus, rather than further arguments for convergence. Unless consensus theorists come up with some convincing argument that can rebut the presumption in favor of convergence, we should favor convergence over consensus by default. But let us suppose that they do come up with some such argument. Let us assume, that is, that consensus theorists manage to show that for any given reason *R* identified via the correct (and suitably conducted) procedure of abstraction, it is never the case that *R* is defeated by private reasons. If sound, an argument of this kind would surely rebut the presumption in favor of convergence: first, since freestanding reasons identified via abstraction cannot be defeated by private reasons, it is never the case that "pro tanto" justified principles are, all things considered, unjustified to some citizens; and for pretty much the same reason, freestanding reasons are by definition shareable; hence, consensus models are not self-defeating because the Freestandingness Thesis turns out to be correct.

In short, if it is the case that freestanding reasons cannot be defeated by private reasons, then consensus theorists catch two birds with one stone: they can maintain that consensus models can both achieve "full justification" (as opposed to a mere "pro tanto", defeasible one) and avoid the charge of being somewhat paradoxical and self-defeating. To use the terminology I hinted at above, a sound argument for consensus must show that private reasons are "bad reasons" compared to freestanding reasons; if this is so, then the former cannot defeat the latter; consequently, freestanding reasons are both shareable and indefeasible.

However, private reasons could be thought to be "bad reasons" both in an *epistemic* and in a *moral* sense. In fact, the phrase "private reasons are bad reasons" can either mean that private reasons lack justificatory *strength*, or it can imply that private reasons are *inappropriate* justificatory grounds. One the first view, the idea that public reasons may be defeated by private reasons necessarily lacks epistemic warrant. On the second view, it is morally inappropriate to advocate private defeaters in public political debate, regardless of their epistemic weight. Thus, consensus models can be either *strength-based* or *appropriateness-based*, depending on whether the arguments supporting them are strength-based (i.e.

aiming to show that private reasons are epistemically weak) or appropriateness-based (i.e. aiming to show that private reasons are morally inappropriate).

Chapter 2 critically reviews four major strength-based arguments for consensus. I shall call them the "top-down argument for consensus", the "social argument for consensus", the "argument from universalization" and the "discourse theoretical argument for consensus". What these arguments seek to show is basically that reasons identified via abstraction have by definition greater epistemic strength than freestanding reasons. As a result, freestanding reasons are both shareable and indefeasible, and it would be an epistemic mistake to believe otherwise. Unfortunately, however, we will see that strength-based arguments for consensus fail, thus leaving the presumption in favor of convergence fully in place.

Chapter 3 verifies whether appropriateness-based arguments for consensus can do the job. While these arguments grant that private reasons might, epistemically speaking, defeat freestanding reasons, they maintain that it is not morally appropriate for reasonable citizens to advocate private reasons in public political debate. In other words, reasonable citizens should *ignore* the fact that freestanding reasons might be non-shareable and defeasible, as allegiance to freestanding reasons is part of what it means to be a reasonable citizen committed to moral standards of appropriateness. To put the point differently, appropriateness-based arguments for consensus suggest that the constituency of public reason should only comprise members who see freestanding reasons as shareable and indefeasible. Those who view freestanding reasons as defeasible may not commit any epistemic mistake, and yet they should not be given a say because their views are morally inappropriate. Freestanding reasons are therefore shareable and indefeasible in the sense that those who believe otherwise, being excluded by the constituency of public reason, are not supposed to share those reasons in the first place.

In chapter 3 I shall consider five appropriateness-based arguments for consensus, which I shall call the "argument form sincerity", the "argument from publicity", the "argument from normative stability", the "argument from reasonable compliance" and the "argument from symmetry". We will see that even these arguments are far from convincing – though toward the end of chapter 3 I shall argue that the convergence model suggested by Gaus should be weakened in an important respect. This will lead me to conclude that a suitably construed convergence model (which I shall dub "symmetrical convergence") is highly preferable to the standard consensus view that most theorists of public reason subscribe to.

II.c Content and method

The convergence model I shall argue for in this book ("symmetrical convergence") has seven fundamental features. First, 1) it presupposes what I shall call the "broad view" of public reason, which holds that all coercive laws must be publicly justified to their addressees. If a law coerces you, you have a right to demand that that law be justified to you. This "broad view" is to be contrasted with the "narrow view" of public reason, according to which laws need not be publicly justified unless they have to do with constitutional essentials or fundamental issues of justice.

Second, 2) I propose to defend a two-step justificatory conception, which starts by identifying potentially justified principles supported by shareable reasons and then verifies whether these principles can gain an "overlapping consensus" of private reasons. Following Gaus, I assume that shared reasoning is an important justificatory tool:[41] by abstracting from citizens' comprehensive doctrines, it helps us bracket disagreement, thus pointing to a set of principles of social cooperation to which all citizens might potentially assent. Still, on a convergence view this is only a first step toward the achievement of public justification. In order to be publicly justified, principles identified via abstraction need to be affirmed by citizens' in the light of their comprehensive, non-public systems of reasons and beliefs. However, third 3), my convergence conception is robust across different accounts of what should could as the correct procedure of abstraction. I assume that in a first stage public reasoning must abstract from citizens' comprehensive doctrines, but I shall not commit myself to any specific procedure of abstraction.

Fourth, 4) the convergence model I shall defend is *procedural*, rather than *substantive*. With this I do not mean, of course, that convergence and the ideal of public reason in general are shorn of any substantive commitments. Quite the contrary, the ideal of public reason is inherently substantive insofar as it requires recognizing others as free and equal moral persons, who should not be forced to do things without an adequate justification. No commitment to publicly justify is possible in the absence of a moral substantive commitment to view coercion as prima facie wrong. Also, the ideal of public reason requires the willingness to cooperate and agree on some principles governing society: anarchists and radical

41 By "shared reasoning" I mean not simply "joint reasoning", but a kinf of reasoning based on public premises and conducted in accordance with public rules of inference and criteria for assessing relevant evidence. See also G. Gaus 2011b: 335. However, I shall generally talk about "freestanding reasoning", rather than "shared reasoning", because the problem is precisely to understand whether freestandingness and shareability are two identical notions, as consensus models based on the Freestandingness Thesis imply.

libertarians will be excluded from our constituency of public reason. However, the conception of public reason I shall defend is procedural (as opposed to substantive) in the following sense: it explains which justificatory procedure we should carry out to assess the legitimacy of principles of justice, but it does not purport to determine in advance which substantive outcomes such a procedure ought to yield.[42]

Of course, public reason is a theory of liberalism. It therefore assumes that some liberal substantive principles can be publicly justified. These will include civil and political rights, rules that assign a certain priority to citizens' basic liberties, and some (perhaps minimal) welfare rights. I do not mean to deny, of course, that this is an extremely plausible conjecture. It is, however, a conjecture which liberals might be committed to revising should citizens have reason to converge on different rules of social cooperation. Justificatory liberals should primarily aim to devise a justificatory procedure that justifies coercion to all members of the public. *This* is, after all, justificatory liberalism's core commitment. However, they should be wary of taking liberal outcomes for granted, assuming that if the justificatory procedure does not lead to standard liberal norms, then it must have been carried out in an inadequate way.

Those who take a procedural stance toward the problem of public justification should be especially wary, in my view, of taking side within much contemporary debate about controversial issues of distributive justice. Thus, while today the terrain of political philosophy is to a large extent organized around those controversial issues, substantive questions of this kind do not loom large in this book. As I see it, justificatory liberalism is best understood as trying to carry the question of political justification to a higher level of abstraction, seeking to specify the formal conditions that arguments in favor of specific principles of distributive justice must meet in order to qualify as publicly justificatory. By the same token, I shall have little to say the proper extent of the liberal state and its substantive commitments. For those who understand liberalism as being committed to a sheer "minimal state",[43] the only tasks of the state are to protect individual liberties and secure an extensive regime of private property rights. On the other side of the dispute, defenders of "welfare state' or "social justice" liberalism challenge the supposed intimate connection between personal liberty and a private property-based market order.[44] For these "new" liberals, property rights are

42 For an overview of the debate about "substantive" and "procedural" justificatory conceptions, see J. Cohen 1997b.

43 R. Nozick 1974.

44 For more on the differences between "old" and "new" liberalism see M. Freeden 1978 and E. F. Paul / F. D. Miller / J. Paul 2007.

a threat to social justice rather than "the guardian of every other right",[45] since they inevitably foster and reify an unjust distribution of political power. Classical liberals *à la* Mill, instead, typically steer a middle way between these two rather radical views. They argue that although property rights are an important tenet of liberalism, measures of social justice such as poor relief, education and health regulations are publicly justifiable.[46]

To be sure, toward the end of chapter 3 I shall deal extensively with issues of property rights and redistribution. There I shall argue that Gaus's convergence model should be amended to a "symmetrical convergence" conception precisely because convergence might incur a peculiar problem when it comes to the justification of principles of distributive justice. This is the fifth feature of the "symmetrical" convergence view I want to defend: unlike convergence, 5) "symmetrical convergence" explicitly constrains the use of private reasons when the issues of distributive justice and property rights are at stake. Again, though, my argument for symmetrical convergence will be concerned, in a rather "procedural" fashion, with how controversies over property rights and social justice should be addressed. It will not attempt to establish which substantive principles of distribution are publicly justified.

Moreover 6), in defending (symmetrical) convergence I shall rephrase the notions of "justification", "reasons", "shareability" etc. in epistemological terms, as I take it that concepts of this kind are inherently epistemological. To say that a coercive law L is publicly justified is to say that every citizen is justified in believing that L is legitimate, and worth endorsing for that reason. And this, in turn, means that an account of public justification must present itself as a moral epistemology, in the sense of an account of the conditions of justified moral belief concerning the legitimacy of political principles.

Surprisingly, though, some justificatory liberals deny this. In particular, "political" liberals such as Rawls, Quong, Larmore and Macedo insist that a suitable theory of public reason should avoid taking side within epistemological issues. The pressing problem, for political liberals, is to obtain a good deal of consensus on political principles in order to secure widespread adherence to them. But because epistemology is itself subject to reasonable and pervasive disagreement, they argue that it would be self-defeating to tie a theory of public justification to some controversial epistemological doctrine, which some reasonable people would inevitably reject. Rawls thus maintains that public justification is a "prac-

45 J. Ely 1992: 26.

46 A classical analysis of the functions of government is provided by John Stuart Mill's *Principles of Political Economy*, book V (1979).

tical" and not an "epistemological" issue,[47] while Larmore, in a related context, claims that "the reasons for the ideal of neutrality" are primarily "*moral*" rather than "*epistemological*".[48]

Of course, political liberalism is a form of justificatory liberalism on my definition: generally speaking, political liberals reject *modus vivendi*, they stress that justification is addressed to reasonable citizens and they insists that a commitment to reason publicly is inextricably intertwined with the ideals of freedom and equality.[49] Still, by downgrading the epistemic question of justification to a quasi-pragmatic problem, political liberals risk losing sight of the essence of public reason. Without an epistemological account of justified moral belief, we cannot determine whether a coercive law is justified to all, for we have no parameter to verify whether citizens have reason to endorse it. At best, we can *observe* that some of them (hopefully, the majority of them) happen to *actually* accept it. Which for political liberals is just as well, for their primary aim is to work out principles that citizens "*regard* as justified".[50] One of the crucial theses of this book is that this political approach is unsatisfactory. Insofar as they take public justification as liberalism's core commitment, justificatory liberals should be wary of treading the path suggested by political liberals.

These remarks about the epistemic dimension of public reason enable me to add an important terminological clarification. In this book, I shall talk about *shareable* reasons, and not about *shared* reasons. For to say that consensus models are concerned only with shared reasons is to suggest, at least implicitly, that on a consensus view public reasoning should draw exclusively on reasons that are *actually affirmed* by all reasonable citizens. To be sure, this seems unavoidable if we accept political liberalism's doctrine of epistemic restraint: without an epistemic theory of justified belief, we can hardly make a distinction between the reasons that are actually shared and the reasons that citizens ought to share if their ways of reasoning fulfilled some (perhaps minimal) epistemic conditions. Again, though, this is implausible. Consensus models must presuppose an epistemic theory of justified beliefs able to determine which reasons are *shareable* (though not necessarily *shared*) and which are not.

Finally, 7) I propose to defend (symmetrical) convergence as a theory of liberalism operating at the level of the traditional state. My discussion of public reason is thus not concerned with the justification of international or transnation-

47 J. Rawls 1993: 44.

48 C. Larmore 1990: 342.

49 To be sure, some political liberals such as B. Ackerman are attracted to loose forms of public justification, which make their views look closer to *modus vivendi* than to justificatory liberalism. As a general rule, however, political liberals are justificatory liberals.

50 S. Macedo 1991: 51.

al forms of political and economical association. To be sure, there is nothing contradictory in a "global" conception of public reason aiming to justify forms of legal or informal interference that go beyond the authority of the traditional state.[51] However, this is a peculiar approach to the question of public justification, which raises questions and problems that I cannot address in this book. To avoid unnecessary complications, then, I shall stick to the traditional view: to ask whether or not a given political proposal is publicly justified is to ask whether or not that proposal deserves to be turned into a binding law of a national state. The question, of course, must be raised as to which reasons citizens owe each other in assessing the legitimacy of any such law. Most theorists of public reason think that citizens owe each other only shareable reasons. We will see that this is not the case.

51 For a "global" conception of public reason see J. Cohen 2010: 319-372.

1. Two models of public reason

1.1. Overview of the argument

In this book I follow a well-trodden path in political philosophy. I start from a general concept and seek to verify which interpretations or conceptions of it are more in tune with its rationale. The general concept I deal with in this book is the idea (and, of course, ideal) of public reason,[52] of which consensus and convergence are two competing interpretations or conceptions. While consensus models hold that justificatory reasons must be public or shareable, convergence models allow diverse private reasons to converge in support of coercive laws. As I stressed in the introduction, most theorists of public reason endorse consensus conceptions, and yet convergence presents itself as a plausible alternative to the prevailing consensus view. The core question I address in this book is whether or not and to what extent the dominant consensus conception is an adequate interpretation of the concept of public reason. In this chapter I lay the basis for my argument about consensus and convergence models of public reason by providing an analytical account of some key concepts. Section §1.2 defines the general concept of public justification as a combination of two fundamental principles. The first principle is normative: it holds that coercive policies and principles *ought* to be publicly justified. I shall call it the "Principle of Political Liberty". The second principle, instead, explains what public justification is, in that it specifies under which conditions a given law can qualify as publicly justified. I shall call it the "Principle of Public Justification". Section §1.3 defines consensus and convergence as two competing interpretations of the general concept of public justification. Section §1.4 argues that consensus models are traversed by an internal tension: on the one hand, they insist that the use of political power must be justified; on the other hand, though, they exclude a priori certain kinds of considerations which could tip the balance of justificatory reasons against coercion. Section §1.5 raises a further worry about consensus models: they insist that private reasons should be expunged from public reasoning and yet private reasons

52 "Idea" and "Ideal" of public reason are obviously not the same thing. The former is a descriptive term. The latter, instead, is normative, in that it implies that public reason expresses a commitment to justify coercion which reasonable citizens should honor. As Rawls notes, public reason is both an idea and an ideal (J. Rawls 1997: 576). Because it is a general idea (i.e. a descriptive concept open to different conceptions), it can be interpreted in different ways. But because it is also an ideal, the right conception of public reason has normative force, in that it commits citizens to justifying their claims to others in a certain way.

are necessary to determine which reasons qualify as shareable. Section §1.6 shows that in order to address these two problems, consensus theorists could adopt two different strategies, which I shall critically examine in the remainder of this book. Section §1.7 concludes.

1.2. Two core principles

1.2.1 The Principle of Political Liberty

The concept of public reason answers two questions. First: *What stands in need of justification*? Second: *What is public justification*? I take it that the following principle captures the liberal response to the first question:

Principle of Political Liberty: Liberty should be the norm; coercion stands in need of justification.

The Principle of Political Liberty rephrases the idea of a fundamental presumption in favor of liberty. Freedom is the normative baseline or default position; coercion, being a deviation from liberty understood as the normative default, always calls for public justification (see Introduction §I.b). The presumption in favor of liberty is best understood on analogy with the presumption of innocence within trial law. The theorist of public reason must assume that coercion is unjustified until a sufficiently compelling case against liberty is provided, just as a judge is committed to assuming that defendant is innocent until defendant is proven guilty beyond a reasonable doubt. Moreover, in both cases the justificatory burden is on those who wish to deviate from the default assumption. The would-be coercer ought to justify her demands to the prospective coerce, while the latter is not required to justify his liberty to the former. Similarly, within trial law the initial burden of proof is not on the defendant but on the plaintiff.

In one formulation or another, the presumption in favor of liberty has been affirmed by most liberal thinkers.[53] More generally, that presumption is an important element of the social contract tradition, in that it expresses the view that the point of departure of political justification is an original point in time at which free and equal individuals are not bound by any antecedently given political obligations. It is the law that calls for justification, and not the original state

53 These include, among many others, J. S. Mill 1979: vol. 21; J. Feinberg 1984: 7-10; S. Benn 1988: 87-90; G. Gaus 2005; 2011: 341-46, J. Rawls 1993:139 and 214-217 and A. Gewirth 1978: chapter 3.

of liberty. Since it simply rephrases the fundamental commitment to publicly justify coercion that lies at the heart of justificatory liberalism, the Principle of Political Liberty does not seem to require much attention. There are, however, many aspects of the Principle of Political Liberty that need to be clarified.

To begin with, it is important to stress that the Principle of Political Liberty is only concerned with the *negative* aspect of freedom. It states that insofar as the state limits citizens' freedom to think, act or move as they see fit, a public justification is required. Let us therefore stipulate that:

1): Andy is free to ϕ if and only if there is no law L such that a) L coerces its addressees either into ϕ-ing or into refraining from ϕ-ing and b) L is legally binding on Andy (i.e., applies to Andy).[54]

On the face of it, this sort of definition presupposes that we can make sense of the idea of coercion. But this seems a tricky task, as much recent literature has witnessed a number of divergent and "essentially contested" interpretations of the concept of coercion. As F. A. Hayek says, I am coerced when the alternatives before me have been so gravely "manipulated" that "the conduct the coercer wants me to choose becomes for me the least painful one".[55] However, philosophers typically hold different views of what should count as a coercive "manipulation".[56] And this, in turn, seems to render the presumption in favor of liberty an unmanageable and ultimately idle concept. I think, however, that we should reject this skeptical conclusion, since the presumption in favor of liberty does not require any comprehensive analysis of coercion, but only its applications to the actions of the state against its citizens.

Many political theorists, ranging from Max Weber to Habermas, from Hans Kelsen to Rawls, have held that at the political level coercion has to do with the threat of legal sanctions. By imposing on Andy a law that says "Do not ϕ!" the state will threaten him with some serious sanctions, which he will incur in case of non-compliance with the law, and which will make ϕ-ing a risky, irrational, or otherwise ineligible option for him.[57] This is a quintessential instance of coer-

54 Clause b) is only meant to rule out the case that Andy is outside the domain of L.

55 F. A. Hayek 1960: 133.

56 For a comprehensive overview of different conceptions of coercion see S. Anderson 2006. Much contemporary debate over the concept of coercion has been spurred by Nozick's path-breaking analytical definition of coercive impositions (R. Nozick 1969).

57 Perhaps one could argue, along with A. Wertheimer (1987) and C. Ryan (1980), that coercion is a "moralized" notion. To say that Andy coerces Bea, on this view, is to say that Andy necessarily wrongs her, perhaps because he violates some rights of hers. By contrast, justified interference, being justified, cannot count as coercive. To use S. Ander-

cion, which does not presuppose any fully-fledged definition of coercive acts. In other words, it is plausible to assume that the presence of legal sanctions is a sufficient though perhaps not necessary condition for a law to count as coercive. The Principle of Political Liberty thus implies that insofar as laws are coercive in this sense, they call for public justification. As Rawls stresses, for the liberal it is "the use of political power" that must be justified, and for Rawls "[p]olitical power is always coercive power backed by the government's use of sanctions".[58]

Of course, the classical Weber-Habermas-Rawls view of coercion is tailored to the national state. It is often charged, quite rightly, that this view cannot account for the fact that transnational or international actors, which typically lack the authority to enforce their decisions coercively, have nonetheless a considerable impact on international politics. This would count as an objection against the classical view, however, only if we endorsed what in the introduction I called a "global" conception of public reason. In the introduction, however, I stressed that in this book I want to stick to the traditional view, according to which public reason is concerned exclusively with the justifiability of state actions (see §I.c above). And as far as the state is concerned, the traditional account of coercion endorsed by Habermas, Rawls and many others does seem to capture adequately the typical modus operandi of political authority. In order for Andy to be free to ϕ, then, it must be the case that the political authority has not enacted any coercive law regulating ϕ, as stated by 1). Another way of putting the point is the following:

2) Andy is free to ϕ if and only if he has neither a legally enforced duty to ϕ nor a legally enforced duty to refrain from ϕ-ing.

son's illuminating example, "if the mafia threatens to destroy your property if you fail to pay protection money, this threat will count as coercive; but if the just, well-regulated state threatens to confiscate your property unless you pay taxes, this threat is arguably not coercive, on this view" (S. Anderson 2006: §3.2). This "moralized" conception of coercion consorts ill with Gaus's view and with public reason liberalism in general. Whereas public reason liberals insist that that coercion can and should be justified through public reasoning, the Wertheimer/Ryan view dismisses the notion of "justified coercion" as a conceptual error. However, this looks like a purely terminological point. It is a point, by the way, which could be easily accommodated, for one could concede that the law ceases to be coercive once it has been publicly justified. However, this would require introducing a new term (say: "coerciveness"), which should be used as a label for legally enforceable yet publicly justifiable impositions, whereas "coercion" would refer exclusively to unjustifiable laws. But this seems an unnecessary terminological complication. For the sake of clarity, then, I shall maintain that citizens are coerced whenever the state threatens them by means of legal sanctions, regardless of whether or not the state is publicly justified in doing so.

58 J. Rawls 1993: 136.

Andy is therefore free to ϕ if he has neither a duty to ϕ nor an opposite duty not to ϕ. As Gaus says, a "moral liberty" is a "no-duty".[59] However, duties entail corresponding rights. Conversely, the core case of rights (an entitlement to make legally enforceable claims on others) carries second-party obligations in its train. To give a straightforward example (in a universe with two people), Andy's duty not to kill Bea entails Bea's right not to be killed, and vice versa. Similarly, Andy's duty to financially support through taxation – say – an occupational policy in favor of women is correlative to Bea's right to avail herself of that policy. Rights are thus inherently coercive, since they are typically paired with others' legally enforceable duties. It thus follows that 1) and 2) are identical with:

3) Andy is free to ϕ if and only if no other citizen has a legal right to demand that he ϕ or refrain from ϕ-ing.

This view is, of course, in tune with Wesley Hohfeld's analysis of liberties and claims.[60] For Hohfeld, Andy has a *liberty* to engage in act ϕ if and only if Bea has no *right* to demand that he refrain from ϕ-ing. On the other hand, the fact that Andy has a mere liberty to engage in act ϕ does not imply that he has a right to ϕ. The distinction between liberty to ϕ and right/claim to ϕ is nicely captured by the classical example of the dollar bill lying on the sidewalk.[61] Bea and Andy are both free to pick it up; yet neither has a right to pick it up; consequently, neither has a duty to refrain from doing so. Hence, should Andy get to the bill first, Bea would have no right to complain.

In sum, the Principle of Political Liberty understands the presumption in favor of liberty in the terms of a presumption against coercion, understood as legal interference backed by the threat of sanctions. As a result, the Principle of Political Liberty requires that public officials publicly justify the institutionalization of a system of legal rights and duties.[62]

59 G. Gaus 2010b: 188.

60 See W. Hohfeld 1913 as well as M. Freeden 1991, chapter 1.

61 See G. Gaus 2000: 186.

62 It is important to stress that only *legal* rights stand in need of justification. In fact, for some theorists of public reason some *moral* rights are not and cannot be publicly justified. Rather, they frame the necessary preconditions for public justification. Rainer Forst advocates this view. He argues that "moral persons have a fundamental right to justification – and a corresponding unconditional duty to justify morally relevant actions" (R. Forst 2012: 21). Hence, even in a state of "naked" or "blameless" liberty, moral persons are under a *duty* of justification, which they must fulfill whenever they lay claims over others. In fact, Forst argues that the commitment to publicly justify could not get off the ground in the first place in the absence of such a fundamental right (R. Forst 2005: 240n). For unless I have a fundamental duty to justify coercion to you, I am not committed to as-

To be sure, the presumption in favor of liberty can itself be couched in the terms of a *legal right*, in the sense of a fundamental right not to be coerced by the state. Of course, this right is not absolute, for coercive laws can be justified. But unless coercion is adequately justified, citizens' right not to be coerced is violated and the use of political power illegitimate. Given the Principle of Political Liberty, public officials have a legal duty to justify the use of political power.

1.2.2 Some misgivings about the presumption in favor of liberty

It is often charged that this understanding of freedom suffers from a "liberal bias", in that it is mainly concerned with restrictions on citizens' "negative" liberty to act as they see fit. Now in a way this is unavoidable, since public reason is a theory of liberalism and not – say – a comprehensive moral account of freedom

signing any relevant moral weight to your original liberty. Forst's point, however, does not count as an objection to the view that rights must always be justified, since the right to justification articulates a purely moral demand. It explains how and why coercion should be justified, but it is not itself coercive. Again, though, only legally enforceable rights stand in need of justification according to justificatory liberalism. Having said that, I must stress that it is questionable whether a commitment to publicly justify really presupposes a right to justification in Forst's sense. Gaus, for instance, denies this. Following Habermas's and Alan Gewirth's argumentative strategy, he argues that a commitment to publicly justify stems from the first-person perspective of moral agents, and not from a prior recognition of the moral status of others. For Habermas, agents are committed to embracing a moral perspective on pain of performative inconsistency (J. Habermas 1990, chapter 3,III), while Gewirth thinks that moral principles can be inferred from the "Principle of Generic Consistency", which compels moral agents to reason from an impartial perspective (A. Gewirth 1978, chapter 3). The key idea is that someone who acts immorally is irrational in a very narrow sense: in some way, she gets caught in contradiction. In a similar vein, Gaus argues that a commitment to publicly justify must be acknowledged on pain of inconsistency. On the one hand, we believe that others are equals. On the other hand, though, we typically claim authority over them. But "how is such a claim to authority consistent with treating others as equal moral persons? At the heart of our moral relations with others is an appeal to authority, yet public reason liberalism insists that we are moral equals. How can a moral equal claim moral authority over another and demand that he is subject to your authority?" (Gaus 2009a: 113). To overcome this impasse, in Gaus's view, you are committed to publicly justifying your demands to others. Only in this way can you claim moral authority over them and at the same time respect them as equals. Yet for all this, you are not committed to seeing those subjected to your demands as having a *right* to justification. In fact, you have no moral *duty* to publicly justify. More simply, you have a compelling *reason* to publicly justify, as you would contradict your own beliefs about moral equality if you failed to do so. In any event, I wish to remain neutral on this point, mainly because in this book I cannot address Forst's own critique of the Habermas-Gaus view. Whether or not public reason presupposes a right to justification, only legal duties stand in need of public justification.

or a theory of democratic legitimacy or will-formation. However, it is worth noting that the Principle of Political Liberty is not insensitive to other conceptions of liberty.

Consider, for instance, Philip Pettit's critique of the liberal understanding of freedom. Pettit has repeatedly insisted that the liberal conception of freedom is short-sighted, in that it rests on the assumption that one is free if one is not interfered with by others. Hence, liberals seem to imply that the fact that Andy *can* interfere with Bea does not in itself limit her freedom. For Pettit, this is a mistake. In his view, Bea is not really free if Andy *could* at any moment constrain her choices if he wished to: Bea would live under the constant possibility that Andy may decide to restrict her liberty, and that would make her unfree. Thus, according to Pettit, "the employer who can fire his employees as whim inclines him" may not actually interfere with his employees, for he may decide not to fire them. Still, on Pettit's view the employees are unfree insofar as their employer *can* interfere with them by virtue of his right to fire them.[63] Now entirely apart from the merits of Pettit's case against the liberal conception of liberty in general, the Principle of Political Liberty can meet his objection in the vast majority of cases. For although the Principle of Political Liberty does equate freedom with the lack of interference, it is by no means concerned with "actual" interference, or with "actual" limitations on negative freedom. Recall that according to 2), Andy is free to ϕ if Bea has no legal *right* to demand that he ϕ if she so wishes. The focus, then, is not on Bea's actual decision to exercise her power over Andy, but rather on her legally recognized entitlement to limit his freedom. To cover Pettit's example, the public reason liberal can point out that insofar as the employer has a legal right to fire his employees, his privileged position of power stands in need of justification, regardless of whether or not he exercises that right.

There is, however, another common objection against the liberal idea that freedom is characterized by the absence of legal interference. If I am prevented by the state from doing what I want, according to liberals, I am to that degree unfree. If, by contrast, no legal constraints prevent me from doing what I want, I am to that degree free. Now for a number of philosophers, ranging from Marxists and socialists to some Christian and even Utilitarian thinkers, this is a one-sided and ideologically biased conception of freedom; the mere lack of coercion, they claim, cannot be a sufficient condition for liberty, although it is of course a necessary one. As a matter of fact, one can be prevented from acting as one sees fit

63 P. Pettit 1996: 581.

by other socially sanctioned obstacles, most notably material inequalities. Isaiah Berlin put this point very clearly:

> It is argued, very plausibly, that if a man is too poor to afford something on which there is no legal ban — a loaf of bread, a journey round the world, recourse to the law courts — he is as little free to have it as he would be if it were forbidden him by law.[64]

To be really free, on this broader view, one must also have the material resources needed to do what one wants. So for instance someone who cannot afford a car is not really free to stop using public transportation according to the conception of liberty Berlin hints at. Now advocates of this broader view of freedom might argue that the classical liberal view sells short the critical potential of public reason, in that it does not demand that material inequalities be justified. But this would be a mistake. It is true that according to the liberal conception of liberty one is free to ϕ even if one is unable to fulfill the material preconditions needed to actually ϕ. If no law prevents people from purchasing vehicles, a homeless person is free to purchase a space shuttle on the liberal understanding of freedom. However, it would be a mistake to think that this conception of liberty is insensitive to inequalities in income and wealth. In fact, schemes of distributions and property protecting and regulating differences in income and wealth presuppose a system of property rights, which, qua legal rights, are coercive. Thus, although the worse off are not necessarily less free than the better off in the sense indicate by Berlin, the latter do owe a justification to the former, as their claims to property stand in need of justification.

In sum, the Principle of Political Liberty seems sufficiently robust across different conceptions of liberty. First, it is not concerned only with actual interference, but more generally with legal rights that entitle citizens to interfere with others. Moreover, the Principle of Political Liberty is entirely consistent with the view that material inequalities stand in need of justification. It is important to emphasize, however, that the Principle of Political Liberty and its underlying presumption in favor of liberty do not imply that *only* coercion stands in need of justification. They hold that coercion must be justified, but they do not exclude that something else may stand in need of justification. Specifically, the presumption in favor of liberty entails no denial of the view that *liberty*, as well as coercion, may call for justification. Some critics of the presumption in favor of liberty seem to overlook this crucial point. For instance, Rainer Forst has argued that the presumption in favor of liberty should be resisted because "there is a standing

64 I. Berlin 1969: 122.

duty to justify morally relevant actions".[65] Once some kinds of action have been identified as morally relevant, one may be under a duty of justification even if one does not interfere, or propose to interfere, with others' freedom. The same line of reasoning applies to legal interference, that is to say, to coercive proposals that might be eventually turned into collectively binding and legally enforced norms.[66]

As Gaus notes, however, liberals do not deny that one may have to justify their liberty. If Bea has provided Andy with some convincing arguments for a law *L* regulating ϕ-ing, he must indeed justify why he should not be subjected to *L*. Gaus thus agrees with Forst that one may have "a case to answer" if one's liberty is identified as "morally relevant".[67] The point, though, is that in any such case the normative priority of liberty is simply relocated to an upper level. To say that Andy has a legal duty to ϕ is simply to say that Bea has already justified to Andy a law requiring ϕ-ing. And this, in turn, presupposes that the presumption in favor of liberty has already been rebutted. Hence, it is always up to the would-be coercer to kick off the justificatory process by providing reasons in support of her claims. To put the point somewhat more elegantly, the presumption in favor of liberty holds that

(I) Unless a law *L* regulating ϕ-ing is publicly justified, Andy should be free to ϕ.

Nonetheless, (I) is distinct from, and by no means entails:

(II) Andy is never committed to publicly justifying his claim that *L* is illegitimate.

And that is because it might be the case that

(III) Bea has provided Andy with a good reason for accepting *L*.

If condition (III) obtains, the presumption in favor of liberty is rebutted. As a result, the justificatory burden is now on Andy, who is not justified in rejecting L

65 R. Forst 2005: 240n.

66 The move from the level of actions to the level of laws regulating actions is not immediate, as there is some significant logical space between these two levels. One difficulty here is that Forst presses on the justification of "morally relevant actions" while at the political level the presumption in favor of liberty only applies to coercive laws, and not to coercive actions. But I set aside this point until chapter 3, §3.6.2.

67 G. Gaus 2005: 275.

until he comes up with a stronger rebutting case against *L*.[68] Again, though, this does not undermine the presumption in favor of liberty, for in the order of justification liberty constitutes the original baseline. Justificatory liberals always start from this default position. They assume that liberty is the moral status quo and seek to verify how and to what extend deviations from the default are publicly justifiable.

These remarks help us better understand the rationale behind the two normative elements of the Principle of Political Liberty. First, that principle holds that "Liberty should be the norm"; second, it claims that "Coercion [though not only coercion] stands in need of justification". The first phrase refers to the default position or justificatory status quo. Liberty should be the norm in the sense that Andy should be considered free to ϕ until an adequate justification for a law preventing him from ϕ-ing has been publicly justified. The second phrase restates the idea that coercion calls for justification but allows that Andy may have to justify his liberty to ϕ for the reason stated above. Both phrases are necessary to articulate the political ideal of freedom underlying the doctrine of public reason. The first phrase is necessary because it reminds us that liberty is the status quo; it thus instructs us to prefer liberty to coercion *a priori* in the absence of an adequate justification, just as a judge should acquit defendants who have not be proven guilty beyond a reasonable doubt. The second phrase is necessary because it reminds us that not only coercion stands in need of justification: once the deviation from the status quo has been justified, the justificatory burden is on those who wish to remain free.

1.2.3 The site of public reason

The Principle of Political Liberty has important implications concerning the site of public reason, where by "site of public reason" I mean the kinds of legislation that must undergo the scrutiny of public justification.[69] Now it follows from the Principle of Political Liberty that the site of public reason should comprise any form of coercive legislation. *L*'s being coercive is a sufficient condition for *L* to stand in need of justification. Surprisingly, though, many justificatory liberals

68 I shall take up this crucial point in chapter 3, §3.6.

69 I talk about "site" instead of "scope" because I already used the latter term to refer to the *national* (as opposed to global) scope of public reason. The conception of public reason I defend is national in scope in the sense that it is only concerned with laws that claim validity within a national state. Now the question must be raised as to whether public reason should address every coercive law binding on a given polity (in which case its site will be *broad*) or only a subset of such laws (in which case its site will be *narrow*).

believe that this is too strong. Specifically, John Rawls (1993), Thomas Scanlon (2003), Peter de Marneffe (1990) and Brian Barry (1995b) claim that the site of public reason ought to be restricted to fundamental issues of justice and basic rights, which means that much normal legislation should be left exempt from the requirements of public justification.

Let us call this the "narrow view" of public reason: coercive laws must be publicly justified unless they regulate non-essential political matters. According to Rawls, such non-essential matters include: "[M]uch tax legislation and many laws regulating property; statutes protecting the environment and controlling pollution; establishing national parks and preserving wilderness areas and animal and plant species; and laying aside funds for museums and the arts".[70] So apparently a piece of coercive legislation that increases tax rates may be legitimately imposed upon tax-payers without an adequate justification.[71] If we accept the Principle of Political Liberty, we must reject this view. As Gaus points out, "[F]ree and equal persons have a right not to be forced or coerced to do things, and so the claim that there were some acts of coercion that simply do not need to be justified must be wrong".[72]

To be sure, defenders of the narrow view do not deny that non-essential matters require some sort of justification. Rather, they claim that laws regulating these issues should be "indirectly" or "derivatively" justified, so to speak. As Scanlon says:

> The basic structure of a society—to which constitutional essentials and questions of basic justice apply…requires a special kind of justification. This is a structure that affects citizens' lives and opportunities in a fundamental way and does so not only without their consent but without their being able to have much influence in the matter. By contrast, in a just political order, while citizens do not consent to every piece of legislation…they do have a fair opportunity to make their opinions heard and affect the outcome through speaking and voting, and through their representatives. If these institutions have the right sort of justification, then this justification also supports legislation enacted through the procedures they define.[73]

It not entirely clear what Scanlon means when he says that the justification of an institutionalized procedure of adjudication indirectly "supports legislation" which is not in itself directly justified, but, essentially, the basic idea seems to be

70 J. Rawls 1993: 214. For a similar view see B. Barry 1995b: 144-45, T. Scanlon 2003 and P. de Marneffe 1990.

71 For other examples related to the narrow view see J. Quong 2011: 275-79.

72 G. Gaus 2011b: 491.

73 T. Scanlon 2003: 163.

this: while constitutional essentials and questions of basic justice must adhere to public reason, minor issues can be settled through democratic procedures; and once a democratic procedure operating in accordance with constitutional essentials has been publicly justified, all its enactments are "derivatively justified". Now surely publicly justified institutions pass on some sort of legitimacy to the laws they enact or contribute to enacting, but it is not immediately clear why such laws should be seen as publicly justified. Yet according to the Principle of Political Liberty coercion must be publicly justified. Therefore, a "derivative" justification is acceptable only if it qualifies as a proper public justification. Let us call this the "Derivative Justification Thesis":

Derivative Justification Thesis: If a) democratic procedure *P* is publicly justified and b) *L* is a result of *P*, then c) *L* is (derivatively) publicly justified.

Unfortunately, the Derivative Justification Thesis is of little help to defenders of the narrow view. If it is true, then the narrow view loses its meaning, for practically all legislation (including legislation concerning non-essential issues) would be publicly justified. If it is false, then the narrow view should be resisted because it conflicts with the Principle of Political Liberty.

1.2.4 Rejecting the Derivative Justification Thesis

However, the Derivative Justification Thesis points to a crucial question: to what extent (if any) can democracy contribute to public justification? The Derivative Justification Thesis provides an extremely strong answer: a publicly justified democracy always justifies all. Suppose a publicly justified procedure *P* allows the majority of voters to impose *L* upon the minority – say via a referendum. Taken literally, the Derivative Justification Thesis implies that *L* would be justified *to all*, including the minority who voted against it. This view rehearses Rousseau's famous claim that "[w]hen a law is proposed in the assembly of the People, what is asked of them is not precisely whether they approve the proposition or reject it, but whether or not it conforms to the general will which is their own… When the opinion contrary to mine prevails, that only proves that I was mistaken".[74] On Rousseau's views, once the general will is revealed it is to be taken as infallible in the strong epistemic sense that if one finds oneself in disa-

74 J. J. Rousseau 1987: IV,2.

greement with it, one must regard oneself as mistaken, and hence change one's beliefs.

This is certainly implausible. The fact that the majority thinks that he is mistaken in – say – opposing the death penalty seems barely a reason for Andy to believe that his deeply held views about human life are flawed. Still, some have insisted that if we could somehow show that Condorcet's jury theorem is applicable to democratic voting procedures, then the Derivative Justification Thesis would indeed be right. As is well known, the key idea behind that theorem is that if each member of a jury is more likely to be right than wrong, then the majority of the jury will also be more likely to be right than wrong. The crucial point is that the probability that the outcome will be correct is an increasing function of the size of the jury. Hence in an electorate of – say – 100.000 citizens, the probability of getting the right outcome skyrockets to over 99%. The shocking upshot is that if Condorcet's jury theorem were applicable to an actual electorate of citizens, democracy would become the voice of God: it would be virtually infallible.[75]

Anyway, we need not worry too much about this devastating conclusion, since the jury theorem has little to do with actual democracy as we know it. In fact, the jury theorem does not work unless each of the following conditions is met. First, (1) voters must be independent and refrain from interfering with each other. Second, (2) people must vote sincerely for what they deem correct, thus avoiding sheer strategic behavior. Third, (3) the choice must be strictly bivalent, in the sense that voters have to choose between no more than two alternatives. Finally, (4) the epistemic competence of the group of voters (the probability of being right across the group) must be above 0.5. Now all these conditions seem hardly applicable to actual democratic procedures;[76] however, it is enough to show that just one of them is unattainable to dismantle the whole architecture of the jury theorem in actual democracies.[77] But if the applicability of Condorcet's jury theorem is put in doubt, then the Derivative Justification Thesis is not warranted.[78]

75 For some receptions of Condorcet's jury theorem see R. Martin 1993, chapters 6 and 7, S. Hurley 1989, D. Black, 1958: 162-165 and L. A. Kornhauser / L. Sager, 1986.

76 For an exhaustive overview of the criticisms raised against claims (1) to (4) see S. Besson / J. L. Martì 2006, chapter 2.

77 Interestingly, the jury theorem is implacable if conditions (1) to (3) are met while (4) is not: in any such case, the probability of getting the right answer plunges to almost zero.

78 It is important to stress that "weak" epistemic conceptions of democracy such as David Estlund's, Joshua Cohen's and Carlos Nino's cannot warrant the Derivative Justification Thesis. Essentially, these weaker views hold that democratic deliberative procedures have more epistemic value than the other non-democratic alternatives, in the sense that democratic majorities are more likely to be right *in general*. But while this can be an argument in favor of democracy, it does not show that voters will *always* "get it right". Rather, the

This is not to deny, of course, that democracy is a fundamental device of adjudication, since public reason may be unable to provide determinate answers to all the questions it addresses. Thus, in the event that "first-order neutrality" (adherence to what public reason justifies) is for some reason impossible or unable to yield determinate results, a publicly justified outcome is still possible thanks to the "second-order neutrality" guaranteed by a fair democratic procedure of adjudication.[79] However, that the task of public reason is to narrow down the list of options from which democratic majorities can choose. As we will see below, voters committed to the ideal of public reason can support permissible proposals over which reasonable people disagree, but they have a strong commitment not to vote for defeated or publicly unjustified proposals. To be sure, public reason does not constrain – let alone "take over" – democracy. It only provides informal and non-enforceable guidelines about how citizens and public officials ought to use their political power. As Rawls says, "that public reason should be so understood and honored is not, of course, a matter of law".[80] Rather, all citizens are under a non-enforceable moral "duty of civility" to adhere to the norms of public reason when debating and voting on relevant political matters.[81]

1.2.5 The principle of public justification

I take it for granted that as justificatory liberals we should endorse the Principle of Political Liberty I have been canvassing so far, as well as its implications concerning the site of public reason. However, that principle is not enough. In fact, once we have established what stands in need of justification, we also need to determine what makes a law publicly justified. We need therefore to turn to our

idea is simply that democracy is preferable to other procedures of adjudication because, over a run of cases, it will yield a higher percentage of correct answers. On this weaker view, though, voters can and will often fail to make the right decision. But if this is the case, then the Derivative Justification Thesis is false because there is no assurance that a publicly justified democratic procedure necessarily justifies coercive laws in a "derivative" fashion.

79 I borrow the distinction from first and second-order neutrality from B. Barry 1995b: 143-145. Here I take "neutrality" to be synonymous with "fairness" or "justificatory impartiality". If a *L* is justified in a neutral fashion, it is justified (i.e., fair) to all.

80 J. Rawls 1993: 213.

81 Ibid. 217. Talk of a "duty civility" seems to presuppose a correspondent "right to justification" in R. Forst's sense, as opposed to a looser moral "commitment" to justification in Habermas's and Gaus's sense (see note 62 above). As I said, however, I want to remain neutral on this point. I thus take it that citizens may be simply morally committed to justifying their demands in public political debate, while they might not be, strictly speaking, under a duty to do so.

second fundamental question: *What is public justification?* In a way, this shift in perspective involves moving from negative to positive liberty, for the question must be now raised as to how Andy's being deprived of part of his negative liberty is consistent with his status of free and equal citizen. To avoid terminological confusion, however, from now on I shall use the term "liberty" or "freedom" only to refer to negative freedom, unless otherwise specified.

So what is public justification? I would conjecture that the following principle offers a fairly robust answer to this question:

Principle of Public Justification: Coercive law *L* is publicly justified if, and only if, every reasonable citizen, taking all good reasons into account, would endorse *L*.

This principle seems promising because it puts together many leading theses that are typically associated with the ideal of public reason. The first is that public reason requires generality: in order to be justified, *L* must present itself as a law which could gain the assent of all those subjected to it. The second idea is that generality does not mean universality: the addressees of public justification are the members of a given society, for the laws and rules of social cooperation are binding only on them. For this reason, the Principle of Public Justification holds that coercive laws must be justified to the citizens subjected to it, and not to humanity at large. The rationale of these two first views is, of course, implicit in the Principle of Political Liberty. Since coercion stands in need of justification, we must focus on the addressees of coercive laws.

Furthermore, the Principle of Public Justification implies that justified laws need not gain the assent of unreasonable people. Here I rely on the classical "Rawlsian" account of the reasonable, according to which reasonable citizens have two features. First, they accept the fact of reasonable pluralism, thus acknowledging that the free use of reason often produces disagreement. Second, they are willing to propose and abide by fair terms of cooperation, provide others are as well. Moreover, the Principle of Public Justification stresses that in assessing the legitimacy of the laws they are subjected to, citizens must draw on "good reasons". As I stressed in the introduction (§I.b), this requirement is crucial to the project of public justification. Unless we can draw a clear line between good and bad reasons, the whole enterprise of public reason falls apart.

Note that to say that citizens must "take good reasons into account" is to conceive of citizens as decent reasoners, who thus do not fall short of some requisite standards of epistemic rationality. Of course, the Principle of Public Justification does not set these standards, which can be more or less demanding. But in the end, this is a virtue of the Principle of Public Justification, which, being part of the general Concept of Public Reason, needs to be robust across different conceptions of epistemic rationality. The Principle of Public Justification simply reminds us that deliberation cannot lead to justified results if deliberators commit (gross) errors of reasoning. Of course, the same is true of the "good reasons" clause. All we know from the Principle of Public Justification is that citizens should rely on good reasons, but this is a formal requirement to which only a specific conception of public reason can give substance.

1.3. Consensus and convergence

1.3.1 The concept of public justification and its conceptions

In sum, both the Principle of Political Liberty and the Principle of Public Justification seem plausible. While the former restates the fundamental presumption in favor of liberty, the latter places some important formal constraints on the way in which citizens should deliberate. Unless Andy is reasonable and willing/able to take all good reasons into account, then *L* may be justified to him despite his belief that *L* is unjustified, and vice versa. At this point, we can formulate the Concept of Public Reason as a combination of the Principle of Political Liberty (A) and the Principle of Public Justification (B):

Concept of Public Reason: (A) Liberty should be the norm; coercion stands in need of justification. (B) Coercive law *L* is publicly justified if, and only if, every reasonable citizen, taking all good reasons into account, would endorse *L*.

Having clarified the Concept of Public Reason, we can define consensus and convergence models of public reason as two competing conceptions of it:

Consensus View of Public Reason (hereafter: "consensus"): (A) Liberty should be the norm; coercion stands in need of justification. (B) Coercive law *L* is publicly justified if, and only if, every reasonable citizen, taking all good reasons into account, would endorse *L*. (C) Only shareable/public reasons are good reasons.

Convergence View of Public Reason (hereafter: "convergence"): (A) Liberty should be the norm; coercion stands in need of justification. (B) Coercive law *L* is publicly justified if, and only if, every reasonable citizen, taking all good reasons into account, would endorse *L*. (C) Both shareable/public and non-shareable/private reasons are good reasons.[82]

On my definition, then, consensus and convergence are in every respect identical but they give two different interpretations of the "good reasons" clause. Clause (C) of the Consensus View of Public Reason expresses what I shall call the *Shareability Requirement*: a consideration that speaks for or against a given law qualifies as a good reason if, and only if, it is shareable; as a result, only public/shareable reasons can be drawn upon in public reasoning. Convergence, by contrast, rejects the Shareability Requirement, as clause (C) of the Convergence View of Public Reason holds that even private/non-shareable reasons are good reasons. Therefore, convergence permits citizens to accept or reject a given law for different private reasons.

1.3.2 Strong and weak consensus

Before proceeding, I want to consider two interpretations of the standard consensus view, which Jonathan Quong has termed "strong" and "weak consensus". Quong has introduced the distinction between weak and strong consensus to respond to James Bohman's and John Dryzek's critique of Rawls's doctrine of public reason. For Bohman and Dryzek, Rawls's conception of public reason is overly restrictive, in a way that risks shrinking the multifaceted "plurality" of real political discourse. In Bohman's view, Rawls presupposes a "singular" account of public reason, which "represents itself as a single norm of public deliberation; in light of this norm, agents come to agree upon some decision for the same publicly accessible reasons".[83] Dryzek concurs: Rawlsian public reason is "singular" because it assumes that "all individuals will reason in the same way".[84] For both Bohman and Dryzek, however, this oversimplified account of political discourse downplays the inherently plural character of democratic deliberation. We should instead embrace what Bohman dubs "plural public reason", where "a single norm of reasonableness is not presupposed in deliberation;

82 On the Convergence View of Public Reason all private reasons are good reasons in the sense that Andy can always judge coercive laws by his non-shareable evaluative standards. This does not mean, of course, that he can foist such standards on Bea, who is in fact equally entitled to rely on hers.

83 J. Bohman 1997: 80.

84 J. Dreyzek 2000: 15.

thus, agents can come to agreement with one another for *different* publicly accessible reasons".[85]

Quong has argued that this criticism is off-target because Rawls's doctrine of public reason does not require citizens to rely on the very same reasons. In fact, Rawls says that

> public reason does not ask us to accept the very same principles of justice, but rather to conduct our fundamental discussions in terms of what we regard as a political conception. We should sincerely think that our view of the matter is based on political values everyone can reasonably be expected to endorse...A vote can be held on a fundamental political question as on any other; and if the question is debated by appeal to political values, and citizens vote their sincere opinion, the ideal [of public reason] is sustained.[86]

According to Quong, this passage proves that that Rawls endorses a "weak" (as opposed to "strong") consensus model, which in his view is not vulnerable to Bohman's and Dryzek's objection. On Quong's definition,

> a *strong consensus* model insists that each person must accept a decision for the very same reasons. A *weak consensus* model merely requires that the reasons each person has for accepting a decision be public or shared reasons (i.e. acceptable to others as sound reasons), but different people may embrace a decision for different public reasons."[87]

Since we have assumed that eligible conceptions of public reason must present themselves as interpretations of the general Concept of Public Reason, "weak" and "strong" must be defined thus:
Strong Consensus View of Public Reason (in short: strong consensus): (A) Liberty should be the norm; coercion stands in need of justification. (B) Coercive law *L* is publicly justified if, and only if, every reasonable citizen, taking all good reasons into account, would endorse *L*. (C) Only public reasons are good reasons; citizens must rely on the very same reasons.

Weak Consensus View of Public Reason (in short: weak consensus): (A) Liberty should be the norm; coercion stands in need of justification. (B) Coercive law *L* is publicly justified if, and only if, every reasonable citizen, taking all good reasons into account, would endorse *L*. (C) Only public reasons are good reasons, though citizens may hold different public reasons.

85 J. Bohman 1997: 83.
86 J. Rawls 1993: 241.
87 J. Quong 2011: 246.

To see more closely what sets apart weak consensus from strong consensus, suppose Andy and Bea have two reasons to accept a given occupational policy *P*. The first reason (*R1*) is that *P* will enhance women's equality; the second reason is that *P* will have significant economic benefits for the worse off in general (*R2*). Now Andy and Bea "have" these two reasons in the sense that they both *share* them. They believe that both *R1* and *R2* are two sound considerations supporting *P*. Suppose, however, that Andy and Bea disagree on their relative degrees of strength. Andy thinks that the beneficial economic impact of *P* is much more relevant than its effect on women's equality. Bea, by contrast, thinks that the value of women's equality far outweighs the pragmatic advantages for the worse off connected with that policy. Now in a way, it seems correct to say that in this case Andy and Bea would actually accept *P* by appealing to two *different* reasons. When asked why in his view *P* is publicly justified, Andy would probably confine himself to saying that it is imperative to implement economically beneficial policies, without even mentioning *R1*. On the other hand, Bea would presumably put this consideration aside and focus instead on the importance of occupational policies that are beneficial to women.

Still, *weak consensus* holds that as long as *R1* and *R2* support the same policy, this would be publicly justified. According to weak consensus citizens must agree on the basis of public reasons, but they need not agree for the *very same public reasons*. On the other hand, *strong consensus* would require citizens to appeal to the very same shareable reasons, whose relative degrees of strength should be themselves agreed upon. Drawing on a similar example, Quong has argued that strong consensus is unduly restrictive, in that it requires citizens to rank different sound public reasons in exactly the same way:

> There seems nothing obviously problematic, for example, in a case where one citizen supports a law prohibiting prayer in public schools on the grounds that allowing it would be a violation of an individual's freedom of religious expression, while another citizen reaches the same conclusion by claiming such a law will effectively violate the state's commitment to establish fair equality of opportunity for all citizens, religious and non-religious alike.[88]

Quong thus concurs with Bohman that public reason must be "plural", as citizens might agree for different "publicly accessible reasons". Indeed, this will be the case more often than not. As Peter Niesen notes, laws and policies are often supported by different "sufficient" (*hinreichende*) reasons, and there is no need to

88 Ibid.

insist that all citizens must order those reasons in the same way.[89] However, weak consensus does limit the plurality of reasons in two important senses. First, and most obviously, it admits only of a plurality of shareable reasons. Consider again the example of a publicly justifiable occupational policy *P*. Although Andy may think that *R2* is the only decisive consideration supporting *P*, he must *share* *R1*, just as Bea must share *R2*. Second, weak consensus allows citizens to rank shareable reasons differently only if these reasons do not conflict with each other.

This second condition is crucial. Weak consensus does not correspond to the view that as long as I advocate shareable reasons, I can order and balance them according to my own evaluative standards. On a consensus view, *all* relevant justificatory reasons (including "strength-affecting" or reason-weighing reasons)[90] ought to be shared, at least in principle. Suppose Andy and Bea discover that, contrary to their earlier assumption, *P* would in fact have a bad economic impact on the worse off, although it would remain beneficial to women. *R2* would now become a shareable reason against *P*, while *R1* would still speak in favor of that policy. Now even under weak consensus, Andy could not be permitted to reject *P* by appealing to his private reasons. Consensus, be it weak or strong, demands that we refrain from advocating our personal views in public justification. Unlike strong consensus, however, weak consensus applies this requirement only to cases in which our personal views tip the balance of publicly relevant reasons. But this cannot be the case if the only public reasons available conclusively support the same law or policy. In any such case, weak consensus allows citizens to judge the strength of non-conflicting reasons according to their own private standards.

I think Quong is right that even if we accepted the Shareability Requirement in general, it would be exceedingly difficult to ascertain a compelling rationale for the strong consensus view. In any event, we need not amend the general formulation of consensus we gave in section §1.3.1, because those who hold the standard Consensus View of Public Reason are not committed to strong consensus. The Consensus View of Public Reason simply holds that citizens should not advocate non-shareable reasons, but of course in many cases (though perhaps not always) there will be no such things as shareable strength-affecting reasons. If Andy and Bea share two reasons *R1* and *R2* for endorsing *P*, but disagree on their relative degrees of strength, the set of public reasons comes down to *R1* and

89 P. Niesen 2002: 49.

90 I borrow the term "strength-affecting reason" from Joseph Raz (1975: 25), although I use it in a slightly different sense. A strength-affecting (or reason-weighing) reason for *R*, on my account, is a reason to believe that *R* is stronger than other reasons conflicting with *R*.

R2. They can only appeal to those reasons on the standard consensus view. If they do, they will conclude that *P* is publicly justified.

The Consensus View of Public Reason, then, is consistent with weak consensus and does not require strong consensus, as it holds that strength-affecting reasons need not be shareable if the reasons they refer to justify the same policy or proposal.[91]

1.3.3 Private and public reasons

Having clarified that "consensus" stands for "weak consensus" rather than for "strong consensus", we can come back to the consensus/convergence dichotomy. To make sense of this dichotomy we need a clear definition of private and public reasons. Apparently, the difference between private and public reasons is easy to grasp: while the latter can be *shared* by all reasonable citizens, the latter are reasonably affirmed by some citizens in the light of their systems of values and beliefs while they are reasonably rejected by others. More formally:

Justificatory View of Shareability: If *R* is a reason for law *L*, *R* is a public/shareable reasons if, and only if, every reasonable citizen would be justified in believing that *R* is a reason justifying *L*.

I call this the Justificatory View of Shareability because it stresses that public reasons must be *justificatory*; it stresses, that is, that public reasons are supposed to justify viz. warrant rational belief in the legitimacy of the law(s) for which they are reasons. Justificatory reasons are often contrasted with explanatory reasons. While the former justify a given rule or course of action by presenting it as legitimate (i.e., morally permissible or even required), the latter simply explain how certain moral and legal rules came about. To give a common example, there are lots of reasons explaining why slavery was legal in the United States, but very few reasons justifying slavery as a legitimate practice. Public reasons are justificatory (as opposed to merely explanatory) because they are not simply meant to explain why laws are enacted or implemented, but first and foremost to justify them to their addressees.

91 None of this vindicates weak consensus against strong consensus. My point is simply that advocates of the Consensus View of Public Reason are not committed to the latter. For this reason, their position need not be vulnerable to the objections that might be leveled against strong consensus.

Notice that the Justificatory View of Shareability is robust across different substantive conceptions of "shareable" reasons. Rawlsians typically equate "shareable reasons" with "political values" that can be affirmed independently of "private" "comprehensive doctrines"; others assume that private reasons reflect "particular interests", as opposed to "common" or "generalizable" interests; others seem to imply that public reasons reflect some "objective" or "true" facts of the world, which exert their normative force upon every rational agents, and are shareable for that reason. I shall come back to some these substantive conceptions of shareability below (§1.6.2), but for the time being it is sufficient to stress that the Justificatory View of Shareability is appealing because it does not commit us to any such substantive conception. It simply holds that if *R* is a shareable reason for *L*, Andy's belief that *R* is not a reason justifying *L* is not justified. Conversely, Andy's being justified in believing that *R* does not justify *L* is a sufficient condition for regarding *R* as non-public.

1.3.4 Three levels of publicness

If we accept the Justificatory View of Shareability, then we can safely assume that the Consensus View of Public Reason is broad and robust enough to encompass the views defended by most theorists of public reason. These include, among many others, Stephen Macedo (2000; 2010; 2011), Charles Larmore (2003), Rainer Forst (2001; 2002; 2012), Thomas Scanlon (2003), Joshua Cohen (1997a), Micah Schwartzman (2011), Jonathan Quong (2011), Samuel Freeman (2007), Jürgen Habermas (1996; 1998) and, to a certain extent, John Rawls.[92] Of course, some theorists of public reason might prefer a slightly different definition of consensus, but essentially the Consensus View of Public Reason systematizes the fundamental assumption which many find uncontroversial: to reason publicly simply *is* to reason in shareable or public terms. Indeed, this assumption is so widespread that some are puzzled by convergence models. Aren't we talking about *public* reason? How can the *private* use of reason be a path toward the achievement of *public* justification?[93] However, this sort of objection confuses

92 I discuss Rawls's complex view in §1.4.2 below.

93 This seems the line of reasoning behind Samuel Freeman's claim that public reason "implies" shared reasoning: "A narrow way to construe this phrase –"justifiable to all for reasons they can accept" – is that it means we can justify laws with one argument for the Catholics, different arguments for Protestants and for Jews, and then other arguments directed to nonbelievers, and so on. But the idea of public reason implies that all should be able to accept the constitution and laws for the same reasons" (S. Freeman 2003: 39).

three different levels at which "publicness" applies.[94] Firstly, publicness can be a property of reason understood as the faculty or ability of a healthy mind to think and make judgments. Secondly, the term "public" can be used with reference to reasons understood as considerations that count in favor of a belief or action. Now I take it that the link between shareability and publicness I have been suggesting so far applies to both levels:

Publicness as a Property of the Use of Reason: Andy uses the faculty of reason publicly if, and only if, he draws shareable conclusions from shareable premises using shareable rules of inference.

Publicness as a Property of Reasons: *R* is a public reason for *L* if, and only if, *R* is a shareable reason for *L*.

Obviously, convergence does not require publicness in these two senses. However, and thirdly, publicness may also be a property of reasoning understood as a commitment to justify coercion *to the public*. Here the focus is neither on the publicness of use of reason nor on the publicness of the reasons one invokes, but rather on the scope of justification:

Publicness as a Property of the Commitment to Justify Coercion to All: Andy's reasoning justifying coercive law *L* is public if, and only if, Andy's reasoning justifies *L* to all his fellow citizens.

Convergence conceptions only require Publicness as a Property of the Commitment to Justify Coercion to All. To say that justification must be public is thus tantamount to saying that it must be universal in scope, at least with respect to a given polity, in that it cannot fail to justify the law to *some* reasonable citizens. Indeed, this is *the* fundamental requirement on which justificatory liberals typically insist. Publicness as a Property of the Commitment to Justify Coercion to All can be achieved under convergence, for Andy may argue that although different citizens have diverse private reasons for endorsing *L*, they *all* have reason for endorsing *L*. Of course, one can legitimately hold both Publicness as a Property of the Use of Reason and Publicness as a Property of Reasons, but there is no necessary connection between the fundamental commitment to publicly justify coercion to all and the Consensus View of Public Reason. In principle, then,

94 "Publicness" should not be confused with "publicity". While the former is a property of reason(s) and reasoning, the latter is a property of laws that are object of common knowledge. See chapter 3, §3.4.

convergence is entirely consistent with the ideal of public reason.

But there is more. In fact, convergence is not only a plausible interpretation of the general Concept of Public Reason; it is a prima facie more plausible than the standard consensus view, for two reasons. First (§1.4), convergence takes account of the full range of citizens' reasons, while consensus expunges from public reasoning a number of reasons which citizens might deem relevant. As a result, consensus models might yield collectively binding results that are not "fully" or "conclusively justified" to all members of the public. Second (§1.5), the Shareability Requirement underpinning the Consensus View of Public Reason looks paradoxical and self-defeating, as it demands that private reasons should not be taken into account, although these are in fact necessary to determine what counts a shareable reason in the first place.[95]

1.4. Conclusiveness as a requirement of public reason

1.4.1 The role of religious reasons

According to Gaus and Jeffrey Stout, convergence gives pride of pride of place to the liberal ideals of toleration and freedom of expression, ideals that consensus conceptions are willy-nilly committed to downplaying. Because they restrict the set of permissible reasons, consensus conceptions inevitably discriminate against some reasonable individuals, in that they ask them to refrain from employing their private reasons in public political advocacy.

This requirement of restraint has struck most faith-friendly critics of public reason liberalism as overkill. Political theorists such as Nicholas Wolterstorff, Philip Quinn, Paul Weithman, Michael Perry and Kent Greenawalt have argued that because public reason liberals impose restrictions on political reasoning that reasonable citizens of faith must regard as unacceptable, public reason fails to respect them as free and equal members of the public. Their complaints hinge upon the view that religious beliefs are so deeply held by those of faith that no switch-over of religiously rooted political convictions onto religiously neutral beliefs is possible. As Wolterstorff puts it, "it belongs to the religious convictions of a good many religious people in our society that they ought to base their decisions concerning fundamental issues of justice on their religious convictions. They do

95 Recall that by "Shareability Requirement" I mean clause (C) of the Consensus View of Public Reason, according to which only shareable/public reasons are good reasons. Given this clause, only shareable/public reasons can be drawn upon in public reasoning (see § 1.3.1 above).

not view it as an option whether or not to do it".[96] In a similar vein, Greenawalt argues that religious beliefs cannot be "disentangled" from one's overall belief system,[97] while Weithman claims that religious citizens cannot be expected to perceive any "pull" from reasons that are not embedded in their deepest religious commitments.[98] Similarly, Michael Perry complains that to "bracket" one's deeply held religious beliefs and values is tantamount to "[annihilating] essential aspects of one's very self".[99] Not only do many religious traditions inform the private conduct of their adherents; they also provide their adherents with encompassing conceptions of justice that they are to use to shape their world. Yet, for all this, public reason requires citizens of faith to put aside their religious conceptions. It requires them, as it were, to check their religious baggage upon entering the public forum. The heart of the so-called "integrity objection" is that in being asked to conduct their political activity in accordance with public reason, religious citizens are being asked to deny or repress a constitutive part of themselves. They are being asked to split themselves into public and private halves. They are being asked, in other words, to alienate or surrender their personal integrity.[100]

Stephen Macedo claims that the "integrity objection" smacks of childish whining: "[C]itizens owe each other reasons that they can share...If some people...feel 'silenced' or 'marginalized' by the fact that some of us believe that it is wrong to seek to shape basic liberties on the basis of religious or metaphysical claims, I can only say 'grow up!".[101] However, many consensus theorists are much more sensitive than Macedo to the objectionably exclusionary character of the Shareability Requirement. Among advocates of consensus, Habermas is perhaps the one who has been most concerned with this problem. Habermas has been at pains to emphasize that the Shareability Requirement need not and should not be regarded as hostile to religious contributions as such, for two main reasons. First, although some tend to equate shareable reasons with secular reasons,[102] public reason should be rather described as neutral among religious and secular doctrines.[103] A consensus-seeking conception of public justification is

96 N. Wolterstorff 1997: 105.
97 K. Greenawalt 1988: 155.
98 P. Weithman 2002: 157.
99 M. Perry 1988: 181-2. See also K. Greenawalt 1995, P. Weithman 1997 and 2002, M. Perry 1991, P. Quinn 1997.
100 The "integrity objection" clearly echoes Michael Sandel's famous criticism of the "unencumbered self" (M. Sandel 1982). For a general overview of various forms in which the "integrity objection" has appeared see P. Neal 2009.
101 S. Macedo 2000: 35.
102 Cfr., for instance, R. Audi 2000.
103 See in particular J. Habermas 2008.

post-religious rather than anti-religious,[104] in that it endeavors to develop a politically viable model of discursive rationality that remains neutral towards science and religion: no tradition (either religious or not) is left out; each tradition must be prepared for public criticism.

Practically speaking, this means that controversial doctrines can be part of public reason only if they are "translated" into public arguments. Specifically, Habermas claims that "all enforceable political decisions *must be formulated* in a language that is equally accessible to all citizens", and "it *must be possible to justify them* in this language as well".[105] Citizens of faith must thus endeavor to present the *content* of their views in terms that secular citizens can accept, while the latter "must open their minds to the possible *truth content* of those presentations".[106] For Habermas, then, citizens may find good reasons to endorse laws which transcend their cultural background only if they are not constrained to eliminate their cultural ethnic-religious roots, but rather advised to translate the dogmatic substances of their doctrines into a language which is equally accessible to all citizens, while secular citizens must get rid of their dogmatic secularism.

Many vivid examples lend plausibility to this interpretation of the "translation proviso". Martin Luther King, Nelson Mandela and Desmond Tutu explicitly appealed to controversial religious doctrines in order to expose injustice. They attacked apartheid systems on explicitly Christian terms in innumerable public places. Their Christian commitments directly shaped their role as influential political leaders driven by the aim of healing profound social rifts. Now the crucial point is that their Christian views were not only intelligible to all, but also translatable into *public* reasons. Anti-apartheid leaders urged to restore public faith in civil justice within a deeply unjust society, and they did so by appealing to compelling shareable reasons, despite the fact that these reasons originally stemmed from religious viewpoints.

In his later works, Rawls himself came to embrace this "translation proviso", which is normally referred to as the "inclusive" or "wide" view of public reason. In *Political Liberalism*, Rawls stated that "the point of the ideal of public reason is that citizens are to conduct their fundamental discussion within a framework … based on values that the others can be reasonably expected to endorse".[107] So formulated, the doctrine of public reason does not clearly prohibit reasoning from both public and non-public reasons, provided the latter (can be reasonably

104 See L. Ceppa 2008: 63-79.
105 J. Habermas 2008a: 126.
106 Ibid.: 132, emphasis added.
107 J. Rawls 1993: 226.

taken to) support or even vicariously replace the former. In his revised account, Rawls has dispelled this ambiguity by endorsing a "wide" or "inclusive" consensus conception.[108] Citizens and public officials may appeal to non-public reasons, "provided that in due course proper political reasons … are presented to support whatever the comprehensive doctrines introduced are said to support".[109]

It is nonetheless obvious that, given reasonable pluralism, the overwhelming majority of private doctrines will fail to pass the threshold of public translatability suggested by Habermas and Rawls, in the sense that they will hardly be able to translate their full contents into public terms. As a result, consensus theorists will end up denying citizens (especially those of faith) permission to appeal to considerations that they deem relevant.[110] For convergence theorists, this is a serious problem:

> For the liberal it must be truly worrying that those with strong religious commitments have become strident critics of public reason liberalism. A foundational liberal principle has

108 J. Rawls 1997: 590-91.

109 Ibid. Many, however, side with Macedo in insisting that "inclusive views" of this kind are too permissive. They are adamant that religious reasons should be expunged from the public square. As Stanley Fish says, "religious propositions must either be excluded from the marketplace or admitted only in ceremonial forms" (S. Fish 1996: 22). Paolo Flores D'Arcais also defends an exclusive view, which explicitly challenges Habermas's "translation proviso". See P. Flores D'Arcais (2007; 2008), as well as Habermas's reply (J. Habermas 2008c).

110 To be sure, consensus models may sometimes accept non-shareable "objections of faith" and "objections of conscience" in general. Consider the case of a pacifist who thinks to have powerful ethical reasons not to serve in the army. It is difficult to see how his views could be *translated* in the sense indicated by Rawls and Habermas. The pacifist does not want to be dragged into the army for one reason and one reason only: he thinks that one should never engage in deliberate acts of violence. But many citizens could find such a radically pacifist view not only unacceptable *per se*, but also unrelated to any relevant public value which could be offered "in due course" to sustain the pacifist's objection. Yet this would strike many as overly restrictive. After all, in liberal states exemptions for ethnical and religious minorities are normally granted, at least in some major cases. As Andrew Lister has recently stressed, however, a consensus conception can account for this: "Exemptions for religious minorities are not justified by the religious views themselves, but by the fact that the people in question sincerely hold these views, and therefore take themselves to be under an overriding obligation not to comply with the laws. The reason that justifies the exemption is respect for religious liberty" (A. Lister 2010: 166). Similarly, Joshua Cohen has stressed that a liberal consensus view must pay heed to "deeply held" ethical and religious beliefs (J. Cohen 1998). For consensus theorists, however, this kind of openness toward non-shareable (and non-translatable) beliefs is warranted only in very limited cases of conscience, such as conscription. Convergence theorists make a much stronger claim: religious, ethical and private reasons in general should play a role in the very justification of the legislative apparatus governing a liberal society.

> been religious freedom; liberalism has taken religious commitment seriously, and has insisted on the importance of people being able to live according to their avowed religious doctrines. But today those with religious commitments are apt to see themselves as critics of liberalism.[111]

Unlike consensus, convergence takes these worries seriously, in that it places few restrictions on the use of religious reasons in public justification. Convergence thus promotes public reason liberalism's foundational political values by expressing greater respect for reasonable pluralism and protecting individual liberty.[112] This seems to create a strong presumption on its behalf.

But for Gaus, the exclusion of religious doctrines is only part of the problem, for two main reasons. First, consensus does not exclude only religious reasons because, as Habermas rightly stresses, not all secular reasons are shareable. Under consensus, *all* private reasons are downgraded to "bad reasons". As a result, a large number of secular and religious objections to laws backed by public reasons would be silenced. Second, and more important, Gaus does not simply claim that convergence is better able than consensus to do justice to liberalism's foundational values such as respect for reasonable pluralism. Rather, he contends that consensus undercuts the very idea of justification, as under consensus citizens are required to abstract from their private evaluative standards (i.e., from reasons and normative considerations that others cannot share), while it is precisely on the basis of those standards that they judge whether or not the law is justified.

The problem, in other words, is essentially *epistemic*. Since under consensus proponents of coercive legislation can dismiss potentially significant objections to their proposals, consensus models run the danger of upholding proposals that some citizens have reason to regard as unjustified to them. But insofar as it allows for defeated (or potentially defeasible) coercive laws being imposed upon the public, consensus undermines the very ideal of public reason. The fundamental aim of public reason is to redeem the coercive character of political authority (Habermas would say: its sheer "facticity") by showing that citizens have reason to abide by its demands. But a theory of public reason cannot perform this fundamental task if it simply "assumes away" a priori some potentially decisive objections to coercion. Gaus's critique is best understood, I think, in the light of Rawls's puzzling doctrine of the overlapping consensus.

111 G. Gaus 2009: 20. For a similar criticism see J. Stout 2004, chapter 3.

112 Consensus prevents citizens from "appealing" to private reasons in the sense that under consensus private reasons cannot be used as grounds for public justification, although consensus models may allow for private objections in cases of conscience (see note 110 above).

1.4.2 Rawls on the overlapping consensus

In Rawls's view, we honor public reason when we judge political issues from a public perspective, embracing a common point of view for settling the terms of our political life. Specifically, Rawls argues that "the nature and contents" of public reason are public in the sense that they are "expressed in public reasoning by a family of reasonable conceptions of political justice reasonably though to satisfy the criterion of reciprocity".[113] Reciprocity is the willingness to cooperate with others on terms all persons can accept. To be more specific, "the criterion of reciprocity requires that when those terms are proposed as the most reasonable terms of fair cooperation, those proposing them must also think it at least reasonable for others to accept them ...".[114] The upshot of this criterion is the liberal principle of legitimacy, according to which "our exercise of political power is proper only when we sincerely believe that the reasons we would offer for our political actions are sufficient [...] and we also reasonably think that other citizens might also reasonably accept those reasons".[115]

Rawls thus thinks that when we justify our proposals to others, we must endeavor to put forward reasons that we sincerely believe are good reasons both *for us* and *for our interlocutors*. In other words, public reasons must, in order to be public, be shareable by all. More generally, Rawls stresses that since "justification is addressed to others who disagree with us", it must always "proceed from some consensus, from premises we and others publicly recognize as true".[116] In this passage, Rawls's appeal to the notion of "truth" is somewhat misleading, but his essential claim is clear enough. What Rawls says is that public reasoning should be conducted within the domain of shareable political values elaborated from resources available in the public political culture, whose affirmation builds on the common ground among reasonable comprehensive doctrines. For Rawls, however, although "a political conception of justice" must "provide a shared public basis for the justification of political and social institutions", it must also be able to gain "the support of an overlapping consensus, that is, a consensus in which it is affirmed by opposing religious, philosophical and moral doctrines...".[117] The enterprise of a political conception of justice is not exhausted by the search for a *public* common ground for adjudicating controversies arising in the public sphere. Rather, it must take account of diverse *private* views stem-

113 J. Rawls 1997: 575.
114 Ibid.: 578.
115 Ibid.
116 J. Rawls 1985: 394.
117 J. Rawls 1987: 421.

ming from controversial "religious, philosophical and moral doctrines", which should be able to affirm that political conception *from their own* points of view. Famously, the justification of the political conception of justice (of which Justice as Fairness is only an example, though Rawls's favorite one) should unfold in two steps:

> Justice as fairness is best presented in two stages. In the first stage it is worked out as a freestanding political (but of course moral) conception for the basic structure of society. Only with this done and its content—its principles of justice and ideals—provisionally on hand do we take up, in the second stage, the problem of whether justice as fairness is sufficiently stable. Unless it is so, it is not a satisfactory political conception of justice and it must be in some way revised.[118]

These two stages presuppose two contrasting forms of reasoning supporting the political principles of a just and stable liberal democracy. The first form draws on public reasons and presents our political principles as those we can all endorse in the light of the political values we can share. The second form of reasoning shows that the political conception can be supported by an "overlapping consensus" of diverse and incompatible doctrines about religious, metaphysical and other philosophical truths. The first form of justification shows that we can endorse the liberal conception of justice for the same reasons. The second describes a process of arriving at the political conception for different, and probably incompatible, reasons.

On Rawls's view, then, *shareable or public reasons* can be fully justificatory only if they turn out to be in some way consistent with diverse *non-shareable reasons* that different reasonable citizens may happen to endorse under reasonable pluralism. More specifically, Rawls's thesis is that private reasons can be set aside only at the *first* stage of political justification, which he dubs "pro tanto justification". At this stage, the political values specified by a shared conception of justice "are suitably ordered, or balanced, so that those values alone give a reasonable answer by public reason to all or nearly all questions concerning constitutionals essentials and basic justice".[119] However, "since political justification is *pro tanto*, it may be overridden by citizen's comprehensive doctrines once

118 J. Rawls 1993: 140-41. Rawls in this passage seems to imply that the overlapping consensus is needed for the sake of "stability", and not in order to achieve "full justification". As we will see below (§1.4.3), some Rawlsians insist on this interpretation, arguing that as far as justification (as opposed to "stability for the right reasons") is concerned, public reasoning should stop at the first stage.

119 J. Rawls 1995: 143.

all values are tallied up".[120] Pro tanto justification must therefore be supplemented with a further twofold justificatory stage, which Rawls describes as a combination of "full justification" and "public justification by political society".[121] Public justification thus takes the form of a two-stage procedure, and is successful only "when all the reasonable members of political society carry out a justification of the shared political conception by embedding it in their several reasonable comprehensive views".[122] What Rawls seems to say is that is not sufficient that a reasonable political conception be justified by appealing to reasons all can accept. Rather, those public reasons must be backed by, or at least turn out not to conflict with, a wide range of reasonable comprehensive doctrines.

Rawls's idea that private reasons can on occasion *override* or *defeat* a publicly shareable argument really looks like a path-breaking departure from the idea that justificatory discourse, qua public, must play out within the boundaries set by a publicly shareable political conception. For Rawls, both consensus and convergence are necessary to make sense of the idea of public justification. Although at a first stage justification must proceed from a pool of sharable public reasons, publicly justified laws must be also supported by *convergent* or *overlapping* reasons. To be sure, pro tanto justification might be employed as a useful heuristic for locating a set of potentially justified principles. Still, given the potential "veto-right" that Rawls's overlapping consensus seems to confer upon comprehensive doctrines, pro tanto justification would end up functioning only as a discovery procedure to uncover convergence points.

1.4.3 Deepening the problem

Now according to Gaus, Rawls's key insight is precisely that while the first justificatory stage is a useful device for identifying "abstract" and "pro tanto" justified principles, it cannot exhaust the process of public justification. For Gaus, shared reasoning is an important justificatory tool, in that it helps identify principles of social cooperation by "abstracting" from citizens' private doctrines. However,

> [u]nless the conclusion of the argument from abstraction can be affirmed in light of a rational and reflective free and equal moral person's full set of evaluative criteria, the abstract justification will be defeated by these other elements of her evaluative set. A theory

120 Ibid.
121 Ibid.: 144.
122 Ibid.

> that is grounded on the importance of evaluative pluralism can bracket some disagreements as a device within the theory to help us see where agreement is possible and progress might be made, but ultimately this agreement only provides Members of the Public with sufficient reasons to endorse a proposed rule if, given all their relevant evaluative standards, it is to be endorsed.[123]

The "argument from abstraction", according to Gaus, serves a fundamental function, as it helps "bracket our disagreements and identify some shared perspective, which provides the grounds for shared reasoning".[124] This is important. As I stressed in the introduction (§II.c), shared reasoning plays a fundamental role, in that it identifies abstract principles that all could potentially embrace. To use Habermas's terminology, shared reasoning is at the core of "moral discourses", in which participants identify which general norms deserve the assent of all.[125] The problem with consensus, however, is that it supposes that public discourse should stop at this general level. Rawls's intuition seems precisely that this view is unduly restrictive: the first consensus stage must be followed by a convergence stage.

Yet Rawlsians typically endorse consensus. They insist that the search for an overlapping consensus should not be understood as a further justificatory stage, in which "pro tanto" justified principles can be "overridden" by citizens' private doctrine: in fact, public justification is already achieved in the first stage, where all shareable reasons are factored in. To be sure, Rawls is adamant that a suitable political conception must indeed "gain an overlapping consensus"[126], which poses an interpretative challenge for consensus-friendly Rawlsians: what, if anything, can explain Rawls's insistence on the second justificatory stage? What is exactly its function? Public reason liberals have come up with a number of different answers, which we can group into four broad categories. The first holds that the overlapping consensus is simply superfluous. Once a political conception has been justified through shared reasoning, public justification has been already achieved. This solution is suggested by both Brian Barry and Mulhall and Swift.[127] The second claims that the overlapping consensus is relevant only for the sake of "stability". Charles Larmore defends a view of this kind.[128] "Stability for the right reasons" is an important value, but on this interpretation the realization of that value is not relevant to the justification of the political conception. A

123 G. Gaus 2011b: 336.
124 Ibid.: 335.
125 See Habermas 1994: 1-18.
126 J. Rawls 1993: 144.
127 B. Barry 1995a; Mulhall/Swift 1996: 240-242.
128 C. Larmore 2003.

third view holds that the overlapping consensus is necessary to justify the shared values on which the first stage relies, rather than the principles of justice it yields. This interpretation is suggested by Jonathan Quong: it is only the conception of the person as free and equal and the "fundamental idea of society as a fair system of social cooperation between free and equal citizens … which should be the subject of the overlapping consensus".[129] Finally, some Rawlsians such as Joshua Cohen and Samuel Freeman argue for a "weak" justificatory function of the overlapping consensus. The idea is that although comprehensive doctrines cannot defeat a conception of justice, failure to achieve an overlapping consensus could provide a reason to make some minor adjustments to the political conception.[130]

Now these interpretations of Rawls's justificatory conception are by no means implausible, since Rawls's own view is notoriously obscure and difficult to ascertain.[131] However, the purpose of this book is not Rawlsian exegesis, so we need not worry too much about the role of the overlapping consensus within Rawls's own conception of public reason. My point is simply that Rawls's doctrine of the overlapping consensus highlights, more or less implicitly, the problem of the dominant consensus view on which Gaus presses:

129 J. Quong 2011: 182.

130 J. Cohen: 273-74. S. Freeman 2007: 350-51.

131 This does not mean that those interpretations are unproblematic, as I argued elsewhere (Zoffoli 2012). Consider the Stability View. On this interpretation of the overlapping consensus, gaining the assent of comprehensive doctrines is important for pragmatic reasons: if it were not backed by an overlapping consensus, the political conception would be less stable because it would not be acceptable to those who demand a comprehensive justification for political conception. The Stability View thus grants that a conception of justice is fair (i.e., justified to all as free and equal moral persons) if and only if it would be endorsed in the "freestanding" stage (it will be recalled from §I,b that a fair principle is nothing but a publicly justified principle). But on Rawls's definition reasonable citizens, qua reasonable, are committed to the (fair) principles of justice identified in the freestanding stage. So won't reasonable citizens, by definition, endorse the conception justified on freestanding grounds? Why "check" with comprehensive doctrines whether they can accept what we already assume is a fair conception? Conversely: doesn't the doctrine of the overlapping consensus risk conferring a veto right upon unreasonable citizens? To be sure, defenders of the Stability View could insist that whether or not a conception of justice is stable depends on whether or not citizens actually endorse it, regardless of whether or not they do so reasonably. But Rawls is adamant that political liberalism is concerned exclusively with reasonable citizens. For this reason, he stresses that "[i]n framing a conception of justice so that it can gain an overlapping consensus, we are not bending it to existing unreason, but to the fact of reasonable pluralism" (J. Rawls 1993: 144). But to accommodate the (unreasonable) demands of those who may refuse to accept a justified (i.e., fair) conception of justice is to bend it to existing unreason. Political liberals must reject the "convergence stage" if its function is to ensure stability by conferring a veto right upon unreasonable citizens.

> [J]ustifying reasons must be conclusive: they must *defeat* other considerations one might have. This conclusiveness requirement is crucial. To see its motivation assume that Alf and Betty are both members of *P*, and Alf proposes law *L*A. Suppose that Alf advances reason *R*1 for Betty to endorse *L*A; although Betty's system of beliefs and values commits her to acknowledging that *R*1 is *a* reason for endorsing *L*A, she also holds that she has reason *R*2 to endorse *L*B over *L*A (where *L*A and *L*B are incompatible alternatives). Suppose that, exercising her reason as a free and equal member of the public, Betty concludes that *R*2 outweighs (or defeats) *R*1, and so she concludes that *L*B is better than *L*A. … [E]xercising her capacities as a free and equal member of the public, Betty concludes that she has more reason to accept *L*B than *L*A. For Alf to *simply* impose *L*A on Betty is inconsistent with treating her as a free and equal member of the public. How could such a law be seen as exemplifying self-legislation by Betty?[132]

In this passage, Gaus and Vallier make an important point, which will play an important role in my argument: they claim that justificatory reasons must be *conclusive*. To hone in on this crucial matter, it is useful to spell out more formally the conclusiveness requirement Gaus and Vallier refer to.

1.4.4 Two kinds of defeaters

For Gaus and Vallier, the conclusiveness requirement demands that justificatory reasons be "undefeated". To illustrate the idea of conclusive justification, then, it necessary to clarify the notion of "defeating reasons" or "defeaters", which has been introduced by J. Pollock and taken up by Gaus.[133] As Pollock and Gaus understand it, a defeater is a reason not to hold a seemingly justified belief. More formally, let us say:

If Andy believes β on account of *R*, *R** is a *defeater* for *R* if, and only if, a) *R** is a reason of Andy's and b) (*R* & *R**) is not a reason for Andy to believe β.

If an argument is defeated, rational belief in its conclusion is no longer warranted. As Pollock argues, however, defeaters can be either *undermining* (or undercutting) or *rebutting* (or overriding). An undercutting defeater undermines the connection between evidence and conclusion, whereas a rebutting defeater only attacks the conclusion by justifying its denial on independent grounds. To illustrate this point, consider a simple example.

132 G. Gaus / K. Vallier 2009: 55.

133 Cf. J. Pollock / J. Cruz 1999: 37-39; G. Gaus 1996: 66-70; G. Gaus 2011b: 245; R. Foley 1987, chapter 1.

Suppose one morning I believe that I woke up one hour earlier than usual. I take this belief of mine to be a reason (call it *R1*) to have a stroll to my office (call this action ϕ), instead of taking the bus as I usually do. As soon as I open my bedroom's window, however, I realize it is raining. The sky is overcast and it looks like the rain will not let up any time soon. I now have a reason (call it *R2*) not to walk, which rebuts my previous reason to walk. Notice that *R2* does not undermine the quality of the evidence on which $R1 \rightarrow \phi$ relies;[134] nor does it point to any logical flaw hidden in the inference from *R1* to ϕ. It is indeed true that I got up earlier than usual. And this is indeed a reason to walk to my office. In other words, $R1 \rightarrow \phi$ remains an epistemically sound inference even after I have discovered that it is raining. The fact that is raining, however, *rebuts* (overrides) my reason to walk by providing me with an independent and stronger reason not to walk.[135] Rebutting defeaters are "stronger" and "overriding" in Joseph Raz's sense: they defeat other reasons by attacking their weight, and not the deliberative route leading to the beliefs for which they are reasons.[136]

An *undermining* defeater, by contrast, would attack the connection between *R1* and ϕ. For instance, I could find out that my clock is not working properly. It thus could turn out that, contrary to my earlier belief, I did not wake up earlier than usual. Alternatively, I could think that, although it is indeed early, I do not feel like walking after all, regardless of the weather. In the first case, $R1 \rightarrow \phi$ would now rest on flawed evidence; in the second case, ϕ would no longer follow from *R1*. In both cases, however, I would end up with a reason to think that there is no sound connection from *R1* to the belief that I should ϕ, for new considerations undermine that very inference. There would not be an independent reason which tips the balance against ϕ despite the fact that ϕ is backed by *R1*.

134 The symbol $\rightarrow$ denotes a justificatory inference and therefore stands for "is a justificatory reason for".

135 By "epistemically sound" inference between I mean a snippet of reasoning which a) starts from reliable premises and b) displays no logical flaws in its overall structure. An epistemically sound inference must not be confused with a sound deductive argument, which proceeds with logical certainty from true premises to true conclusions. An epistemically sound inference need not be sound in this strict sense. In fact, it may well lead to conclusions that a moral agent has, all things considered, reason to deem false, for there might be a more compelling deliberative path justifying the opposite conclusion. In other words, an epistemically sound inference can be rebutted. By contrast, a sound deductive argument cannot be rebutted, since its soundness guarantees the truth of its conclusion, to which the rational agent affirming that argument is committed. In focusing on an epistemic (as opposed to deductive) definition of soundness, I side with informal logicians who take justificatory discourse to rest on "ampliative" arguments, whose conclusions do not follow with deductive certainty, and whose overall strength depends on how well one has taken all the relevant information and possible defeaters into account.

136 J. Raz 1975: 25-28.

Rather, I would lack a reason to ϕ in the first place. Another way of putting the point is that if a reason is *undermined,* it turns out to be merely *prima facie*. Despite its initial plausibility, it was never a sound reason in the first place. By contrast, a *rebutted* reason is a *pro tanto* reason. It is indeed a reason, and yet it is overridden by some stronger considerations. Here I rely on S. Kagan's well-known contrast between "prima facie" and "pro tanto reasons". Unlike a prima facie reason, "a pro tanto reason has genuine weight, but nonetheless may be outweighed by other considerations".[137] By contrast, "a prima facie reason appears to be a reason, but may actually not be a reason at all". [138]

In my examples I have talked about reasons for action, and not about reasons for belief. However, undermined and rebutted reasons for belief essentially share the same features of undermined and rebutted reasons for action. If a reason for belief is undermined, it does not lead to the belief for which it seems (or seemed) to be a reason. If a reason for belief is rebutted, one has reason to hold the opposite belief. More formally, let us thus say that

If Andy believes β on account of R, R^* is an *undermining defeater* for R if, and only if, a) R^* is a defeater for R and b) R^* is a reason for Andy to believe that R does not support β.

By contrast,

If Andy believes β on account of R, R^* is a *rebutting defeater* for R if, and only if, a) R^* is a defeater for R and b) R^* is a reason for Andy to believe $\sim\beta$.

With these definitions in the background, we can better understand which reasons qualify as conclusive. In order to verify whether a given reason R justifying belief β is conclusive, we need to understand whether it defeats (either by means of rebuttal or undercutting) the set of reasons against β:

Conclusive Justification (CJ): Belief β is conclusively justified to Bea if, and only if, the set of reasons Bea has for accepting β defeats the set of reasons she has for rejecting β.

If R defeats any reasons Bea has for not holding β, then β is conclusively justified to her. Conversely, if R is defeated by reasons for not holding β in her belief

137 S. Kagan 1989: 17n. However, "pro tanto" reasons should not be confused with a "pro tanto" justification in Rawls's sense. See §1.5.7 below.

138 Ibid.

system (and these reasons are not themselves defeated), then β is conclusively unjustified to her.

1.4.5 Conclusive justification

According to Kurt Baier, definitions of conclusiveness such as CJ are too weak. He writes: "Suppose I know that a given coin has a strong bias, and this is a reason for thinking it will come up heads more than five times during the next ten throws, *and that there is no other fact that overrules this reason.* Still, it is not conclusive".[139] To get clearer on Baier's critique, consider a similar example. Suppose Andy has some reason to believe that a certain event occurred because a reliable eyewitness told him so (call this belief β). Imagine further that he no reasons to believe otherwise since he was not there. But this does not necessarily entail that he has conclusive reason to hold that belief – all he has is a tiny piece of evidence, which, however reliable, seems far from conclusive. Baier's intuition seems to be that in addition to a relational dimension (*R* must defeat any conflicting reasons), there must be a further independent standard (*R* must be supported by a certain amount of evidence). If *R* falls short of that standard it is not conclusive, even if it defeats all conflicting reasons.

Now Baier is absolutely correct that not every degree of evidence is sufficient to justify a given belief β. On closer inspection, however, CJ is not vulnerable to his objection, since CJ holds that in order to count as a conclusive reason, *R* must overrule *any defeater*, including rules like "Do not to believe β until the evidence supporting it is sufficient". To cover Baier's example, one could take the rule "Do not make judgments of certainty (or non-probabilistic claims) based on probabilistic grounds" as a defeater which overrules the reason for believing that the coin will come up heads more than five times out of ten. In Baier's example and in our example of the eyewitness, then, the problem is that although some tiny pieces of evidence could speak in favor of certain beliefs, they fail to pass a minimal threshold for credible belief. Again, though, the threshold is implicit in CJ, in that it can be cast in the form of a defeating rule: "Do not endorse *P* until the set of reasons supporting it meets the minimal justificatory threshold".

Baier's point is interesting, however, because it suggests introducing a third kind of defeaters, which Pollock and Gaus do not seem to take into account. Consider again the case of the eyewitness. The eyewitness' testimony is defeated according to the definition of defeating reasons we gave above (§1.4.4). Recall

139 K. Baier 1995: 70n.

that if Andy believes β on account of *R*, *R** is a defeater for *R* if, and only if, a) *R** is a reason of Andy's and b) (*R* & *R**) is not a reason for Andy to believe β. This is the case in our example: given the fact that the eyewitness' testimony is too weak, Andy has no reason to believe β (i.e., that the event it reported occurred). Still, the eyewitness' testimony is not undermined. Nor, importantly, should Andy believe that the event reported by the eyewitness did not occur. Rather, he should suspend judgment because he lacks sufficient information to form a considered opinion on that matter. In other words, the "minimal justificatory threshold" acts neither as an undermining defeater (for it does not undercut the inference leading to the belief in question) nor as a rebutting defeater (for it does not justify the opposite belief). Rather, the threshold works as a "suspending defeater", as I shall call it:

If Andy believes β on account of *R*, *R** is a *suspending defeater* for *R* if, and only if, a) *R** is a defeater for *R* and b) *R** is a reason for Andy to suspend judgment on β.

Once we grant that CJ requires taking account not only of rebutting and undermining defeaters, but also of reasons for suspending judgment, we should reject Baier's claim that accounts of conclusive justification such as CJ are too weak, for the reasons stated above. But perhaps one could raise the exact opposite objection, arguing that CJ is too strong. It is too strong, one could object, because the very notion of "conclusive justification" seems synonymous with that of "final" or "irrefutable" justification. It seems, in other words, that in order to be conclusively justified in endorsing β, Andy should be a fully rational Hercules with unlimited cognitive faculties, for he should be able to scrutinize each and every possible consideration that might speak for or against β. The problem with this objection, though, is that it assumes that according to CJ rational agents are expected to have access to all relevant reasons. If, however, we deny this strong requirement, then "*L* is conclusively justified to Andy" will mean something like "taking all realistically accessible reasons into account, Andy should endorse *L*". This account of conclusiveness would fall well short of the extremely demanding ideal of full rationality that the objection bestows on CJ. But I defer this point until chapter 2 (§2.7.2).

1.4.6 The Conclusiveness Thesis

In sum, CJ seems a plausible account of conclusive justification. But should we turn it into a strict *requirement* of public justification? Should we maintain that justificatory reasons *ought to* be conclusive in the sense indicated by CJ? As I see it, there is strong reason to answer in the affirmative. Consider: Bea receives a phone call from Andy, who says: "You should collect me from the airport tomorrow morning because you owe me a favor". Bea is in some way moved by Andy's remark, but she replies: "I know I owe you a favor but I cannot make it to the airport tomorrow morning because I need to take my mother to the hospital". Now imagine Andy agrees that Bea's reasoning is sound, at least from her perspective. He knows that, all things considered, Bea has *more* reason to go to care about her mother than to do him a favor. In other words, he acknowledges that the reason he gave her is defeated (in this case: rebutted) by stronger considerations. But if this is so, then it would be stubborn and disrespectful for Andy to insist that she should indeed pick him up.

We can extend the same line of reasoning to the level of public justification. In order to justify *L* to Bea, Andy cannot simply point out to her that she has some reasons for accepting *L*, as these reasons could be defeated by some more compelling reasons against *L*. Rather, Andy must reasonably substantiate the claim that that her set of reasons in support of *L* defeats, on the balance, her set of reasons against *L*. In other words, Bea must have conclusive reason to believe that *L* is better than no law at all:

Conclusiveness Thesis (CT): Coercive law *L* is justified to Bea only if she has conclusive reason to rank *L* over liberty.

CT is implicit in Gaus's thesis that "Principle/policy P is justified if and only if everyone has reasonable grounds for accepting it over all challenges to it".[140] The qualification "over all challenges to it" is decisive, for it points to the fact that, in order to be justified to Bea, *L* must be supported by a set of reasons which conclusively defeat any objections to *L*.

It is important to stress that according to CT, justificatory reasons must conclusively justify coercion over liberty; they need not conclusively justify some specific coercive law over other coercive proposals. Hence, CT is to be contrasted with the following thesis:

140 G. Gaus 2003: 214.

Radical Conclusiveness Thesis (RCT): Coercive law *L* is justified to Bea if, and only if, she has conclusive reason to rank *L* over any other eligible options.

RCT looks difficult to meet. In fact, the crux of public reason is to select among options that cannot be conclusively defeated, and this appears clearly when it comes to the interpretation of abstract rights and principles.[141] Take, for instance, the right to free speech. In its abstract formulation, that right is certainly publicly justified to all. But this means that although Bea and Andy can share the "concept" of the right to free speech, they will almost certainly disagree on which "conception" better spells out the content of that concept. They will disagree on the meaning of "speech", on the qualification "free", on what is actually encompassed by the right to free speech, on whether or not and to what extent this right admits of exceptions and so on.

In cases of this kind, then, the problem is that while a general principle is conclusively justified, its interpretations are inconclusively justified: they are all permissible, in the sense that none of them is conclusively defeated; however, none of them is conclusively justified over the others. In Gaus's terminology, this is an instance of "nested inconclusiveness". Nested inconclusiveness occurs when four conditions are met. First, there must be a set of "competing interpretations of a more general, victoriously justified, notion" such as a general principle P:[142] "P has been publicly justified" but "is open to interpretations P_1, P_2 and P_3, none of which has been publicly justified".[143] Second, only one member of the set can be chosen. Third, because the options are interpretations of a "victoriously justified notion", rejection of every member is conclusively unjustified. Finally, none of the possible interpretations are justified over the others.

Now if we accept RCT, we seem committed to the view that whenever none of the interpretations of a conclusively justified principle can be conclusively justified over the others, then public reason should suspend judgment, thereby justifying no principle at all. This is certainly implausible. Since in cases of nested inconclusiveness citizens have conclusive reason to rank P over no law at all, they must resort to some democratic procedure of adjudication, which will select some interpretation of it. Perhaps, though, one could still defend RCT by arguing that if the majority of voters chose – say – P_1, then P_1 would be conclusively justified. While prior to taking a vote none of the interpretations of P was conclusively justified, the outcome of a suitably conducted procedure of adjudication

141 For more on this point see A. Williams 2000 and M. Schwartzman 2004.

142 G. Gaus 1996: 158. Here the term "notion" is normatively loaded, so to speak, as it refers to normative concepts.

143 G. Gaus 2003: 216.

conclusively justifies the interpretation favored by the majority – it counts as a reason which conclusively tips the balance in favor of a previously inconclusively unjustified principle. This line of reasoning is problematic, however, because we have rejected the Derivative Justification Thesis (see §1.2.4 above). Consequently, if P_1 wins the day, the minority cannot be expected to regard P_1 as conclusively justified over P_2 and P_3 because there is no guarantee that democratic procedures of adjudication will always yield epistemically justified results. More modestly, the minority should regard P_1 as a reasonable and legitimate principle if a) no alternative to P_1 is conclusively justified over the others, b) P_1 is better than no principle at all and that c) the democratic procedure through which P_1 won the day is reasonably fair. However, none of this entails that P_1 is as such epistemically superior to all other eligible options.

The reason why CT is preferable to RCT is that it does not require that a given coercive law be conclusively justified over other eligible options; it only demands that coercion be conclusively justified over liberty. [144] Consider again the case in which citizens have conclusive reason to rank P over no law but no conclusive reason to accept any specific ranking of its interpretations, P_1, P_2 and P_3. Now if considered together, P_1, P_2 and P_3 are inconclusively justified, in the sense that none is more justified than the others. But we "zoom in", as it were, and consider them in isolation, each of these interpretations is conclusively justified over liberty, for each of them is better than no law at all. Of course, P_1, P_2 and P_3 meet CT to the same extent, so even in this case a democratic procedure of adjudication is needed to settle the issue. CT thus assigns an important role to democracy, but it also sets limits to it. While democracy is necessary to choose among equally permissible principles, voters committed to the ideal of public reason should not support proposals which cannot be conclusively justified over liberty. The task of public reason is to identify an "eligible set" of proposals, which should not comprise coercive laws that some citizens have reason to regard as worse than no law at all.

1.4.7 A first presumption in favor of convergence

With these considerations in the background, we can better understand where the (first) problem with consensus models lies. I started by highlighting a general worry about the Shareability Requirement, namely, that it expunges from the

144 By "coercion" here (and in this book in general) I mean coercive laws (*L1, L2, L3, ... Ln*) which can be understood as interpretations (P1, P2, P3, ... Pn) of a more general principle P.

domain of public reason a number of reasons (especially religious reasons) to which some citizens might assign primary importance (§1.4.1). On one reading, Rawls's doctrine of an "overlapping consensus of reasonable comprehensive doctrines" seems meant to address this fundamental problem: while shared reasoning plays an important role in identifying principles of social cooperation, these are not "fully" justified unless in a second justificatory stage citizens' private reasons converge in their support (§1.4.2). Still, Rawlsians typically maintain that this reading of Rawls is mistaken; they insist that the "overlapping consensus" should play no role in justifying principle of social cooperation (§1.4.3). If we do away with the second stage suggested by Rawls, however, our conception of public justification will incur a decisive problem. In fact, reasons justifying coercion should be conclusive (§1.4.6), which means that they should not be defeated (§1.4.3 – 1.4.5). Yet as the example suggested by Gaus and Vallier indicates, shareable reasons may be defeated by private reasons. Consensus models, however, fail to take private defeaters into account, insisting that once all public reasons have been factored in, public justification has been achieved. But if this is so, then consensus is open to the charge of falling foul of CT. As a result, it may fail to exclude from the optimal set of proposals potentially defeated coercive laws, thereby undermining the very ideal of public reason. By contrast, convergence models insist that public justification cannot be achieved until *all* relevant reasons (both public and private) have been taken into account. Unlike consensus, convergence does not risk violating the fundamental conclusiveness requirement expressed by CT. This seems to establish a strong presumption in favor of convergence.

1.5 Can consensus models consistently exclude private reasons?

1.5.1 The Freestandingness Thesis

Thus far, I have argued that convergence is prima facie preferable to consensus because the latter may not live up to public reason's conclusiveness requirement. This, however, is only part of the problem. To see why, we need to come back to our definition of public reasons. According to the Justificatory View of Shareability (§1.3.3), *R* is a public/shareable reasons for endorsing law *L* if, and only if, every reasonable citizen would be justified in believing that *R* is a reason justifying *L*. Now justificatory liberals typically couple this formal definition with another view of shareability, which I shall call the Freestandingness Thesis (hereafter: FT). Essentially, FT holds that public reasons are "freestanding" considerations that can be identified in isolation from private reasons, to wit, by bracketing citizens' comprehensive doctrines. To give a formal definition of FT, let *U* be the full set of considerations arrived at by abstracting from citizens' comprehensive doctrines and Ω be the correct procedure of abstraction. We then obtain:

Freestandingness Thesis (FT): A reason is public/shareable if, and only if, it is freestanding. *R* is a freestanding reason for endorsing law *L* if, and only if, a) Ω (if carried out properly) leads to *U* and b) $R \rightarrow L$ is part of *U*.

Now in principle the Justificatory View of Shareability and FT are fully compatible. The former gives a formal definition of what public reasons are, while the latter explains how public reasons can be identified. If we affirm FT, we will claim that Ω (if carried out properly) leads to a set of freestanding reasons which all citizens are justified in regarding as justificatory. As the Justificatory View of Shareability states, these reasons will be shareable or public.

However, affirming the Justificatory View of Shareability does not entail endorsing FT. One could hold the former and yet deny that reasons identified via abstraction are necessarily shareable in the sense expressed by the Justificatory View of Shareability. In this section, I want to make exactly this claim: FT should be resisted because *U* may not comprise reasons which all are committed to sharing. Essentially, the problem with FT is that in order to consistently claim that *R* is a public reason, one must show that *R* is not defeated by private reasons. If some reasonable citizen has private defeaters for *R*, I shall argue, *R* is not a public reason, even if *R* is arrived at through Ω. Being part of *U*, then, is not a sufficient reason for being shareable – nor, as we will see, a necessary one. This is a major problem for consensus models. For once FT is rejected, the Shareability Requirement they hinge upon turns out to be paradoxical and self-defeating: to rely on shareable reasons, as the Shareability Requirement demands, already requires bringing private reasons into the picture, for these are necessary to determine what counts as a shareable reason in the first place.

Interestingly, even critics of consensus such as Gaus, K. Vallier and J. Stout accept FT. What these critics claim is not that freestanding reasons are not shareable, but rather that private reasons should be taken into account in a separate justificatory stage, whereby the strength of the "freestanding" argument is assessed in the light of citizens' comprehensive doctrines. The convergence stage is thus necessary to ensure that public justification meet the conclusiveness requirement: freestanding reasons are shareable but they may not be conclusive because they may be defeated. In this section I argue that in addition to being open to this charge, consensus models incur a second, deeper problem: freestanding reasons are not necessarily shareable because those who have private defeaters for those reasons are not justified in (let alone committed to) sharing them.

1.5.2 Procedures of abstraction

Before turning to my substantive critique of FT, some preliminary remarks about Ω are in order. Although both consensus and convergence theorists typically affirm FT, they give different interpretations of Ω. In this section, and in this book in general, I shall be concerned mainly with three such interpretations, namely Rawls's 1), Gaus's 2) and Habermas's 3).

On Rawls's view, Ω is a stand in for the mechanism of abstraction of the "original position", presented as a "political" device of representation. The "original position" is constructed out of some core "political" ideas latent in liberal societies, namely freedom, equality, fairness, and society as a fair system of social cooperation. Political ideas of this kind, for Rawls, are to be contrasted with philosophical, moral and religious views affirmed by citizens in the light of their "comprehensive" doctrines. Generally speaking, on the Rawlsian account comprehensive doctrines have three core features. First, they are unrestricted in scope, as they can provide their adherents with any sort of "philosophical", "moral" and "religious" reasons for action and beliefs.[145] Second, comprehensive doctrines must be internally articulated in a consistent manner, at least "loosely" so.[146] Finally, and most obviously, a comprehensive doctrine is never affirmed by all reasonable citizens in a liberal society. By contrast, a "political conception" is "freestanding" with respect from comprehensive doctrines, in the sense that is worked out independently of any such doctrine and thus "expounded apart from … any wider background".[147]

2) In defining Ω, instead, Gaus starts from the assumption that citizens hold different belief systems. Gaus's notion of "belief system" is very close to the Rawlsian definition of comprehensive doctrines we gave above. In particular, belief systems as Gaus defines them are characterized by the second feature displayed by comprehensive doctrines, namely internal consistency. To determine whether or not a given belief β is part of Andy's belief system, one needs to verify to what extent β is consistent with his present set of reasons and beliefs.[148] But despite the close similarity between the Rawlsian idea of "comprehensive doctrines" and Gaus's notion of "belief systems", Gaus does not understand Ω as a procedure for isolating "political" reasons from "comprehensive doctrines", for three reasons. First, Gaus is critical of Rawls's sharp distinction between "com-

145 J. Rawls 1993: 13.
146 Ibid.
147 Ibid.: 12.
148 See chapter 2, §2.4.1 – 2.4.2.

prehensive doctrines" and "political conception(s)", which he deems elusive.[149] In his view, freestanding reasons are shareable but they need not be, strictly speaking, political in Rawls's sense; for instance, they may draw on "comprehensive" philosophical or moral notions and yet be abstract enough to be part of *U*. Second, the very structure of Ω is modeled after the fundamental "comprehensive" notion of "agency", which he borrows from S. Benn. According to Benn and Gaus, an agent is somebody who acts in accordance with his thoughts and convictions and sees his actions as results of his own decisions.[150] While Rawls wishes to remain neutral on moral and philosophically bulky ideas and commitments of this kind, Gaus implies that the idea of agency lies at the heart of Ω, in the sense that it would lead to moral principles that fully protect citizens' status as "agents". Finally, on Gaus's view Ω cannot lead to purely political results because Ω (and public reason in general) presupposes an epistemic account of justified beliefs, while Rawls insists that epistemology is a controversial branch of philosophy, on which a "political" conception should remain silent.[151]

3) According to Habermas's discourse-theory, instead, *U* would comprise only reasons that can gain the assent of all participants in justificatory discourses. For Habermas, the main function of reasons is to support validity claims raised in communicative contexts. Validity claims such as "*N* is right" or "*p* is true" are *universal*, in a twofold sense. First, since they are raised in almost any speech situation, they are universal formal features of communication as such. Second, and more importantly, they do not claim validity for the speaker as such. Nor do they aspire to be valid for some specific group of speakers. Rather, they claim *universal validity*. With her utterance the speaker transcends the specific communicative context in which the utterance is made, in that she claims, at least implicitly, that each and every possible speaker should recognize that – say – *N* is right.

Essentially, then, Ω should be understood as a discursive procedure. Specifically, Ω teases out reasons that reflect, and can be unanimously affirmed from, a universalistic standpoint. As a general rule, this means that *U* will essentially comprise *moral* or "reciprocally and generally" endorsable considerations,[152] which express "generalizable interests" in a Kantian fashion.[153] Freestanding reasons are therefore mainly moral reasons arrived at through a discourse-theoretical Kantian version of Ω. Moral reasons must not be confused with *ethi-*

149 See G. Gaus 2003: 177-204.

150 See S. Benn 1988: 87-90 and G. Gaus 2011b: 337-41. Gaus specifies that the idea of "agency" is weaker and less demanding than that of "personal autonomy" (Ibid.).

151 See chapter 3, §3.3.

152 R. Forst 2002.

153 J. Habermas 1990.

cal reasons. While for Habermas moral reasons are shareable because they are affirmed from an impartial, universalistic viewpoint, ethical reasons reflect controversial conceptions of the "good life", over which citizens of liberal democracies disagree. Thus, the function of Ω is to work out a set of freestanding, moral considerations which all could affirm if they embraced a universalistic moral perspective detached from their particular ethical backgrounds.[154] Although Habermas's conception differs in many respects from Gaus's,[155] it shares something close to Gaus's threefold critique of Rawls's "political" stance. First, Habermas is skeptical about Rawls's attempt to draw a clear line between comprehensive doctrines and political conception(s). Second, as Rawls himself stresses, Habermas's conception rests on the comprehensive controversial assumption that the obsolete notion of metaphysical truth should be replaced with that of discursively sanctioned validity.[156] Finally, Habermas's discourse theory presupposes an epistemic account of justified belief, which ties epistemic justifiability of validity claims to their discursive acceptability.[157] For both Gaus and Habermas, then, Ω is not a purely "political" device and does not aim to yield purely "political" results.

This overview is important, especially because in this book I shall deal extensively with the three conceptions I have sketched.[158] Furthermore, this overview enables me to make a general point of clarification: while the terms "comprehensive doctrine", "belief system" and "ethical conception" are not identical, they basically contain things of the same kind, namely, "private" or "non-shareable" conceptions of the good, values and commitments. Although Rawls, Gaus and Habermas defend different procedures of abstraction, they start from similar views of what should count as a "private" doctrine. As a general rule, therefore, I shall use the terms "comprehensive doctrine", "belief system" and "ethical conception" interchangeably. Bear in mind, moreover, that I intend to defend a two-step justificatory procedure: at a first stage, shared reasoning identifies potential-

154 However Habermas is explicit that at the political level moral argumentation always plays out against a background of rights and duties justified through the application of the principle of discourse to the domain of legal rights (J. Habermas 1996, chapter 3). Rainer Forst, instead, argues that moral arguments should play a much more direct role in the very justification of political principles (R. Forst 2012, chapter I.4). More on this point in chapter 2, §2.5.2.

155 See chapter 2, §2.5 – 2.6.

156 J. Rawls 1995. However, Habermas has a slightly different take on this point in his later works. See chapter 2, §2.5.2.

157 See chapter 2, §2.5.1 – 2.5.3.

158 In the following chapter I shall also consider a fourth and much more radical substantive conception of shareability, according to which shareable reasons reflect true facts about the world. See chapter 2, §2.3 – 2.4.

ly justified principles of social cooperation; at a second stage, these principles need to gain an "overlapping consensus" of private doctrines. Now Rawls, Gaus, and Habermas suggest three different ways in which this second stage might be put into practice. On Rawls's view, this second stage searches for an "overlapping consensus" supporting a pro tanto justified political conception. On Gaus's view, private "evaluative standards" need to converge in support of the outcome of abstract principles protecting agency. [159] A discourse-theoretical convergence conception (which Habermas explicitly rejects arguing for a consensus view) would instead claim that moral reasons need to be backed by, and embedded into, ethical considerations. Finally, it is crucial to my ongoing argument to stress that Rawls, Gaus and Habermas endorse FT. Although they give different interpretations of Ω (and consequently, of what should count as a freestanding reason), they agree that freestanding reasons are shareable, as FT states. As we are about to see, however, there is no necessary link between freestandingness and shareability.

1.5.3 Undermined freestanding reasons are not shareable

To see where the problem with FT lies, let us imagine a constituency of public reason whose members agree that $R \rightarrow L$ is part of *U*. The members of our constituency need not endorse the same version of Ω; nor do they need to agree on the substantive contours of *U*. They do agree, however, that if they bracketed their private doctrines, they would believe that *R* justifies *L*. For simplicity, imagine that our constituency is limited to two members, Andy and Bea. Suppose that according to Bea, $R \rightarrow L$ is powerful enough to establish an all-things-considered case for *L*. Andy, instead, protests that *R* is defeated within his comprehensive doctrine. Consider a first way in which he could make this sort of claim:

Case A) Andy affirms a utilitarian doctrine which instructs him to accept collectively binding laws if and only if these are likely to increase average utility. However, *R* says nothing about whether or not *L* will increase average utility. As a result, he has a private reason R^* to believe that there is no connection from *R* to the conclusion that *L* is justified.

Note that, by stipulation, Andy does not deny that $R \rightarrow L$ can be arrived at through

159 G. Gaus 2011b: 276-91.

Ω, which he deems an acceptable mechanism of abstraction. In criticizing *R*→*L*, then, Andy reasons from the perspective of "you and me", as Rawls would say: [160] Andy takes the conclusion of the procedure of abstraction as given but claims that they do not cohere with his utilitarian convictions, to which he assigns paramount importance. Now in case A), *R** defeats *R*, since in Andy's view (*R* & *R**) is not a reason to endorse *L*. Specifically, *R** acts an *undermining defeater* against *R*, which, it will be recalled, shows that there is no sound inference from *R* to the belief for which it purports to be a reason. Given his comprehensive doctrine, Andy maintains that the belief "*L* is better than no law at all" is synonymous with "*L* would bring about more units of utility than no law at all". But because *R* says nothing about the impact of *L* on average utility, Andy is committed to the view that *R* cannot warrant any sensible conclusion about the legitimacy of coercive laws. In other words, *R** undermines the very inference form *R* to *L* by discarding the implicit premise "Legitimate laws need not be grounded in the principle of average utility", on which *R*→*L* relies, as false. Notice, though, that Andy need not reject *L* altogether. In fact, it might be that

Case B) Andy accepts *L* despite his belief that *R** undermines *R*, because he thinks *L* is likely to increase average utility.

What Andy claims both in case A) and in case B), however, is that *R* is definitely not the kind of reason that justifies *L* to him because *R* is undermined.

Now defenders of FT are committed to the view that in cases A) and B) *R* is shared by Andy. Although *R* is undermined from his perspective, *R*→*L* is part of *U*. And according to FT, this is a necessary and sufficient condition for *R* to be a public reason, which all, including Andy, are committed to sharing. But this seems clearly false. Once it has been defeated by *R**, *R* is no longer a reason at all from Andy's perspective. It is difficult to see how one could consistently believe that *R* is undermined and still regard it as a reason, since undermined reasons simply fail to provide grounds for holding the beliefs they support. Recall that undermined reasons are merely prima facie reason in S. Kagan's sense: they appear to be reason, but on closer inspection they turn out to be no reasons at all. Recall the example we gave above (§1.4.4): I discover that my alarm clock is not working properly, and this discovery undermines my previous belief that I have time to walk to my office. Surely it would be odd to say that I still have reason to walk, despite the fact that that reason is undermined. It seems in fact natural to assume that because it rests on an assumption which I now know is false, my

160 J. Rawls 1993: 28.

previous reason to walk is no longer a reason at all in my view. Importantly, undermined reasons are not merely "bad reasons". Rather, they are not reasons at all because the conclusions they purport to justify simply do not follow from their premises.

In sum, FT seems false when it comes to freestanding reasons that are subject to private undermining defeaters. In cases A) and B), *R* is not shareable despite the fact that it is part of *U*, because *R* is not a reason of Andy's. I do not mean to deny, of course, that *R* is a reason for Bea despite *R**, as *R** is not part of Bea's belief system. My point is simply that as soon as an undermining defeater for *R* enters Andy's belief system, *R* should no longer be considered a reason of his. Contrary to FT, then, in cases A) and B) *R* turns out to be not a public reason, but a private reason of Bea's.

1.5.4 Rebutted freestanding reasons are not shareable

My argument thus far implies that unless there is an epistemically sound inference from *R* to β in Andy's belief system, *R* cannot be shared by Andy because it is not a reason of his. Some think that *R*'s being an epistemically sound consideration in this sense is not only a necessary condition for *R* to count as a reason, but also a sufficient one. As I see it, Scanlon defends a view of this kind when he argues that on his "minimal" definition a reason is simply a "consideration that counts in favor of something".[161] If we interpret the phrase "*R* counts in favor of belief β" as being synonymous with "there is an epistemically sound inference from *R* to β", then Scanlon endorses the following definition of reasons for belief:

Minimal View of Reasons: If Andy believes β on account of *R*, *R* is a reason of Andy's if, and only if, there is no reason *R** such that a) *R** is a reason of Andy's and b) *R** undermines *R*.

Now if the Minimal View of Reasons is correct, then FT is false with respect to undermined freestanding reasons but (apparently) true with respect to rebutted freestanding reasons. In other words, it seems that according to the Minimal View of Reasons *R* would still be shared by Andy in the following case:

Case C) Andy affirms a religious comprehensive doctrine. He thinks that *R* ex-

161 T. Scanlon 1998: 17.

presses an important value, and that this value constitutes a things-being-equal reason for *L*. However, he also thinks that *L* is inconsistent with his religious views about social justice. This is an overriding reason *R** for Andy to reject *L*.

While in cases A) and B) Andy denies that there is a sound inference from *R* to *L*, in case C) he grants that *R* supports *L* and yet claims that he has a stronger independent reason to endorse ~*L*. In other words, in case C) *R** rebuts or overrides *R*. Now defenders of the Minimal View of Reasons might claim that in case C) Andy has a reason *R* to support *L*, since *R* is not undermined by *R**. Thus, in case C) *R** does not deprive *R* of the epistemic property of shareability despite the fact that the former defeats the latter. There are, however, two problems with this view. First, 1) the Minimal View of Reasons is questionable. Second, 2) if we look at the matter more closely we will see that even those who affirm the Minimal View of Reasons are not necessarily committed to the view that in case C) *R* is shareable. Let me begin with the first problem.

1) As Benn points out, reasons must be understood as "commitments", in that they exert normative force on rational agents by "committing" them to endorsing the beliefs for which they are reasons.[162] But of course, nothing in case C) commits Andy to believing that *L* is legitimate. In fact, Andy ought to hold the exact opposite belief. And this is so because Andy should know that *R* points to a conclusion which he has reason to deem false. This is important. Reasons for belief are standardly truth-centered, in the sense that they aim to justify true beliefs. But this means that if *R* supports a belief I have reason to deem false, then I cannot consistently regard *R* as a reason of mine, because I know that *R* fails to do what reasons for belief are supposed to do, namely, justify (or commit to holding) true beliefs.

This is not to deny, of course, that I may have reason to hold false beliefs.[163] The point is rather that *R* cannot be a reason for me to believe β as long as I have a justified belief that β is false. Should physicists discover that some particles travel at a higher speed than light, most of my current beliefs about particle physics would prove false. Still, as long as I justifiably (though perhaps mistakenly) believe that nothing is faster than light, no consideration purporting to rebut this belief of mine can figure as a proper reason in my belief system. By the same token, in case C) Andy should not merely assign greater weight to *R** that to *R*. Rather, he should discard the latter as a truth-averse consideration, which, as such, cannot count as a reason for him.

162 S. Benn 1988: 22-42. For a similar view see K. Baier 1975: 57-86.
163 See chapter 2, §2.3.

Perhaps one might retort that my argument does not show that rebutted reasons are not reasons, but only that they are "bad reasons": insofar as they are not undermined, one could insist, rebutted reasons are still reasons in the sense that they still commit to the beliefs for which they are reasons; however, they are bad reasons in the sense that they are trumped by "better" conflicting commitments. However, this sort of rejoinder is problematic. To see why, recall that we have already admitted that undermined reasons are not reasons at all. We have admitted, that is, that it is more appropriate to label them as "non-reasons", rather than as "bad reasons". According to the objection I have sketched, instead, rebutted reasons raise to the level, as it were, of reasons, though of course of bad ones. However, if rebutted reasons are "bad reasons", they are "bad" in the most pejorative sense: they instruct one to accept what one has reason to reject. Undermined reasons, by contrast, do not necessarily point to beliefs that one has reason to deem false. In case A), *R* is undermined, but this does not mean that *L* is necessarily unjustified to Andy. In fact, as case B) shows, *R*'s being undermined is entirely consistent with Andy's being justified in accepting *L* all things considered. In cases A) and B), *R** shows that *R* is not a reason for *L*, but it does not present itself as a reason for *~L*. In case C), by contrast, *R* speaks in favor of what from Andy's perspective is an admittedly false belief.

Given the truth-oriented character of reasons for belief, rebutted reasons are in an important respect "worse", so to speak, than undermined reasons. But because we already established that undermined reasons are "non-reasons", rather than "bad reasons", it seems that rebutted reasons are not reasons at all, either. All this suggests replacing the Minimal View of Reasons with

Expanded View of Reasons: If Andy believes β on account of *R*, *R* is a reason of Andy's if, and only if, a) Andy has no undermining defeaters for *R** and b) β is, all things considered, the thing Andy ought to believe.

If the Expanded View of Reasons is correct, then FT is false not only with respect to undermined reasons, but also with respect to rebutted ones. In case C), *R* is not shareable despite the fact that it is part of *U*, because *R* is not a reason of Andy's. Of course, even in this case *R* is a reason for Bea despite *R**, as *R** is not part of Bea's belief system. Contrary to FT, however, *R* turns out to be not a public reason, but a private reason of Bea's.

2) Interestingly, however, one can maintain that *R* is not shareable in case C) even if one affirms the Minimal View of Reasons. To see why, remember our original formal definition of shareable reasons, which I called the Justificatory View of Shareability. Above (§1.3.3) I stressed that the Justificatory View of Shareability is concerned with *justificatory reasons*, that is to say, with reasons

justifying belief. It follows that unless Andy thinks *R* is a reason justifying *L*, he does not share it as a reason in the sense indicated by the Justificatory View of Shareability. But of course, in case C) Andy cannot possibly think that, as he knows that *R* fails to justify *L*. True, *R* is not merely an "explanatory" reason, as it does aim to simply explain – say – why *L* may come about or be actually implemented as a matter of contingent fact. Rather, *R* aims at justifying *L*, in the sense that it presents itself as a reason for believing that *L* is legitimate. However, *R* fails to perform this task from Andy's standpoint. Although *R* aspires, as it were, to be justificatory, it is not actually a justificatory reason to Andy because Andy has reason to reject as unjustified the belief for which *R* is a reason. To put it differently, *R* is a things-being-equal justificatory reason. It *would* justify *L* to Andy things being equal, that is, if Andy had no stronger, overriding reason to believe that *L* is in fact unjustified. But as soon as Andy comes to endorse such an overriding reason, *R* ceases to be justificatory from Andy's standpoint because, all things considered, *R* turns out to be unable to justify *L* to him.

In case C), then, *R* is not shareable according to the Justificatory View of Shareability because Andy is not committed to regarding *R* as a reason justifying *L*. However, and this is the interesting bit, denying that *R* is shareable in case C) entails no denial of the Minimal View of Reasons. In fact, although the Minimal View of Reasons holds that considerations that are not undermined are reasons, it does not imply that such reasons are justificatory. Thus, although defenders of the Minimal View of Reasons could insist that in case C) Andy shares *R* as a *reason simpliciter*, they should nonetheless maintain that he does not share *R* as a *justificatory reason*. But because the Justificatory View of Shareability holds that being justificatory is a necessary condition for being a public reason, it follows that in case C) *R* is not public, regardless of whether or not the Minimal View of Reasons is correct. The Justificatory View of Shareability, then, establishes a case for rejecting FT even when it comes to rebutted freestanding reasons. A reason may be part of *U* and yet be private, for it might be subject to other people's private rebutting defeaters, which would downgrade it to a non-justificatory reason.

1.5.5 Suspended freestanding reasons are not shareable

Now consider suspending defeaters (see §1.4.5 above). Recall that if *R** is a defeater that suspends *R*, Andy is committed to suspending judgment on whether or not the belief supported by *R* is justified. To come back to our case, Andy might claim that the freestanding reason *R* for *L* is suspended by some private reason of his:

Case D) Andy affirms a utilitarian doctrine, according to which collectively binding laws can be justified on non-utilitarian grounds, provided they do not reduce average utility, not even by few units. However, Andy does not have enough evidence to ascertain whether *L* will live up to this sort of expectation. Andy has therefore a private reason *R** to suspend judgment on the legitimacy of *L*.[164]

Our twofold argument about the non-shareability of rebutted reasons can be smoothly extended to case D). If we affirm the Expanded View of Reasons, we will say that *R* is not a reason in the first place, since *R* does not commit Andy to endorsing the belief for which it purports to be a reason. As a result, *R* cannot possibly be viewed as a reason Andy can share. If we affirm the Minimal View of Reason, instead, we will maintain that *R* is indeed shared by Andy as a reason, since it is not undermined by *R**. Still, it cannot be a shareable reason in the sense indicated by the fundamental Justificatory View of Shareability, since *R* is not a justificatory reason. Either way, suspended freestanding reasons are not shareable, for the same reason why rebutted freestanding reasons are not shareable.

1.5.6 Weak Shareability Requirement?

At this point, we have strong reason to think that FT is false. The fact that *R* is part of *U* is not a sufficient condition for *R* to be a shareable reason because if *R* is defeated by *R** in Andy's belief system, Andy will reasonably claim that *R* is not a (justificatory) reason of his. It seems, then, that FT should be replaced with

Weak Freestandingness Thesis (WFT): *R* is a public reason for endorsing law *L* if, and only if, a) *R* is freestanding in the sense described by FT and b) *R* is not defeated by private reasons.

164 An interesting question is whether *L* could be legitimately imposed upon Andy in this case. It might seem that it could, for Andy views *L* and ~*L* as equally justified. Given the presumption in favor of liberty, however, we should resist this conclusion. Remember that the presumption in favor of liberty is analogous to the presumption of innocence within trial law (§1.2.1): in case of uncertainty, the theorist of public reason should favor liberty over coercion, just as a judge should acquit defendants who have not be prove guilty beyond a reasonable doubt (*in dubio pro reo*). Thus, unless all citizens happen to be willing to endorse laws backed by suspended reasons, the theorist of public reason must assume that suspended reasons fail to publicly justify coercion.

On the face of it, WFT is not implausible. Given the depth of reasonable pluralism, it may be useful to first bracket disagreement by means of (some) abstraction procedure and then verify whether the reasons comprised by (our version of) *U* can be shared by all members of the public in the light of their comprehensive doctrines. However, being part of *U* (however we may define it) does not seem, strictly speaking, a necessary condition for being a public reason. Suppose we get rid of any abstraction procedure and focus from the outset on comprehensive doctrines. Suppose we find out that all such doctrines endorse a given set of laws for the same reason *R*. In this case we would conclude, without any reference to Ω or *U*, that *R* is a shareable reason. It follows that WFT should be amended to

Undefeated Public Reasons Thesis (UPRT): *R* is a public reason for endorsing law *L* if, and only if, *R* is a reason on the Expanded View of Reasons (or a reason that all reasonable citizens could regard as justificatory in the sense indicated by the Justificatory View of Shareability).

UPRT is shorn of any reference to Ω and *U*. All UPRT requires is that *R* be an undefeated justificatory reason. But if FT is replaced with UPRT, then consensus models seem untenable. It is impossible to delineate a justificatory procedure that draws exclusively on public or shareable reasons, as the Shareability Requirement demands, for the simple fact that it is impossible to determine whether or not *R* is public or shareable until all potential private defeaters for *R* have been factored in. It seems, then, that only convergence is a tenable conception of public reason. But this is not quite right. In fact, one could insist the following conception could withstand our criticism while retaining some sort of shareability requirement:

Negative Convergence View of Public Reason (in short: negative convergence): (A) Liberty should be the norm; coercion stands in need of justification. (B) Coercive law *L* is publicly justified if, and only if, every reasonable citizen, taking all good reasons into account, would endorse *L*. (C) Public reasons are good reasons. Private reasons are good reasons unless they justify coercion.

On this alternative view there must be, as it were, a "negative" convergence on *L*, in the sense that citizens can legitimately reject *L* if they have strong *private objections* to *L*. This view allows for significant room for private reason, as it holds coercive laws must always be consistent with (though not necessarily backed by) citizens' private doctrines and beliefs. Still, clause (C) of the Negative Convergence View of Public Reason does express a shareability requirement, though this is weaker that the one affirmed by the Consensus View of Public Reason. In fact, the standard Shareability Requirement of consensus models applies both to reasons for *accepting* coercion and to reasons for *rejecting* it. Thus consensus holds that private reasons can neither defeat nor justify coercion, while convergence rejects the Shareability Requirement altogether, allowing private reasons to act both as defeaters of coercion and as reasons justifying coercion. Negative convergence, instead, rests on a weaker, asymmetrical Shareability Requirement, which rules out as bad reasons only private reasons justifying coercion, but not private reasons against coercion.

Now apparently, such a Weak Shareability Requirement would not be vulnerable to the criticism I have put forward in this section. In fact, this requirement does not deny that private reasons should be accounted for as potential defeaters. However, it claims that private reasons can never be used as grounds for accepting coercive laws. In other words, the weaker Shareability Requirement may concede that taking account of private defeaters is necessary to determine which reasons are public, but it denies that coercive laws can be justified by an "overlapping consensus" of private doctrines.[165]

Yet on closer inspection even the weaker Shareability Requirement is untenable. To see why, consider the following development of case D), in which *R* is suspended (see §1.5.5 above):

Case E) Andy affirms a utilitarian doctrine, according to which collectively binding laws can be justified on non-utilitarian grounds, provided they do not reduce average utility, not even by few units. At first, though, Andy does not have enough evidence to ascertain whether *L* will live up to this expectation. He takes this to be a suspending defeater *R** for *R*. But Andy thinks over the matter more carefully and concludes that *L* will not reduce average utility. Because his comprehensive doctrine holds that *L* can be justified on non-utilitarian grounds, and because he thinks that *R* speaks in favor of *L*, he accepts *L*.

In case E), Andy's suspending defeater *R** for *R* is itself defeated by his belief (call it *R***) that *L* is consistent with the principle of average utility. Taken together, *R*** and *R* provide him with a reason to endorse *L*, though taken in isolation they are unable to warrant his endorsing *L*. This is a key point: in case E) Andy shares *R* as a public reason only because *R*** sustains it. Without *R***, *R* would not be a (justificatory) reason for Andy. Ultimately, then, it is *R*** that turns *R* into a public reason, which he can share will his fellow citizen Bea. Note

165 Incidentally, negative convergence is also immune to the charge of violating the conclusiveness requirement, since it discards as unjustified all proposals backed by public reasons for which citizens have private defeaters.

that a similar situation could occur if *R* were rebutted. Consider the following development of case C) (see §1.5.4 above):

Case F) Andy affirms a religious comprehensive doctrine. He thinks that *R* expresses an important value, and that this value constitutes a things-being-equal reason for *L*. At first, though, he rejects *L* because he thinks that *L* is inconsistent with his religious views about social justice. He takes this to be a rebutting defeater *R* for *R**. Scanning his belief system, however, Andy discovers another reason *R*** that rebuts *R**; this reason is that although *L* falls short of his ideal of social justice, *L* would still be better than no law at all. [166]

Even in this case, *R* is shareable only insofar as it is backed by *R***, which defeats *R**. Since situations like case E) or case F) could eventuate, one cannot consistently claim that *R* is a public reason for *L* unless one shows that *L* is backed by an overlapping consensus of private doctrines. But because it disallows all appeals to private reasons for accepting coercive laws, the Weak Shareability Requirement affirmed by the Negative Convergence View of Public Reason makes it impossible to verify whether allegedly shareable reasons are public.

1.5.7 A twofold presumption in favor of convergence

I conclude that the Shareability Requirement (even in its weaker variant) looks inherently paradoxical and self-defeating. To work out principles of social cooperation grounded on public reasons, one needs to have an account of what public reasons are. But as soon as one sets out to determine which reasons are public, one is bound to delve carefully into citizens' comprehensive doctrines. To reach this conclusion, I have tried to refute FT. If *R* is defeated by private reasons, then *R* is not shareable, even if *R* is part of *U*. Of course, in cases A) to E) Andy's defeaters are private. They are defeaters from his perspective but not from Bea's. But this means that if *R** is a private defeater of Andy's (which is not itself defeated)[167], then *R* is downgraded to a private reason of Bea's, as opposed to a public reason of all. Hence, FT is false: *R*'s being freestanding is neither a neces-

166 It will be recalled from §1.4.6 that insofar as *L* is better than liberty or no law at all, then *L* is acceptable from the standpoint of public reason.

167 If *R** itself defeated, then *R* may be a public reason, as cases E) and F) remind us. While in those cases Andy has a private defeater *R** for *R*, *R*** commits him to sharing *R* all things considered.

sary nor a sufficient condition for *R* to be a public reason. As UPRT states, a reason is public if and only if it is not defeated by citizens' private reasons.

My argument against FT strengthens the presumption in favor of convergence, which now appears to be twofold. On the one hand, consensus models are problematic because they exclude potentially decisive private defeaters. As a result, the Consensus View of Public Reason may not always live up to public reason's conclusiveness requirement. On the other hand, consensus models insist that private reasons should not be taken into account despite the fact that private reasons are necessary to determine which reasons are public.

Three important remarks before proceeding. First, talk of "private defeaters" seems to suggest that the only function of private reasons is to defeat (some of) the coercive laws supported by freestanding reasons. But this view is consistent with the Negative Convergence View of Public Reason, and not with the Convergence View of Public Reason. On the latter view, as cases B), E) and F) suggest, private reasons may well end up replacing or strengthening the "pro tanto" justification of coercion. In case B), Andy accepts *L* despite the fact that *R* is undermined (see §1.5.3 above); in cases E) and F) he accepts *L* because the (suspending and rebutting) defeaters for *R* are themselves defeated. To be sure, above (§1.4.7) I stressed that the main problem with consensus is that insofar as it exclude private reasons, it risks upholding laws that some citizens may have reason to reject. Still, the fact that my argument focuses on private defeaters should not be taken to imply that the only function of private reasons is to defeat coercion. Private reasons, on the convergence view I want to defend, may both defeat and justify coercion.

The second remark is terminological. Above (§1.4.4) I introduced S. Kagan's definition of "pro tanto" reasons, according to which a pro tanto reason has genuine weight (it cannot be undermined), but may overridden by stronger considerations (it can be rebutted). It is important not to confuse this narrow understanding of pro tanto reasons with the broader notion of "pro tanto justification" or "pro tanto justificatory stage", which I borrow from Rawls. By "pro tanto justification" or "pro tanto justificatory stage" I mean the freestanding reasoning led by Ω and aiming at spelling out the content of *U*. The pro tanto justificatory stage is the first stage of the two-step justificatory procedure. Now the reasons comprised by *U* are pro tanto in the sense that they could be defeated at the second stage, in which citizens' private reasons are taken into account. "Pro tanto justification" thus means defeasible justification based on reasons comprised by *U*. However, freestanding reasons may be defeated in three ways: they can be undermined, rebutted or suspended. Therefore, freestanding reasons are not "pro tanto" reasons in S. Kagan's narrow sense, as Kagan seems to imply that pro tanto reasons cannot be undermined.

Finally, since freestanding reasons may be defeated, they may not be reasons at all. They are certainly not reasons if they are undermined. If we accept the Expanded View of Reason, we should say the same of both suspended and rebutted reasons. To avoid unnecessary complications, however, I shall regularly talk of "freestanding reasons" even if these are defeated.

1.6 Two families of arguments for consensus

1.6.1 A challenge for consensus

Thus far, I have not tried to establish a conclusive case for convergence, but only a presumption in its favor, which can of course be rebutted. Suppose consensus theorists come up with an argument which warrants the following claim:

If *R* is a reason identified via the correct (and suitably conducted) procedure of abstraction Ω, there is no *R** such that a) *R** is a private reason and b) *R** can be legitimately advocated as a defeater for *R*.

If sound, an argument of this kind would surely rebut the twofold presumption in favor of convergence I have described: first, since freestanding reasons identified via abstraction cannot be defeated by private reasons, it is never the case that "pro tanto" justified principles are, all things considered, unjustified to some citizens; and for pretty much the same reason, freestanding reasons are by definition shareable; hence, consensus models are not self-defeating because the Freestandingness Thesis turns out to be correct. Thus, if freestanding reasons cannot be defeated by private reasons, then consensus theorists catch two birds with one stone: they can maintain that consensus models can both achieve conclusive justification (as opposed to a mere "pro tanto", defeasible one) and avoid the charge of being somewhat paradoxical and self-defeating.

Remember that according to clause (C) of the Consensus View of Public Reason (the Shareability Requirement), only shareable reasons are "good reasons", while the Convergence View of Public Reason holds that even private reasons are good reasons. Now consensus theorists could reasonably claim that private reasons are bad reasons precisely because they cannot defeat freestanding reasons. Hence, the argument consensus theorists must be after can also be described as trying to substantiate the following claim:

If *R* is a reason identified via a correct (and suitably conducted) procedure of abstraction Ω, there is no *R** such that a) *R** is a private reason and b) *R** is a *good* reason, which, as such, can be legitimately advocated as a defeater for *R*.

Again, this claim would warrant the thesis that freestanding reasons are both conclusive and shareable, thereby rebutting the twofold presumption in favor of convergence. Still, the fact that such a presumption is in place shifts the justificatory burden onto consensus theorists. For this reason, this book is devoted to analyzing arguments for consensus, rather than further arguments for convergence. Consensus theorists cannot simply *assume* that citizens committed to the ideal of public reason should reason in shareable terms. Rather, they must come up with some convincing argument explaining why private reasons are in fact bad reasons, which, as such, cannot defeat freestanding reasons. Unless they can do this, we should favor convergence over consensus.

It is important to distinguish two very different ways in which private reasons could be thought to be "bad reasons". In fact, the phrase "private reasons are bad reasons" can either mean that private reasons lack justificatory *strength*, or it can imply that private reasons are *inappropriate* justificatory grounds. If we question the strength of a reason, we ask ourselves to what extent it commits us to endorsing the belief for which it is a reason. This is first and foremost an epistemic question concerning the beliefs we have sufficient reason to hold. By contrast, if we question the appropriateness of a reason, we ask ourselves whether or not it would be convenient or right to actually use that reason in a given justificatory context. This is, in a broad sense, a purely moral question about the reasons we are permitted to advocate when we want to justify certain claims to certain people. Thus consensus models can be either *strength-based* or *appropriateness-based*, depending on whether the arguments supporting them are strength-based (i.e., aiming to show that private reasons are weak) or appropriateness-based (i.e., aiming to show that private reasons are inappropriate). It is now crucial to get clearer on these two families of arguments for consensus.

1.6.2 Strength-based arguments for consensus

The following examples can help us understand what exactly strength-based arguments for consensus seek to show:

Case 1) Andy is charged with murder. The prosecutor points to a complex web of circumstantial evidence against Andy, which allegedly demonstrates his implication in the crime. After carefully revising all the information and evidence available, however, Justice Bea concludes that Andy did not commit the crime he is accused of. Justice Bea acquits Andy.

In this case, Bea does the right thing for an obvious reason: she is convinced that Andy is innocent. She holds that the circumstantial evidence against Andy is definitely not *strong* enough to provide a conclusive case for his conviction. Now according to strength-based arguments for consensus, private reasons are bad reasons just as the evidence against Andy is a bad ground for conviction in case 1). Citizens should view private reasons as *lacking epistemic strength compared to freestanding reasons*, just as in case 1) Bea should believe that the reasons corroborating the charge against Andy are defeated by stronger considerations. 168

In chapter 2 (§2.2.1) I shall distinguish between two different strength-based arguments for consensus. *Radical strength-based arguments for consensus* seek to show that private reasons are always defeated by the very fact that they are private: if *R* is a private reason within a given belief system *S*, then *S* must comprise a defeater for *R*; and this follows automatically from the fact that *R* is private. Radical arguments of this kind, then, seek to show that my claim that freestanding reasons may be defeated by private reasons is false. On a radical strength-based view, there can be no such thing as a reason that is justificatory for some citizens but not for others. If *R* is a sound reason, *R* is, *mutatis mutandis*, a justificatory reason for all. Conversely, if *R* is not a reason for some, then it is not a justificatory reason for anyone. *Moderate strength-based arguments for consensus* are weaker. They reject the radical claim that unless Andy's reason *R* for accepting *L* is freestanding, then Andy must have a defeater for *R*. Rather, they seek to show that freestanding reasons are always defeated by freestanding reasons. Private reasons, on this more moderate view, are defeated when they conflict with freestanding reasons; they are not defeated by definition. However, we need not elaborate too much on the difference between moderate and radical arguments, since sometimes strength-based arguments for consensus are open to both interpretations. All we need to stress is that strength-based arguments have two interrelated features: first, they contend that private reasons are "bad reasons" in a strictly epistemic sense; second, they hold that private reasons are defeated, either by definition or by freestanding reasons.

168 There are two related questions here. The first is whether Bea should believe that Andy is innocent. The second is how Bea should act given her beliefs, to wit, whether she should acquit him or not. As we will see below (§1.6.3), these two issues are independent because a judge could legitimately make decisions that run counter her beliefs about the case. I must thank Jens Steffek and Maria Paola Ferretti for pressing me on this point.

1.6.3 Appropriateness-based arguments for consensus

Appropriateness-based arguments for consensus claim that while private reasons may well have undefeated epistemic weight, they are inappropriate justificatory grounds. To see what sets apart strength from appropriateness, consider the following case:

Case 2) Andy is charged with murder. The prosecutor convincingly shows that enough circumstantial evidence corroborates the charge beyond a reasonable doubt. Eventually, though, it turns out that that much of that evidence was obtained by illegal means. As such, it is no longer admissible in court. Justice Bea acquits Andy.

Even in this case, Bea does the right thing, but for a peculiar reason. In the cases we have discussed so far, Bea acknowledges that although some evidence might still speak against Andy, she has stronger reason to believe that Andy did not commit the crime he is accused of. In case 2), instead, Bea is still convinced that Andy is guilty. While in case 1) Bea *is committed to revising her beliefs*, which turn out to be unjustified, in case 2) she is compelled to *ignore her justified beliefs*. In case 2), Bea would probably regret to acquit Andy, whom she has conclusive reason to believe guilty. Still, acquitting him is the *appropriate* thing to do. She must pretend, as it were, that much of the evidence the prosecutor collected never existed. Given what trial law prescribes, it would not be legally appropriate to use it as a ground for conviction.

Now appropriateness-based consensus models would require of Bea as a citizen what case 2) would require of her as a judge. As a member of the public committed to the ideal of public reason, Bea should put aside her private beliefs for the same reason why Justice Bea should ignore a mishandled piece of evidence in a courtroom. The idea that certain reasons and arguments are inappropriate in political contexts is nicely captured, I think, by Bruce Ackerman's notion of a conversational self-restraint.[169] Some issues should be crossed off the political agenda. It would be inappropriate to touch on certain topics, especially if doing so involves advocating our private views. After all, almost any conversational context involves some sort of self-restraint, which is normally associated with, and specified by, the social role or institutional office that one holds. Clearly there are things that judges, congressmen, priests or deans cannot say. So why shouldn't the members of the public be burdened with a similar principle of re-

169 See B. A. Ackerman 1980: 117-19.

straint? Perhaps there are indeed arguments that civic-minded citizens should avoid bringing up. And maybe an appropriateness-based argument for consensus could manage to show that such inappropriate arguments comprise all non-shareable reasons.

Some think that a principle of conversational restraint is presupposed, at least implicitly, by Rawls's thesis that citizens are under a "duty of civility", which morally compels them "to explain to one another ... how the principles and policies they advocate and vote for can be supported by the political values of public reason".[170] This seems to lead directly to what Christopher Eberle calls "the principle of restraint": "A citizen should not support any coercive law for which he lacks a public justification", meaning that the "good citizen" simply ignores his non-public doctrines.[171] On this reading, duty of civility and Shareability Requirement really look appropriateness-based, since they appear to entail some kind of self-imposed conversational restraint: regardless of whether or not their private reasons are strong or even conclusive, citizens committed to the ideal of public reason should abstain from appealing to them. They should rather endeavor to "give arguments that all reasonable citizens might agree to".[172]

On an appropriateness-based consensus view, reasonable citizens should *ignore* the fact that freestanding reasons might be non-shareable and defeasible, as allegiance to freestanding reasons is part of what it means to be a citizen committed to the ideal of public reason. To put the point differently, appropriateness-based arguments for consensus suggest that the constituency of public reason should only comprise members who see freestanding reasons as shareable and conclusive. Those who view freestanding reasons as defeasible may not commit any epistemic mistake, and yet they should not be given a say because their views are morally inappropriate. In a way, then, even on an appropriateness-based consensus view freestanding reasons are shareable and conclusive: for those who believe otherwise, being excluded by the constituency of public reason, are not supposed to share those reasons in the first place.

170 J. Rawls 1993: 217.

171 C. Eberle 2002: 68. It is important to stress, however, that "restraint" applies to the domain of public justification, where the members of a suitably idealized constituency of public reason justify their proposal to one another. Restraint does not apply to the broader domain of the public sphere, in which actual citizens in flesh and blood exchange information. I shall take up this point in chapter 3, §3.4.2.

172 J. Rawls 1998: 620.

1.6.4 Limits of appropriateness-based arguments for consensus

Remember the problem. Consensus theorists must substantiate the Shareability Requirement, according to which only freestanding reasons are good reasons. This, I have argued, can be done in two ways. One can either claim that private reasons are weak considerations or insist that they should be ignored on grounds of inappropriateness. Now strength-based arguments for consensus, if sound, would clearly rebut the presumption in favor of convergence. If private reasons lack epistemic strength, then proposals backed by freestanding reasons necessarily meet CT, for it can never be the case that private reasons defeat public reasons. By the same token, freestanding reasons are necessarily sharable, in addition to being conclusive.

As I shall argue in the next chapter, however, strength-based arguments for consensus should be resisted. In any event, as we will see in chapter 3, public reason liberals (especially political liberals) are normally more attracted to appropriateness-based consensus model. The obvious problem with appropriateness-based arguments for consensus, though, is that they ask citizens to ignore reasons they might deem decisive. Of course, Bea could be impressed by an appropriateness-based argument for consensus. She could thus be willing to ignore her private reasons in the context of public justification. Yet the strength of those reasons would remain unaltered. She might still believe that some of the normative conclusions arrived at through shared reasoning are not conclusively justified to her, for they might be weakened or even overridden by her private reasons. And of course, she could maintain that whenever shared reasoning yields results that she regards as defeated, she does not really share the reasons supporting those results. In other words, she could maintain that shared reasoning is in fact nothing but a *freestanding reasoning*: it abstracts from her private views but does not lead to results she has reason to share. To simply claim that citizens should put aside decisive reasons (or, which is the same, that only citizens who are actually willing to do so should be part of our constituency of public reason) is to ignore the problem, not to solve it.

Still, it would be a mistake to hastily dismiss appropriateness-based arguments for consensus a priori. True, appropriateness-based consensus risks imposing unjustified laws, but this could be a tolerable price to pay should consensus fare much better then convergence with respect to other desiderata of public reason. Consider, for instance, the category of the "reasonable", which is typically seen as freestanding with respect to that of "epistemic rationality".[173] In ascribing cer-

173 This can mean two things: first, that reasonableness is a moral property of persons and not an epistemic property of beliefs; second, that although reasonableness is a property of

tain features to reasonable citizens, we assume that they will reason in a certain way and abide by certain rules of conduct. Thus being reasonable may well entail ignoring some relevant reasons, not because these lack epistemic weight, but simply because we assume that the "good" or "reasonable" citizen does not rely upon them in public political advocacy.

In effect, we will see that some appropriateness-based arguments for consensus press convergence on very this point. They claim that under convergence citizens are permitted to act unreasonably and hence that the Convergence View of Public Reason is traversed by an internal tension. On the one hand, convergence upholds the Principle of Public Justification, which states that coercion is justified only if all *reasonable* citizens could endorse it; on the other hand, though, clause (C) of the Convergence View of Public Reason permits citizens to rely on reasons which reasonable citizens should refrain from advocating. It seems safe to assume that if convergence were indeed likely to downplay the reasonableness requirement or other fundamental values, then we should favor consensus over convergence, regardless of whether or not private reasons might defeat, epistemically speaking, freestanding reasons. Unfortunately, chapter 3 will show that no such appropriateness-based argument manages to rebut the twofold presumption in favor of convergence.

1.7 Summary

In this first chapter I set the stage for my argument about consensus and convergence models of public reason. I began by describing the general Concept of Public Reason as a combination of two fundamental principles (§1.1). The first principle, which I called the Principle of Political Liberty, holds that liberty should be the norm, while all use of political power backed by the threat of legal sanctions stands in need of justification. After defining the Principle of Political Liberty (§1.2.1), I tried to identify and dispel some misunderstandings about the "liberal" presumption against coercion and its underlying conception of liberty (§1.2.2).

First, the Principle of Political Liberty it is not concerned only with actual interference, but more generally with legal rights that entitle citizens to interfere with others. Moreover, the Principle of Political Liberty does not view a state of formal liberties tainted by material inequalities as the status quo. Quite the contrary, I explained that the Principle of Political Liberty is entirely consistent with

both persons and beliefs, a belief need not be epistemically justified or epistemically rational in order to count as reasonable. See chapter 3, §3.3.4.

the view that material inequalities stand in need of justification. Furthermore, the Principle of Political Liberty and its underlying presumption in favor of liberty do not imply that only coercion stands in need of justification. Although it states that liberty should be the norm, the Principle of Political Liberty shifts the justificatory burden onto those who reject coercive laws that have been already justified. In discussing the Principle of Political Liberty I also stressed that all coercive laws need to be justified. This led me to reject the "narrow view" of public reason, which limits the site of public reason to fundamental issues of justice and constitutional essentials (§1.2.3). Moreover, I rejected the Derivative Justification Thesis, arguing that public justification may not be achieved derivatively, to wit, by means of publicly justified democratic procedures (§1.2.4).

The second principle comprised by the general concept of public justification is the Principle of Public Justification, according to which a coercive law is publicly justified if and only if all reasonable citizens, taking all good reasons into account, would endorse it (§1.2.5). The consensus/convergence distinction came into play at this point (§1.3.1). The dominant consensus view insists that only public or shareable reasons are good reasons – although I clarified that consensus theorists are not committed to "strong consensus", according to which citizens must accept laws for the very same reasons (§1.3.2). The alternative convergence conception, instead, holds that even private reasons qualify as good reasons.

After defining the concepts of "public reasons" (§1.3.3) and "publicness" (§1.3.4), I tried to show that despite its minority status, convergence is prima facie preferable to consensus. To begin with, convergence expunges from the domain of public reason a number of reasons (especially religious reasons) to which some citizens might assign primary importance (§1.4.1). Starting from Rawls's suggestions about the need for an "overlapping consensus" (§1.4.2 – 1.4.3), I argued that the exclusion of private reasons is problematic because reasons justifying coercion should be conclusive (§1.4.6), which means that they should not be defeated (§1.4.4 – 1.4.5). But since consensus fails to take private defeaters into account, it is open to the charge of falling foul of the conclusiveness requirement. I argued that this establishes a first presumption in favor of convergence (§1.4.7).

Then I sought to strengthen the presumption in favor of convergence by introducing the Freestandingness Thesis or FT (§1.5.1), which I then criticized. Although both consensus and convergence theorists endorse it (§1.5.2), FT seems false, which means that the Shareability Requirement advocated by consensus models is paradoxical and self-defeating. Since freestanding reasons might be undermined (§1.5.3), rebutted (§1.5.4) or suspended (§1.5.5) (in short: defeated) by private reasons, and since defeated reasons do not qualify as shareable (justificatory) reasons, the Shareability Requirement would make it impossible to determine which reasons are public (§1.5.6).

I thus argued that that there is a strong, twofold presumption in favor of convergence, which, however, might be rebutted (§1.5.7). In fact, if there were an argument showing that private reasons are "bad reasons", it would make little sense to claim that freestanding reasons might be neither conclusive nor shareable (§1.6.1). Specifically, one could still defend consensus if one managed to show that private reasons are either epistemically weak (§1.6.2) or morally inappropriate (§1.6.3 – 1.6.4). In the next chapter I shall examine the first strategy.

2. Strength-based arguments for consensus

2.1. Overview of the argument

Consensus models are prima facie problematic because they may violate public reason's conclusiveness requirement (§1.4) and because they overlook the fact that private reasons play a major role in determining which reasons are public (§1.5). Both problems, I have argued, stem from the fact that "freestanding" justifications might be defeated by private reasons. In the previous chapter (§1.6.1) I argued that to dodge this fatal objection consensus theorists must show that private reasons are "bad" reasons, which, as such, cannot defeat freestanding reasons. In this chapter I propose to critically review the arguments for consensus (strength-based arguments) which seek to show that private reasons are "bad" in an epistemic sense: they lack epistemic weight compared to freestanding reasons; as a result, the latter are always conclusive and shareable/public. In this chapter I shall sketch an epistemic account of justification which undermines this sort of arguments in general. Specifically, I shall argue that theorists of public reason should embrace a "pluralist" epistemology, which is explicitly defended by Gaus. Once we accept epistemic pluralism, a strength-based defense of consensus is no longer a viable option.

This chapter is organized in the following way. Section §2.2 offers an overview of four major strength-based arguments purporting to justify the Shareability Requirement on epistemic grounds. I shall call them the "top-down argument for consensus", the "social argument for consensus", the "argument from universalization" and the "discourse-theoretical argument for consensus". Sections §2.3 and §2.4 argue that the top-down argument for consensus should be resisted. Sections from §2.5 to §2.8 refute the other three arguments. However, I will be primarily concerned with the implications of the discourse-theoretical argument for consensus. I shall argue that although that argument has real bite, it fails to appreciate a crucial asymmetry between a discursive redemption of truth-claims and the public justification of rightness-claims. In defending this thesis, I shall compare Habermas's discourse-theoretical approach to public justification with Gaus's moderately "relativistic" conception of reasons. Drawing on his "weakly externalist" conception of "open justification", I shall argue not only that strength-based arguments for consensus fail, but also that discourse theory itself should allow for some sort of relativism of reasons. In particular, I shall argue that Gaus's "relativism of reasons" (or, as I shall say, "epistemic pluralism") can be rephrased in the terms of a plurality of ethical discourses, which can yield a number of private yet properly justificatory reasons. Section §2.9 concludes.

2.2. Four conceptions of objectivity

2.2.1 Public reasons as objective reasons

In the previous chapter (§1.6.1) I anticipated that strength-based arguments for consensus can be either radical or moderate. They are radical if they seek to show that private reasons are defeated by the very fact that they are private: if *R* is a private reason within a given belief system *S*, it follows from the fact that *R* is private that *S* must comprise a defeater for *R*. They are moderate if they claim that although private reasons are not defeated by the fact that they are private, they are always defeated by conflicting freestanding reasons: if *R* is a private reason within a given belief system *S*, *R* is undefeated only if *S* does not comprise any freestanding reason *R** that conflicts with *R*, as any such freestanding reason would defeat *R*. In short: on a radical view, private reasons are defeated by definition; on a moderate view, they are defeated only when they conflict with freestanding reasons. Either way, though, strength-based arguments for consensus defend a very strong thesis. Why should we think that private reasons are by definition defeated? One answer would seem to come from Christine Korsgaard's intuition that the idea of a private reason is somewhat contradictory, since reasons are by definition "inherently shareable".[174] Korsgaard draws both on Kant's universalization principle and on analogies to Wittgenstein's private language argument. On the one hand, practical reasons are "inherently shareable" because they offer, in a Kantian fashion, common grounds for endorsing universally binding norms of action. On the other hand, reasons are "inherently shareable" and essentially public because the idea of a private reason is as incoherent as that of a private and essentially incommunicable language. Hence, "the only reasons that are possible are the reasons we can share".[175]

Now although strength-based arguments for consensus (especially radical ones, as we will see) are substantially in tune with this line of reasoning, Korsgaard's view is unable to rebut the second bit of the presumption in favor of convergence, which draws on the intuition that freestanding reasons may not be shareable. Imagine that Andy endorses Korsgaard's radical (and highly controversial) conception of reasons. Would he necessarily contradict himself if he insisted that *R** defeats a freestanding reason *R* despite the fact that *R** is not public? No, because Andy would merely claim that *R* is as private as *R** – it is not a reason *he* can share as justificatory, for the reasons canvassed in chapter 1, §1.5.3 – 1.5.5. Andy could therefore conclude that although *R**, being private, is

174 C. Korsgaard 1996b: 135.
175 C. Korsgaard 1996a: 301.

not a reason, by the same token R is not a reason, either: Andy and Bea would simply lack proper reasons to adjudicate the issue. Andy, then, could consistently hold both Korsgaard's conception and the view that freestanding reasons may not be shared by all.

To rebut the presumption in favor of convergence on epistemic grounds, one cannot simply insist that reasons are by definition shareable. One must rather come up with a strength-based argument which can show that *freestanding* reasons are by definition shareable *because* they cannot be defeated by private reasons (which also implies, again, that freestanding reasons are necessarily conclusive). So we are back to the obvious question about strength-based arguments for consensus: Why should we think that private reasons are defeated, either by definition or by freestanding reasons? As I see it, both radical and moderate strength-based arguments attempt to answer this question along the following lines: freestanding reasons necessarily enjoy a superior epistemic status because they are *objective*, while private reasons are intrinsically *subjective*. Specifically, the arguments for consensus that I term "strength-based" share two core premises: the first premise is that there is some correct version of Ω, which, if carried out properly, determines which reasons are freestanding/objective (I). The second premise is that subjective reasons are defeated (II). The basic line of reasoning behind a strength-based argument for consensus, then, runs as follows:

(I) There is some procedure of abstraction Ω for identifying the set of freestanding reasons U (where freestanding reasons are objective reasons)
(II) Subjective/private reasons are defeated[176]
Therefore,
(T1) If R is freestanding, it cannot be defeated by non-freestanding reasons
Therefore,
(T2) Freestanding reasons are both shareable and conclusive.

Radical and moderate arguments view the priority of objective reasons expressed by (II) in two different ways. On a radical view, objective/freestanding reasons have more epistemic weight because private reasons are always defeated by the very fact that they are private:

(I) There is some procedure of abstraction Ω for identifying the set of freestanding reasons U (where freestanding reasons are objective reasons)

176 Strength-based arguments (both radical and moderate) simply hold that private reasons are defeated; they need not determine in which sense they are defeated. Thus in premise (II) "defeated" may mean undermined, rebutted or suspended.

(II) If R is not objective, it is defeated by definition (i.e., by the fact that it is private)[177]
Therefore,
(T1) If R is freestanding, it cannot be defeated by non-freestanding reasons
Therefore,
(T2) Freestanding reasons are both shareable and conclusive.

A moderate argument, instead, would point out that although you may in principle have subjective justificatory reasons, you are committed to viewing those reasons as defeated whenever they conflict with freestanding, objective considerations. Stripped to its essentials, then, a moderate strength-based argument for consensus displays the following structure:

(I) There is some procedure of abstraction Ω for identifying the set of freestanding reasons U (where freestanding reasons are objective reasons)
(II) If a) R is a freestanding reason while R^* is a private reason and b) R and R^* conflict, then R defeats R^*.[178]
Therefore,
(T1) If R is freestanding, it cannot be defeated by non-freestanding reasons
Therefore,
(T2) Freestanding reasons are both shareable and conclusive.

Of course, different variants on these two argumentative patterns are possible, depending on how one interprets the idea of freestandingness. In chapter 1 (§1.5.2) I introduced three major interpretations of the procedure of abstraction Ω leading to U (which, it will be recalled, stands for the full set of freestanding reasons): Rawls's, Gaus's and Habermas's. Of these three views, however, only Habermas's is compatible with a strength-based defense of consensus, in that it equates freestanding reasons with (provisionally) objective reasons. In addition to Habermas's conception, in this chapter I shall introduce two further conceptions of objectivity, which, in turn, buttress two further conceptions of freestandingness. The "top-down argument for consensus" (1) rests on a "metaphysical" conception of objectivity. The "social argument for consensus" (2) holds that objectivity is an inescapable feature of rationality understood as a social and linguistically mediated process. I shall also consider the "argument from universalization" (3), which understands objectivity/freestandingness in a Kantian fashion. This conception of objectivity and freestandingness is in some important respects

177 The fact that R is private may undermine, rebut or suspend R. See note 176 above.
178 Again, R may undermine, rebut or suspend R^* (see note 176 above).

close to Habermas's (§1.6.2); however, it does not necessarily presuppose Habermas's overall discourse-theoretical account of justification. Lastly, as already mentioned, Habermas's "discourse-theoretical argument for consensus" (4) interprets objectivity in terms of intersubjective agreement, placing primary emphasis on the priority of "moral" over "ethical" reasons.

2.2.2 Four strength-based arguments for consensus

(1) The top-down argument for consensus rests on the implicit assumption that Ω should be understood as a procedure for discovering true facts about the world, which *U* casts in the form of objective reasons. If a consideration is not comprised by *U*, on this view, it is not actually a reason, as it does not reflect an objectively sound inference which applies to all rational agents. Joseph Raz and Steven Wall suggest this line of reasoning. In their view, for instance, to say that one has a reason not to lie is to say that one's reason would not conform to some objective moral facts if one thought that it is permissible to lie. But if freestanding reasons are real entities that each and every fully rational agent would recognize, they are by definition shareable or public. As Wall says, the top-down argument implies that "if a citizen believes that there is a moral reason for him to support the legal enactment of a coercive drug policy for his society, then he must also believe that there is a moral reason for his fellow citizens to do so as well".[179] The top-down argument is clearly a radical (as opposed to moderate) strength-based argument for consensus, in that it dismisses the idea of "private reasons" as a conceptual error. One cannot consistently claim both that a) *R** is a reason and that b) *R** is private, according to the top-down argument for consensus. If b) is the case, then *R** is not a reason (it is by definition defeated), for it is not a consideration that reflects true facts about the world.

(2) The social argument for consensus is close to Korsgaard's view. This strength-based argument is radical. It starts from Wittgenstein's observation that unless ruler and rule-follower agree on what a rule actually implies and on what it means to correctly follow it, the rule will always be open to countless subjective interpretations. Indeed, "no course of action could be determined by a rule, because every course of action can be made out to accord with the rule".[180] Now for Korsgaard and many others, reasons and linguistic meanings share a crucial feature with rules: they are "normative" concepts, in that they take the form of ought-statements. By saying "this is a reason for you to believe *L*", I point to the

179 S. Wall 2010: 134.
180 L. Wittgenstein 2001: 201.

fact that you *ought* to do so. Drawing on this intuition, Kurt Baier holds that reasons are "directive", in the sense that they "direct us to believe something, that is, to "perform" in a certain way".[181] But if this is so, then the addressee of justification and the rule-follower find themselves in the same situation: they can come up with nearly any explanation of what a reason is, and of what it means to act on it. To avoid this problem, Korsgaard takes up Wittgenstein's intuition. In order to determine whether or not Andy is acting on reason *R*, we need to verify whether or not Andy relies on a socially sanctioned *viz.* shareable interpretation of *R*: "To act on a reason is already, essentially, to act on a consideration whose normative force may be shared with others".[182] Note that here Korsgaard does not simply claim that reasons are by definition shareable. As I stressed above, this would not be enough to justify consensus (§2.2.1). Rather, Korsgaard's claim is that only socially recognized norms provide reasons *because* they are shareable. To use our terminology, the social argument for consensus interprets Ω as a procedure for identifying socially binding rules of action, which are "freestanding" in the sense that they apply to all members of society, irrespective of the particular worldviews these may happen to affirm. As such, freestanding reasons are "socially" objective, as it were. Consequently, they are inherently shareable and conclusive, while the very idea of a "subjective" reason borders on incoherence.

(3) The argument from universalization rests on another assumption defended by Korsgaard, in that it holds that proper practical reasons must pass some threshold of universalization in a Kantian fashion. Here Ω works as a universalization procedure, while *U* comprises only reasons that everyone could endorse from a detached, universalistic perspective. In order to count as a proper moral reason for *L*, on this view, *R* must be objective or impartial, and hence sharable. Thomas Nagel rephrases the notion of impartiality in the terms of an objective "view from nowhere".[183] By subjecting their agent-relative reasons to Nagel's method of objectivity, moral agents assess them from increasingly impersonal points of view, which are distinct from their original "private" standpoints and which provide reasons independent of those standpoints. Because agent-relative reasons are by definition bound to the perspective of some specific moral agents, only agent-neutral impartial reasons can count as proper reasons. However, the most classical versions of the argument from universalization are to be found in

181 K. Baier 1995: 45. A similar assumption, which I sought to defend, is implicit in Benn's claim that reasons should be understood as normative "commitments". See chapter 1, §1.5.4.

182 C. Korsgaard 1996b: 136.

183 T. Nagel 1986.

"Kantian constructivist" approaches to justification. So for instance in Rawls's "original position" the veil of ignorance guarantees reasonableness by holding back information that would impugn the parties' impartiality. Despite their purposive-rational attitude, the parties are forced by the veil of ignorance to reason on the basis of shareable impartial reasons: "Since the differences among the parties are unknown to them, and everyone is equally rational and similarly situated, each is convinced by *the same arguments*".[184] The argument from universalization often takes a radical form: unless ϕ-ing in circumstances C is justified by freestanding reasons that all should share, then there is no reason at all to propose a norm that requires ϕ-ing in circumstances C; conversely, if R is a reason that speaks against a universalizable norm L, then R is not actually a reason. However, moderate variants of this strength-based argument for consensus are possible. Moreover, as we will see in the next chapter, there are even weaker versions of this argument, which seem to imply that non-universalizable reasons are morally "inappropriate", rather than epistemically weak (see chapter 3, §3.5.3).

(4) The discourse-theoretical argument for consensus is heavily indebted to the Kantian interpretation of Ω and U, which Habermas rephrases in discursive terms. To be sure, for Habermas "moral discourses" led by the principle of universalization are only part of the discursive enterprise of justification, which also includes "pragmatic", "ethical" and "empirical" discourses.[185] However, Habermas argues that the primary aim of Ω is to identify "moral" freestanding reasons, as opposed to "ethical" ones. Importantly, Habermas suggests that justificatory discourses (especially moral discourses) lead to inherently shareable freestanding considerations, to which all should assent and assign paramount weight, because these considerations are (provisionally) objective. The reason for this lies in the fundamental assumption that with their validity claims, speakers implicitly aim to gain the assent of an unrestricted audience. To do so, they seek to ground their claims in good reasons. Thus "the speaker refers with his validity claim to a potential of reasons that could be brought to bear for it".[186] And in Habermas's view, the reasons that could be brought to bear for a validity claim are evaluated in terms of their *intersubjective acceptability*. The justificatory potential of a reason is therefore entirely dependent on its being acceptable by all participants in rational discourses. Since some kinds of reasons (especially moral reasons) are by definition acceptable to all participants in justificatory discourses, only these kinds of reasons redeem, in a fallible and post-metaphysical manner, the old

184 J. Rawls 1971: 139, emphasis mine.

185 See §2.6.2 below.

186 J. Habermas 1992: 77.

metaphysical idea of an antecedently given, transcendent realm of moral truths. In sum, freestanding reasons are (provisionally) objective reasons that would be accepted by all in certain justificatory discourses. Therefore, they are shareable and conclusive. The discourse-theoretical argument for consensus can be interpreted both in a radical and in a moderate fashion, and it is in fact unclear which interpretation better reflects Habermas's own view (more on this ambiguity in §2.8.1 below).

In what follows, it will be important to bear in mind the two strength-based argumentative patterns I have sketched above (§2.2.1). Those two patterns stress that radical and moderate strength-based arguments for consensus share two core premises. The first premise is that there is some correct version of Ω, which, if carried out properly, identifies objective reasons (which are freestanding and are therefore part of *U*) (I). The second premise is that subjective/private reasons are defeated (II). Now in this chapter I shall not challenge the first premise. That is, I shall not argue against the general idea that freestandingness should be equated with some conception of objectivity. Rather, I shall argue that even if we assume that freestanding reasons are objective reasons, strength-based arguments for consensus fail because the second premise is unwarranted. That is, no strength-based argument for consensus (be it radical or moderate) manages to show that private reasons are defeated either by the fact that they are private or by freestanding reasons.

2.3. The top-down argument for consensus

2.3.1 The basic argument

The top-down argument for consensus, it will be recalled, holds that reasons are inherently shareable because they reflect some objective features of the world. In its basic formulation, the argument runs as follows:

(I) Ω discovers objective/freestanding reasons which reflect true facts about the world.
(II) If *R* is not objective, it is defeated by definition (i.e., by the fact that it is private)
Therefore,
(T1) If *R* is freestanding/objective, it cannot be defeated by non-freestanding/subjective reasons.
Therefore,
(T2) Freestanding reasons are both shareable and conclusive.

The problem with this argument is readily apparent: under conditions of reasonable pluralism, people have different conceptions of the "objective truth". As Hobbes said, people naturally aim at "right reason" – they insist that their reasoning reveals the truth, thus entrenching in a dogmatic defense of what *they* believe to be the truth. In his doctoral dissertation, Rawls already warned against this "authoritarian" stance toward the problem of justification. "Authoritarian" views, according to Rawls, appeal to "exalted entities" such as objective moral truths, without providing adequate grounds for accepting them.[187] Why should Bea's beliefs about the objective truth count more than Andy's? Why couldn't Andy, too, take an authoritarian stance and impose on Bea what he takes to be the truth? It is hard to see how Bea's insistence that her reason determines right reason for all can be made consistent with her commitment to treat Andy as a free and equal fellow citizen.

It is not accidental that defenders of the top-down argument for consensus, such as Raz and Wall, typically endorse perfectionist conceptions of liberalism. While justificatory liberals insist that coercion must be justified on grounds that all free and equal citizens can accept, perfectionists understand the state as having a license to enact coercive policies which in some way reflect and are grounded in citizens' "true" reasons and commitments.

Convergence theorists might be tempted to reject this paternalistic line of reasoning by denying (I). In this way, they would endorse a skeptical position about the incommensurability of ultimate values akin to Berlin's (see Introduction, I.a). While empirical knowledge can be backed by objective facts that serve as a check or test of its correctness, skeptics typically believe that normative judgments fall short of the requirement of objectivity implied by (I). This has led many to think that it is hopelessly utopian to search for an independent objective criterion able to determine the correctness of normative and evaluative judgments. Now some convergence theorists could be attracted to this relativistic line of reasoning. For once objectivity has been dismantled as a naïve attempt to overcome the irresolvable relativism of privatized worldviews, the only viable solution to the problem of political justification is to identify convergence points among essentially private conceptions of the right and the good.

Even this approach is problematic, however, and it is crucial to see why. In the introduction I stressed that justificatory liberalism steers a middle way between perfectionist liberalism *à la* Raz and Wall and Berlin's pluralistic liberalism. While the former appeals to the "positive" dimension of liberty to impose unjustified restrictions on negative freedom, the latter dismisses the idea of posi-

187 J. Rawls 1955: 608–9.

tive freedom altogether, thus ruling out a priori the possibility of a Kantian reconciliation between freedom and coercion. Yet for all this, perfectionist and pluralistic liberalism share a crucial feature: they defend a *metaphysical thesis* concerning the existence of reasons for accepting or rejecting coercion.

On my definition, metaphysical conceptions purport to determine which reasons *exist*. They ask: how can we determine whether $R \rightarrow \beta$ is a sound inference? *Is there* a sound reason to accept β? These are metaphysical questions in the sense that they are in principle neutral on whether or not R is a reason that actual agents can be reasonably said to *have*. A metaphysical conception does not, as such, explain why Andy, as a rational agent in flesh and blood, is committed to believing β on account of R. It simply holds that, if $R \rightarrow \beta$ is sound, there is a reason to believe β. Metaphysical approaches are to be contrasted with *epistemic* conceptions of the reasons that citizens *have*. If we judge $R \rightarrow \beta$ from an epistemic perspective (as opposed to a metaphysical one), we will no longer ask whether or not that inference is, as such, sound – or, which is the same, whether or not there is a reason R to accept β. Rather, we will ask whether or not Andy is epistemically justified in holding β on account of R. As Gaus and Robert Audi stress, these are two distinct questions.[188] It is one thing to say that the moral rule "if Bea is in pain, then Bea should be assisted" in conjunction with the fact that Bea is in pain is a reason to assist her. It is another thing to say that Andy is committed to assisting Bea if she is in pain because he has a reason to do so. The former thesis is (according to my terminology) "metaphysical" in that it holds there is a sound reason to assist people in pain. The latter statement holds instead that Andy has such a reason, and hence that the demand that he assist Bea is epistemically justified to him.

Now to deny (I) is to take sides within a metaphysical dispute concerning the reasons that there are. According to this metaphysical conception of reasons, to which advocates of pluralistic liberalism are sympathetic, it makes simply no sense to say that there are such things as objectively sound reasons. But justificatory liberals need not deny (I). For even if the metaphysical views expressed by (I) and (II) were true, the epistemic conclusion about the reasons that rational agents have would not follow. Because (I) is a metaphysical claim about the reasons that there are, (I) and (II) can only warrant the metaphysical conclusion that:

(III) Only objective reasons arrived at through Ω exist. Such reasons are shareable and conclusive.

188 R. Audi 2001: 53-5; G. Gaus 2011b: 231.

This is a metaphysical view, in that it holds that the good reasons that *exist* are shareable. It is crucial to note, however, that defenders of the top-down argument for consensus cannot content themselves with (III). Remember the issue. We must develop an account of public justification that explains how the law can be justified to its addressees. But to say that the law must be justified *to* Andy is to say that he must *have* sufficient reason to accept it. To say that there are only shareable reasons, as stated by (III), is not enough. The top-down argument for consensus must in some way show that its metaphysical premises lead to the epistemic conclusion that all rational agents have the same reasons. In effect, (T2) should be understood as an epistemic (as opposed to metaphysical) thesis. According to (T2), it will be recalled, if only objectively sound reasons are proper reasons, then justificatory reasons are shared by all rational agents (and seen by all as conclusive). Unlike (I), (II), and (III), then, (T2) is an epistemic thesis concerning the reasons that people can be said to have. So the fact that freestanding reasons apply equally to all rational agents does not mean that any such agent can be reasonably said to have those reasons. It simply means that *there is* no such thing as a proper private reason, as stated by (III). Thus, the inference from (I) and (II) to (T2) would be warranted only if something like the following claim figured among the premises of the argument:

(II*) Andy has a reason R to accept β if and only if R is an objective reason for β.

If (II*) were granted, then (T2) would indeed follow. Of course, in this case the epistemic question concerning the reasons that rational agents have would collapse into, and be parasitic upon, the more fundamental metaphysical question concerning the reasons that there are. Once we have established, by means of some discovery or construction procedure, that R is an objectively sound reason for β, we have *eo ipso* proved that each and every similarly situated rational agent is epistemically justified in accepting β on account of R. In other words, if *there is* a reason for accepting β that applies to all rational agents, then any such agent *has* a reason for, and is committed to, accepting β. In what follows, I shall offer a streamlined version of Gaus's arguments, which I find compelling, against claims such as (II). This will lead me to sketch a pluralistic epistemic conception which resists the view that the reasons that one has can be in some way inferred from the reasons that there are.

2.3.2 Strong externalism

In order to introduce (II*) as a further premise, defenders of the top-down argument for consensus must endorse a strongly externalist conception of reasons. As Gaus puts it, strong externalism holds that "whether Andy is justified in believing β ... ultimately depends on whether there simply are good reasons for believing β. And whether there simply are good reasons for believing β does not depend on the nature of Andy's perspective, but is an external, entirely objective, matter".[189]

Defenders of the top-down argument for consensus are, of course, aware that some strongly externalist epistemic conception is necessary to their argument. In fact, Wall and Raz explicitly subscribe to strong externalism. In particular, Raz makes a distinction between "facts" and "beliefs", arguing that only the former, and not the latter, can be reasons. Facts are about true state of affairs, while beliefs are mental states about facts. But of course, beliefs can be true or false. So how can one's beliefs about what is the case be relevant if beliefs can be false? If it is a fact that there is a reason for accepting β, then Bea *has* that reason simply by virtue of being a rational agent responsive to reasons. Thus, if β is to be justified to Bea, all Andy has to do is point out to her that there are some objectively sound reasons which conclusively support β. Whether or not this brings about her belief that these reasons are in fact sound adds nothing to the force of Andy's justification.

Although Raz admits that "in order to be guided by what is the case a person must come to believe that it is the case", he maintains that "it is the fact and not the belief in it which should guide him and which is a reason".[190] He adds: "Justification and evaluation depend on how things really were at the time. . . . Justifications (at least some kinds of justifications) do not depend on the agents' perspective, and do not depend on the reasons for which agents acted".[191] If, for instance, I see that the door is locked, I will have a justified belief that I cannot enter the room without a proper key. Raz recognizes that if I did not actually come to believe that the door is locked, I would not actually realize to have a reason – say – to look for a proper key. His point, however, is that I would nonetheless *have* that reason, although I would not realize it. And this is because reasons reflect facts, and it is a fact that the door is locked. As (III) implies, if $R \rightarrow \beta$ is an objectively sound reason, then any rational agent has a reason to accept β. If objectively sound reasons exist, they are necessarily shared (i.e. possessed) by all.

189 G. Gaus 1996: 32.
190 J. Raz 1975: 17.
191 J. Raz 1998: 31.

Similarly, Wall insists that if a "fully rational version of yourself would accept" my reasons, then I can consistently claim that you *have* in fact reason to agree with me.[192]

But strong externalism seems obviously problematic. Taken literally, it implies that because some mathematicians in the late 20th century came up with some very sophisticated proofs of Fermat's last theorem, Andy necessarily has a reason to believe that that theorem is correct. But if Andy is a clumsy moral philosopher, rather than an experienced mathematician, he will probably see the proofs of Fermat's last theorem as nothing but abstruse mathematical formulations that in some way belong together. It would be bizarre to insist that simply because there are conclusive proofs of the theorem, Andy has reason to accept it. Andy can be reasonably said to have a reason to accept the theorem only if he can in some way see its proofs as justificatory. Gaus makes a similar example. Strong externalism

> implies that Aristotle, when writing on physics, had – possessed – a reason to embrace particle physics, because particle physics is true. But surely he did not have any such reason; to see *R* as a reason is to see it as justificatory, but Aristotle simply could not employ his rationality in a way that could lead him to see the facts supporting particle physics as justificatory (he could not even understand these facts)".[193]

In order to count as justificatory reasons, according to Gaus, facts must in some way be turned into beliefs: "Facts become reasons when they enter into cognitive systems with inferential norms and are able to *justify* acceptance of a belief".[194] The same line of reasoning applies to practical reasoning. To rephrase Bernard Williams's famous example, Andy may have some objective, external reasons to join the army although "he has no motivation to join the army at all, and all his desires lead in another direction: he hates everything about military life and what it means".[195] Williams, however, rejects this view with an argument that in some way echoes Gaus's worries about the potential lack of intelligibility of external facts. What can we mean, Williams asks, by saying that Andy has a reason to join the army, if not the fact that he actually believes that he should join the ar-

192 S. Wall 2010: 135.

193 G. Gaus 2011b: 232. Indeed, it seems that "[o]n a strongly externalist conception of reasons there could be a fact *F* that was a reason to accept *β*, even if humans were incapable of recognizing *F*, conceiving of it, and so on … I do not doubt that such facts exist …, but it is mysterious what could be meant by saying that they provide *reasons* to believe *β*. "Reasons for whom?" is the proper query" (G. Gaus 1996: 35).

194 Ibid.

195 B. Williams 1981: 106.

my? Andy's family might insist that Andy should indeed join the army, perhaps arguing that "all his male ancestors were soldiers", and that "family pride requires him to do the same".[196] However, since these arguments strike Andy as old fashioned and ultimately silly, it is rather odd to say that he *has* a reason to join the army.

Similarly, it may well be true that people in pain should be assisted, and hence that there is a reason for Andy to assist Bea if she is in pain. But if none of Andy's moral beliefs commit him to embracing the moral rule that people in pain should be assisted, it makes little sense to say that he has a reason to comply with it.[197] Scanlon objects that in cases of this kind an observer could and should insist that Andy is committing a moral error.[198] If Bea is crying out for help, it is objectively wrong not to assist her. But this sort of complaint would be a restatement of a metaphysical thesis. Andy would commit a moral error because his moral beliefs would not conform to some moral facts, which can be either discovered by intuition or constructed through a suitable moral procedure. This is fine. But if we endorsed strong externalism, we should take a further step. We should maintain that Andy already has a reason to do what he thinks there is no reason to do. This seems implausible. The epistemic question concerning the reasons people have cannot collapse into the metaphysical question concerning the reasons that there are.[199]

2.3.3 Moderate externalism

It might be objected, however, that the top-down argument for consensus does not necessarily presuppose such a strongly externalist account of justification. For one could try replacing (II*) with
(II**) Unless there is an objectively sound reason in support of β, Andy cannot have a reason to accept β.[200]

What sets apart (II**) from (II*) is that the former, unlike the latter, takes objective soundness as a necessary yet not sufficient condition. This could be described as a *moderately* externalist view. Unlike strong externalism, moderate

196 Ibid.
197 As I anticipated in chapter 1 (§1.4.5), only realistically accessible reasons should be taken into account in defining what one has (conclusive) reason to believe. See also §2.7.2 below.
198 T. Scanlon 1998: Appendix.
199 For a similar view see R. Martin 1993: 77-82.
200 See G. Gaus 2011b: 244.

externalism grants that some objectively sound reasons might not be reasons of Andy's. However, if Andy has a reason, it is must be objectively sound. On this view, the fact that there are conclusive proofs of Fermat's last theorem is not a sufficient condition for holding that Andy has reason to accept it. If, however, Andy has a reason to accept the theorem, it is necessary that that reason be objectively sound. Observe that if (II*) were replaced with (II**), the inference from (I) and (II) to (T2) would still be warranted, since the notion of "justificatory private reason" would still make no sense. Although objectively sound reasons may not be epistemically justified to all, no rational agent is epistemically justified in holding unsound reasons.

But even moderate externalism should be resisted according to Gaus. Suppose "Alf and Betty are lovers. [...]. Alf has seen receipts of little-out-of-the-way hotels in her pocketbook (and he hasn't visited such hotels with Betty [...]), she has been working late every night for two months now, she keeps calling him "Dearest Frank", and the like".[201] Few would deny that in this case Alf would be justified in believing that Betty is unfaithful. But now imagine that Alf hires a private detective, whose "report explains away all of the evidence that pointed so strongly to Betty's unfaithfulness. It turns out that every night she stayed at work late to write a romantic novel. Since the romantic novel took place in little-out-of-the-way hotels, she visited them (alone) as part of her research. And the central character – modeled, it turns out, after Alf – is named Frank".[202] It turns out that Alf's belief about Betty's unfaithfulness was not supported by (true) facts. Yet before hiring the private detective, Alf was unaware of the fact that Betty was not actually cheating on him. Quite the contrary, there was some telling evidence that pointed to Betty's unfaithfulness. Again, it seems obvious to assume that before hiring the private detective Alf had indeed reason to believe that Betty was having an affair. Contrary to what moderate externalism holds, then, *R's* being objectively sound is not even a necessary condition for *R* to be a reason that rational agents can possess. In fact, "a person can have impeccable reason to believe what is false".[203] The same is true of evaluative judgments. To come back to Williams's example, if Andy's beliefs about military life commit him to believing that he should not join the army, he definitely has a reason not to join the army, regardless of whether or not that reason is "real".

201 G. Gaus 1996: 66.
202 Ibid.: 67-8.
203 Ibid.: 38.

2.3.4 Internalism

Now it seems that by rejecting both moderate and strong externalism, one must embrace an internalist conception of justification or "Reason Affirmation Thesis",[204] according to which Andy's actually affirming *R* is a necessary and sufficient condition for *R* to be a reason of Andy's. Unless Andy actually believes that he should assist people in pain, he has no reason to do so. Conversely, the bare fact that he thinks that people in pain should be assisted shows that he has a reason to do so. Now it is obvious that if internalism were correct, then the top-down argument for consensus would fail. As people embrace any sort of reasons and beliefs, not all reasons will be shared. Indeed, there might be no public or shared reasons at all, since Andy's and Bea's actual beliefs might not overlap in any significant respect.

Now Gaus thinks that, in a way, internalism is on the right track, in that it makes a clear distinction between the question concerning the reasons that there are and the question concerning the reasons that rational agents have. To answer the latter question we must start from what actual agents believe; and by doing so we may end up discovering a substantial gap between the "real" objective reasons that exist and the reasons that actual agents have. But the obvious problem with internalism is that it seems committed to the counterintuitive view that plainly crazy, vicious and contradictory beliefs are justificatory with respect to Andy as long as he actually holds them. Suppose that Andy can by no means conceive of a bird that cannot fly. Although Bea insists that overwhelming evidence shows that penguins cannot fly, Andy feels unmoved. He raves about the unreliability of that evidence, which, he claims, must by fake. All he knows is that any birds he has seen can fly, and because penguins are birds, he cannot believe that they cannot fly. Now although this is what Andy actually believes, we would not say, I think, that he really has a reason to believe that penguins can fly.

To rescue his internalist conception of reasons from this obvious objection, Williams has introduced the notion of a "sound deliberative route". To use Williams's own example, imagine that Andy, who absolutely loves gin, is about to drink a glass of petrol, which he erroneously takes to be gin.[205] Now internalists seem committed to maintaining that Andy has indeed reason to drink petrol, since nothing within his actual "subjective motivational set" speaks against that

204 G. Gaus 2011b: 233.
205 B. Williams 1981: 102.

option.[206] But Williams denies this to be the case. He stresses that internalism does not correspond to the view that, unless Andy actually has a given motive, he cannot have an (internal) reason corresponding to that motive. Rather, the view is that we can attribute to Andy only reasons that he *could come to have* by following "a sound deliberative route".[207] In other words, Andy may simply fail to notice some relevant information, which, we take it, would certainly lead him to change his mind. As a general rule, then, the notion of a "sound deliberative route" attempts to explain Andy's reliance on bizarre beliefs by pointing to a temporary failure to appreciate relevant evidence.

But because Andy can hold bizarre unjustified beliefs, his actually affirming *R* cannot be a sufficient condition for *R* to be a reason of Andy's. Nor can it be necessary. Once Bea has provided him with extensive evidence that penguins cannot fly, Andy has a reason to revise his beliefs, no matter if he insists on rejecting Bea's criticism.[208] As Gaus points out, "to say what reasons actual Alf now has, we have to consider the reasons that Alf would arrive at if he followed certain sound deliberative routes *from his present reason set*".[209] The qualifica-

206 It worth stressing that, given his Humean understanding of practical rationality, Williams maintains that one's "subjective motivational set" must include one's desires to act. The first reason is that in this way we can get around the thorny controversy between Humeans and anti-Humeans over the role of *desires* in practical reasoning. Humeans typically maintain that because reason must have the power to motivate, and because motivations require wants, reasons for action must be grounded in desires (See on this S. Gosepath (ed.) 1999; E. J. Bond 1983: 27-41). As Hume famously declared, "Reason is, and ought only to be, the slave of passions" (D. Hume 1978: 414). So even if Andy managed to bring about Bea's actual belief that *L* is justified, she might nonetheless have no actual reason to act in accordance with *L* – she might not want or desire to comply with *L*. To be sure, Humeans normally grant that desires do not and cannot figure among the reasons for *belief*. As Bernard Williams recognizes, if one is aware of the fact that *p* is true, one is rationally committed to believing *p*. Conversely, one cannot consistently *want* to believe *p* unless one already believes that *p* is true (B. Williams 1973: 136-51). To use Williams's own example, someone who says "I know for sure that my son died in a car accident but I want to believe that he is actually alive" is trapped in some sort of soothing yet clearly irrational self-deception. Williams, however, insists that there is an asymmetry between belief and action. While beliefs do not and cannot be grounded in desires, reasons for actions must in some way reflect some desires to act. Now although I think that this orthodox Humean approach incurs some serious problems, we need not tackle this issue here, since justification has mainly to do with reasons for belief. For our purposes, then, it is sufficient to interpret "S" as the set of one's beliefs, which, in turn, can provide one with internal reasons for endorsing further beliefs.

207 B. Williams 1995: 35.

208 To show that affirming a reason is not a necessary condition, Gaus rephrases Mill's famous example of the dangerous bridge: "[A] person who is about to cross a dangerous bridge has a reason *R* not to cross it, even if he does not know that it is dangerous and so could not presently affirm *R*" (G. Gaus 2011b: 234).

209 Ibid., emphasis mine.

tion "from his present reason set" is crucial, because, as Williams himself recognizes, the idea of a "sound deliberative route" could be exploited by externalists in a way that could blur the boundary between internalism and strong externalism. What externalists like Raz might argue is that *R* is a reason of Andy's if *R* is what "*any rational deliberator as such*"[210] would accept. Consider some examples we mentioned above. We argued that Bea cannot really justify Fermat's theorem to Andy if he is not an experienced mathematician. But an externalist could contend that Andy *would* believe (indeed, *any* rational deliberator would believe) that the theorem is correct if he took some advanced math classes. Similarly, Alf could be said to have a reason to believe in Betty's faithfulness even before hiring the private detective. After all, the detective's report provided him with the evidence needed to engage in "sound deliberation". If he had access to that evidence, he would definitely believe that Betty was faithful all along.

But this criticism is overstated. There seems in fact to be a crucial difference between lacking evidence and failing to appreciate available evidence. Before hiring the private detective, Alf had no evidence to believe in Betty's faithfulness. Indeed, he had reason to hold the opposite belief. But once the detective's report has rebutted his original belief, he is committed to changing his mind. The same is true of the example of Fermat's last theorem. Although Andy would accept the latest proofs of the theorem if he were an experience mathematician, he cannot be said to have a reason to accept them if he lacks the appropriate conceptual tools. By contrast, he would act irrationally if he mastered mathematics but still refused to accept the sophisticated proofs of the theorem. What I want to suggest is that the idea of a sound deliberative route should be interpreted as aiming at both ironing out inconsistencies among one's existing beliefs and achieving a reasonable amount of internal coherence.[211] The intuitive thought is that if $R \rightarrow \beta$ is justified to Andy in the light of his existing beliefs, he has reason to believe β. Only in this case can Bea attribute *R* to Andy (i.e., maintain that *R* is a reason Andy *has*) despite the fact that he happens to reject $R \rightarrow \beta$.

210 B. Williams 1995: 54.

211 Consistency and coherence and not the same thing. Coherence presupposes consistency but, additionally, requires that the belief system be sufficiently elaborated and thus take the form of a complex web of beliefs. See G. Gaus 2011b: 241.

2.4. Open justification

2.4.1 Open vs. closed justification

Gaus's notion of "open justification" fleshes out elegantly this rough intuition. Both "closed justification" and "open justification" take Andy's "current belief system as the point of departure". But while the former takes Andy's current belief system as the "alfa and omega" of what he has reason to accept and reject, the latter asks whether Andy would be committed to endorsing further reasons and beliefs in the light of "extensive criticism and additional information" made available by Bea.[212] On open justification, "we treat [one's system of beliefs and reasons] as open to new information and arguments and, from this external perspective, mak[e] judgments about what would then be justified in [one's system of beliefs and reasons]".[213] Gaus argues that the idea of open justification presupposes a *weakly externalist* conception of reasons.

Since justification must be open, we must in some way endorse an externalist conception of reasons. Bea's criticism can lead Andy to revise his belief system by providing him with new reasons and beliefs that are external to his current system. Externalism, however, must be weak. This view fits well with Williams's influential account of internal reasons, although Gaus, unlike Williams, is mainly concerned with reasons for belief rather than with reasons for action. Gaus basically agrees with Williams that in order for a person to have a reason for belief, there must be a sound deliberative route from the person's subjective motivational set to the consideration which allegedly provides the reason to believe. Weak externalism thus maintains that although Bea can demand that Andy accept reasons that are external to his current belief system, Bea's reasons (no matter how good they are in her view) can enter Andy's system only if they can be recognized as such by him given all his conceptual resources. Andy must be able to see them as reasons that can fit within his belief system, which may differ in many respects from Bea's.

2.4.2 Open justification and internal coherence

One might wonder, however, what the term "extensive criticism and additional information" actually means, or, to put it differently, what degree of "openness"

212 G. Gaus 1996: 32.

213 Ibid. 31. For a slightly different and somewhat weaker definition of open justification see G. Gaus 2011b: 248-53.

can be reasonably demanded from one's belief system. We can begin by distinguishing two ways in which Andy could criticize Bea's system of reasons and beliefs. The first kind of criticism bears on considerations of coherence. The second (and much stronger) type of criticism points to the quality of the evidence on which Bea's beliefs are based. Suppose Bea holds a belief system which comprises three main sets of beliefs: *S1*, *S2* and *S3*. Despite her willingness to develop a tenable system, Bea has failed to notice two problems. First, she has overlooked the fact that one of the members of *S1* is at odds with a member of *S2*. Second, she is not aware of the fact that *S3* could be rebutted by new empirical evidence. Now, if Bea, scanning her own beliefs in good faith, is truly unaware of these problems, then her belief system would be justified under closed justification. Under open justification, instead, external arguments could compel her to modify her system, even if she should actually fail to appreciate their strength. For instance, Andy could point out to Bea that her current sets *S1* and *S2* are not entirely compatible, whereas Charlie could present her with new evidence able to rebut *S3*. Now both types of criticism seem compatible with (and indeed, required by) the idea of open justification. It is hard to see how Bea's belief system could be openly justified if she refused to modify incoherent or flawed beliefs. The second type of criticism, however, is potentially very strong, in a way that could make it incompatible with the idea of open justification. In order to be acceptable to Bea, this second line of criticism must, I think, come down to the first and more modest one, which points to the internal coherence of her belief system.

To see why, suppose Andy and Charlie criticize Bea's belief in the existence of God. Following a "coherentist" approach, Andy could scan Bea's belief system looking for contradictory beliefs – for beliefs, that is, that could commit her to abandoning her belief in God. Charlie, however, could take a more radical stance. He could argue that even if her belief in God were internally consistent, she should nonetheless be agnostic on that issue. One should be agnostic – so Charlie's argument might go – with respect to views for which there is neither a compelling proof nor a compelling refutation, and good enough arguments on both sides of the debate to believe that the issue is not settled. But because God's existence can be neither proved nor disproved, Bea should give up her belief that God exists. It is easy to imagine how Bea could reply to this sort of critique. She could contend that her beliefs rely on evidence (say a holy book) which, from her perspective, conclusively justifies her views. This simple example shows that under open justification epistemic critiques must be part of a broader coherentist line of criticism. For if open justification allowed for something stronger than "weak" considerations of coherence, it would be hard to see how one's system of reasons and beliefs could still be the "point of departure" of open justification.

Charlie's arguments would make sense to Bea only if they pointed to the fact that the evidence she relies on is incompatible with her criteria for assessing evidence and information.

It might be objected that this "coherentist" reading would make open justification a circular process. On the one hand, Bea's system of reasons and beliefs is openly justified only if it is able to withstand external criticism. On the other hand, however, any such criticism must take Bea's current belief system as a point of departure. One way of avoiding this problem could be to say that each belief system must comprise at least one permanent set of beliefs, whose plausibility must be taken for granted. In this way, Andy's criticism would always be bound to a fixed point of reference internal to Bea's belief system. So for instance in criticizing Bea's religious beliefs Andy should recognize that her rules for assessing evidence are members of the fixed set. Alternatively, one could argue that although each criticism presupposes fixed points of references, these points may vary on a case-by-case basis. Whenever Andy sets out to criticize one of Bea's beliefs, he must assume some of them as a given point of reference, but these need not be part of a fixed set. Rather, beliefs that are assumed as a fixed point of reference at time t1 could become the object of criticism at time t2, and vice versa. On this reading, Andy could indeed criticize Bea's reliance on "religious" evidence, but to do so he should assume other beliefs of hers as a temporary point of reference. On both views, open justification would be an open-ended yet non-circular process, in which all criticism comes down to considerations of coherence based on either provisional or fixed points of reference, which are internal to the current system under scrutiny.

Both views are, I think, necessary to make sense of the idea of open justification. Yet the first view, which holds that open justification must presuppose some fixed points of reference, might appear too strong. As Quine famously argued, although some beliefs are so firmly entrenched at the center of our web of beliefs that we ordinarily (and mistakenly) consider them to be analytic truths, none of them are unrevisable.[214] But this seems to imply that, contrary to the first view, there can be no constant viz. unrevisable points of reference in one's belief system. The first view, though, should not be equated with the strong thesis that some beliefs are unrevisable. Rather, it should be read as pointing to the fact that since some beliefs are much more deeply held than others, it makes sense, as a general rule, to take them as fixed points of reference. Open justification starts from a given sets of beliefs in an effort to enhance internal consistency and coherence, which may require revising or even dropping some beliefs of the

214 W. v. O. Quine 1951.

original set. But given its coherentist character, open justification is conservative; it tends to sacrifice as little as possible of the evidential support that one's overall system of beliefs has. Things being equal, then, open justification tends to favor consistency- and coherence-based adjustments that do not involve revising or dropping those beliefs upon which a good deal of one's current web of beliefs currently hinges. Imagine, for instance, that Bea holds the following beliefs:

(a) God exists;
(b) Abortion is wrong;
(c) I do not honor God if I do not go to church on Sunday morning.

While (c) and, to a certain extent, (b), seem theoretically amendable under open justification, (a) really looks like a fundamental belief, which can serve as a constant point of reference for coherentist criticism (assuming of course Bea is a religious person who has no doubt about the existence of God but is in principle willing to revise and reconsider her beliefs about the everyday practices dictated by her creed). Again, though, (a) need not be taken as an unrevisable dogmatic truth. More simply, we can imagine that nothing of what Andy may say will ever reasonably persuade Bea that God does not exist. Should (a) ever conflict with another belief of hers X, she will always favor, things being equal, revising or dropping X rather than (a). Under open justification, then, Andy can probably only try to show that holding (a) commits Bea to accepting or dropping other beliefs of hers. On the other hand, however, beliefs such as (b) and (c) seem good candidates for the second view, according to which points of reference may vary on a case-by-case basis. Andy might temporarily take – say – (b) as a plausible belief and argue that other beliefs that Bea holds are inconsistent with (b), while in other contexts he could set out to criticize (b) by using different points of reference which are internal to Bea's current belief system.

2.4.3 Rejecting the top-down argument for consensus

Of course, these highly speculative remarks hardly contribute to understanding what can actually count as an openly justified belief. And maybe it is altogether impossible to spell out the idea of open justification in any greater detail, because, as Gaus says, "full explication of the idea of open justification would require […] a counterfactual test".[215] Moreover, Gaus has recently stressed that the

215 G. Gaus 1996: 31.

amount of internal coherence that can be required of one's belief system depends on one's cognitive capacities. To begin with, Gaus warns against the myth of full coherence: "To see instantaneously and costlessly all the implications of all one's beliefs and to render them maximally coherent is so far beyond human cognitive capacities that it is hard to see such beings as even the most idealized versions of ourselves"[216]. Our beliefs are so complex and intricate that none of us could ever aspire to fully coherentize their belief system – let alone "instantaneously and costlessly". Within certain bounds, inconsistencies and ignorance about implications must be tolerated. Moreover, these bounds need not be the same for every person, since people's cognitive capacities may significantly differ. It would be unreasonable, for instance, to demand that an average (or below average) reasoner achieve the same amount of internal consistency that can be required of – say – a sophisticated logician.

We can pass over these complications, however, since the basic idea behind the idea of open justification is clear enough. Although only openly justified belief systems can provide proper justificatory reasons, open justification must always take one's actual belief system as the point of departure. And because people hold different beliefs sets, especially with respect to evaluative judgments and ethical convictions, there will be a number of different and ultimately incompatible "points of departure". Consequently, what is openly justified to Andy may not be openly justified to others: "Given Alf's perspective ... it is possible that he has no reason to believe β, while given our belief system, we do".[217]

This leads to what Gaus calls "moderate relativism of reason". As it should have been clear all along, Gaus's relativism of reasons is (on my definition) an epistemic thesis and should not be confused with the metaphysical claim that objectively sound reasons do not exist.[218] To avoid confusion, however, we can use the term "epistemic pluralism", which is to be contrasted with "metaphysical relativism of reasons". As Gaus emphasizes, "relativism of reasons" does not entail "relativism of truth".[219] Rather, the point is that people may be epistemically justified in holding different reasons and beliefs. The upshot is that because the reasons that one has always stem from one's "subjective" belief systems, reasons are intrinsically "private" or "subjective", and only ephemerally "shareable" or "objective". This explains why the top-down argument for consensus fails. Recall that the original version of the metaphysical argument for consensus is

216 G. Gaus 2011b: 239.
217 G. Gaus 1996: 39.
218 On the other hand, it should also not be confused with moral relativism or value pluralism, according to which all moral claims are equally valid.
219 Ibid.

flawed, in that it purports to infer the epistemic conclusion that reasons are necessarily shareable and conclusive (T2) from a metaphysical conception of the reasons that there are. If no further premises are added, the argument can at best prove that *there are* only shareable reasons (III).

I argued, however, that (III), being a metaphysical thesis, falls short of what a theory of public justification needs. As the primary aim of any such theory is to determine which reasons people *have* to accept the law, the top-down argument for consensus must in some way jump to an epistemic conclusion such as (T2). We saw that the top-down argument for consensus could do this only if either (II*) or (II**) were added to its premises. But Gaus convincingly argues that both claims should be resisted on epistemic grounds. Additionally, I tried to show that by rejecting both (II*) and (II**) one need not embrace a sheer internalist conception of reasons. Rather, one should employ a weakly externalist standard of idealization which conceives of citizens as rational agents committed to a certain degree of internal consistency and coherence. Weak externalism leads to what I have called epistemic pluralism. But once epistemic pluralism is granted, the reasons that rational agents have need not, and in most cases will not, reflect objectively sound reasons. Yet it is precisely by appeal to the reasons that people have that we should publicly justify the law. Therefore, the best understanding of reasons does not entail anything as to their automatic shareability.

2.5. The discourse-theoretical argument: a radical version

2.5.1 The basic (radical) argument

Let us now turn to Habermas's defense of consensus. Habermas would also reject the line of reasoning behind the top-down argument for consensus, though for slightly different reasons. Moreover, as we will see, his discourse-theoretical epistemic conception could be described as weakly externalist in Gaus's sense. Yet discourse theory rejects the link between weak externalism and relativism of reasons. The discourse-theoretical argument for consensus can be couched both in a radical and in a moderate form. The radical version holds that private reasons are not proper justificatory reasons because they cannot be shared by all participants in justificatory discourses. The moderate version is more complex, and I will consider it below (§2.8). The structure of the radical discourse-theoretical argument for consensus is the following:

(I) *R* is a (provisionally)[220] objective (i.e., freestanding) reason if, and only if, it could be accepted as sound by all competent[221] participants in unrestricted[222] rational discourses, through which Ω is carried out.
(II) If *R* is not (provisionally) objective/freestanding, it is defeated by definition (i.e., by the fact that it is private).
Therefore,
(T1) If *R* is objective/freestanding, it cannot be defeated by subjective/non-freestanding reasons.
Therefore,
(T2) Freestanding reasons are both shareable and conclusive.

Like all strength-based arguments for consensus, this discourse-theoretical defense of consensus rests on the assumption, expressed by (I), that the procedure of abstraction Ω should in some way lead to objective results, and hence that freestandingness should be understood in terms of objectivity. Now as I argued above in defending Gaus's pluralistic epistemology, (I) must be understood as an epistemic premise, which is independent of the metaphysical thesis concerning the reasons that there are. Besides, Gaus points out that if we want to work out a viable epistemic account of justification which does not risk loosening its grip on reality, we must abandon the utopian aspiration to build up a theory of rationality from scratch. We must start from where we are and work our way toward improving our existing standards of rationality:

220 Objectivity is always "provisional" because deliberation is always open to potential objections; thus a consensus is only reached on the proviso that someone may, in the future, raise valid objections. By "provisionality" here I mean essentially "fallibility" *viz.* constant openness to potentially decisive objections. For a more comprehensive and systematic understanding of provisionality within Kantian critical theory see E. Ellis 2004; 2008.

221 The qualification "competent" should not be taken to introduce some dubious idealization. It only serves the function of avoiding some major counterintuitive implications, especially when it comes to technical or scientific questions. Recall the Fermat's theorem's example. Given his incompetence in mathematics, Andy would not be justified in accepting the latest proofs of the theorem. He would not share them as reasons for accepting it. But this does not make those proofs less objective. Hence the claim that inferences are objective only if they are shared by "competent speakers".

222 The qualification "unrestricted" is important. For Habermas, not all discourses seek objectivity. "Ethical" or "Ethical-existential" are in fact solely concerned with the self-clarification of the values and life histories shared by a given group or community. They are concerned with the question "What is good for us?", and not with the question "What deserves to be endorsed as a valid claim?". Since they abandon the aspiration to objectivity, such discourses are "restricted" to a limited number of participants sharing a common background of values and commitments.

> Our problem as reasoners is to think things through the best we can in a world in which cognitive capacities are limited, and we cannot think forever. Because fully idealized conceptions of rationality assume away the very context in which reasoning occurs and the problems it addresses, they are useless to us and our real problems as rational agents. We must begin with real rationality.[223]

Habermas's view is somewhat similar. The fundamental insight of his post-metaphysical approach is that we always start from "within". There is no way to circumvent our own way of life or form of life or to grasp reality "from without" – let alone "from nowhere". We start from within our own position of historically situated and socially bounded agents. In a way, then, Habermas's post-metaphysical approach rejects naïve objectivism just as Gaus dismisses "fully idealized conceptions of rationality [which] assume away the very context in which reasoning occurs".[224]

Yet Habermas takes a step further. Recall that while Gaus rejects strong and moderate externalism on pragmatically-flavored epistemic grounds, he remains neutral on the metaphysical question concerning the reasons that there are. Whether or not objectively sound reasons would be available to some idealized ourselves, it is imperative not to conflate allegedly justificatory facts with the reasons that the actual ourselves are justified in holding. Habermas, by contrast, tackles directly that metaphysical issue. For Habermas, arguments like the top-down argument for consensus are flawed in the stronger sense that their *premises* are false, at least with respect to practical rationality. On Habermas's post-metaphysical view, moral objectivity can no longer be hypostatized into a realm of antecedently given truths to which reason must *conform*. Rather, moral objectivity must be seen as something that post-metaphysical reason tentatively *strives for*. This is important. While post-metaphysical thinking "discharges everything that has to do with content into the realm of the contingent", it hopes to show that "even the borders of allegedly incommensurable worlds prove to be penetrable in the empirical medium of mutual understanding".[225] Thus, rather than separating the metaphysical question concerning the reasons that there are from the epistemic question concerning the reasons that we have, we should interpret the former in the light of the latter. Unlike Gaus's, Habermas's view is, as it were, bottom-up. We should start from the reasons that we have to retrieve and reconstruct, in a provisional and fallible way, the metaphysical legacy. In a way, then, constructivists are on the right track according to Habermas. They are wrong, to

223 G. Gaus 2011b: 260

224 Ibid.: 261.

225 J. Habermas 1992: 116.

be sure, in assuming that moral objectivity can be achieved once for all by abstracting away our situated perspective. Yet they point to a valuable insight, since post-metaphysical reason should be indeed understood as undertaking the quest for some sort of objectivity.

2.5.2 Some important remarks

Three important preliminary remarks before proceeding. First, it is important not to confuse Habermas's attempt to redeem the metaphysical idea of truth through discursive consensus with his earlier consensus theory of truth, from which he later retreated. On a consensus theory of truth, "the universal-pragmatic meaning of truth … is determined by the demand of reaching a rational consensus".[226] In other words, truth is brought about by rational discourses that aim at universal consensus among participants. Now Habermas is convinced that this view is problematic and should be replaced with a "pragmatic epistemological realism", [227] which sees the world, rather than ideal consensus, as the truth-maker. Whether or not a proposition is true does not depend on whether it could gain the assent of participants in justificatory discourses. In fact, its truth will depend on whether or not it conforms to the world. Still, although ideal consensus is not the truth maker, it serves the fundamental pragmatic function of testing the plausibility of truth-claims that some participants may plausibly contest. Discourse becomes necessary when the beliefs on which we rely in everyday practice (and which we believe reflect true facts about the world) lose their unproblematic status as the result of practical difficulties, or when unexpected circumstances end up throwing them into question. Cases of this kind call for an empirical inquiry through which truth-claims are submitted to critical testing. The important point is that such a critical testing, for Habermas, can only be carried out by means of rational discourses. In short, discourse does not create truth; rather, it helps us discover which prima facie controversial truth-claims deserve to be regarded as true. When the objectivity of the external world is put in doubt, discourses kick in with the aim of reconstructing objectivity in intersubjective terms.

Second, although Habermas's analysis of empirical "truth-claims" will play a major role in my argument, I will be primarily concerned with "rightness-claims", which refer to the validity of ought-statements (see §2.6.2 below). [228]

226 J. Habermas 2001: 89.

227 J. Habermas 2003: 7.

228 However, for Habermas these two kinds of claims are related because, in an important respect, rightness claims are "truth-analogous" (see §2.6.3 – 2.6.4 below).

Below (§2.6.4) we will see that when it comes to rightness-claims, the discourse-theoretical argument for consensus defends the priority of freestanding/objective reasons by rehearsing the fundamental intuition that lies at the heart of the "argument from universalization": if a moral norm is valid for all, it must be justifiable to all with the same reasons. These idea has been elegantly developed by Rainer Forst (2002; 2012), who has repeatedly insisted that the "general and reciprocal" acceptability of norms requires a deeper "general and reciprocal" acceptability of the reasons justifying those norms. In a nutshell, the idea is that the shareability of norms must reflect the shareability of reasons.

Finally, I must emphasize that my discussion will deliberately oversimplify Habermas's overall account of political justification. Habermas summarizes his idealized conception of practical discourse in the "discourse principle" (D), according to which a rule of action is justified, and thus valid, only when all those affected by it could accept it in a reasonable discourse. In *Between Facts and Norms* Habermas links principle D with an analysis of the demands inherent in modern legal systems, which he describes in the light of the history of Western modernization. He starts with the sociological assumption that modern law is fundamentally concerned with the definition and protection of individual rights in their various institutional contexts. However, such rights are expressions of freedom only if citizens can also understand themselves as the authors of the laws that interpret their rights – that is to say, only if the laws that protect private autonomy also issue from citizens' self-legislating exercise of public autonomy. Therefore, the various rights to individual freedom must also include rights of political participation. As Habermas understands the relation between private and public autonomy, each is "co-original"; conceptually, each presupposes the other in the sense that each can be fully realized only if the other is fully realized. Now Habermas claims that this co-original relationship enables his discourse theory to combine the best insights of the civic republican and classical liberal traditions of democracy. Specifically, Habermas regards rights of liberty and political participation as an abstract system of basic rights generated by reflection on the nature of principle D in contexts shaped by the functional demands on modern law (or the "form" of positive law). Because such rights are abstract, each polity must further interpret and flesh them out for its particular historical circumstances, while the system of rights constitutes a minimum set of normative institutional conditions for any legitimate modern political order. In other words, Habermas understands political justification as an interpretive enterprise, in the sense that by justifying collectively binding laws, participants interpret and flesh out the rights and duties that the theorists has already justified by applying principle D to the "form" of positive law. For simplicity, however, I shall consider discourse as a means for justifying collectively binding laws, without elaborating on the question of how discourse could and should relate to (and serve an interpretative function with respect to) the abstract scheme of rights.

2.5.3 Post-metaphysical objectivity

Let us now come back to the (radical) discourse-theoretical argument for consensus I sketched in §2.5.1. I trust it is not necessary to expand on the well-known battery of philosophical arguments through which Habermas defends his post-metaphysical shift in our conception of reason. For our purposes, it is sufficient to emphasize that for Habermas post-metaphysical reason is rooted within discursive processes of argumentation and dialogue in which the claims implicit in ordinary speech acts are tested for their rational justifiability. Reason thus appears in the weaker form of an essentially finite and fallible procedural medium oriented toward intersubjective agreement. It should no longer be located in an ideal realm independent of us, but instead in the idealizations we necessarily make while communicating and acting. Alleged objective facts now appear in the form of contentious validity claims, which call for discursive redemption and validation. According to Habermas, then, a detranscendentalized post-metaphysical concept of reason is the key to reformulating objectivity in a radically disenchanted world of "privatized gods and demons".[229] Thus, as (I) stresses, objectivity should be understood in terms of intersubjective agreement.

For Habermas, post-metaphysical thinking and communication mutually ground each other. On the one hand, post-metaphysical thinking is inherently discursive and communicative because it regards intersubjective agreement as the only standard of objectivity that survives the fall of metaphysics. But on the other hand, everyday communication, from which the ideal of discourse is derived,[230] is itself inherently post-metaphysical. The point is not simply that metaphysics is flawed, and hence that it ought to be replaced with discursive rationality. Habermas's thesis is also that in everyday interaction we *do already* in some way take a post-metaphysical stance toward the problem of justification.

229 J. Habermas 1988: 261.

230 Discourse is not the same as communication. The former is rather constructed out of the latter, positing as counterfactual assumptions the idealizations implicit in everyday communication. Discourses kick in when ordinary communication fails to reconcile the actions of the speaker with the expectations of the hearer. In any such case, speaker and hearer shift reflexive levels, from ordinary speech to discourse. While "communication remains embedded in a context of action … discourses transcend the compulsions of action", in the sense that they turn the claims implicit in the speaker's actions into validity claims seeking rational validation (J. Habermas 1973: 19).

As Gaus says, "beliefs about objectivity – what it is and how is to be achieved – are justified in the same way as any other beliefs, namely, in relation to one's system of reasons and beliefs".[231] Habermas would wholeheartedly agree. It is precisely our inescapable understanding of communicative agency that commits us to regarding intersubjective agreement as the ultimate standard of objectivity, and this is perfectly consistent with our believing that "true" objectivity lies beyond discourses. Since we implicitly subordinate our validity claims (including those arising out of our beliefs about objectivity) to discursive validation, intersubjective "objectivity" is always presupposed as a constitutive element of our everyday communicative action.

Gaus, however, seems to reject (I), for two related reasons. First, (1) given its tendency to achieve universality, the quest for objectivity seems to tread the path against which Gaus warns: "In a way ... seeking objectivity in interpersonal agreement is an effort to get outside our own systems of reasons and beliefs".[232] The ideal of intersubjective agreement could thus risk raising the low level of idealization employed by his weakly externalist conception of reasons. Second, (2) if we understand objectivity in terms of intersubjective agreement and hold that rational agents are committed to objectivity, then we have to conclude that Andy is not justified in holding non-freestanding beliefs. But the whole point of Gaus's epistemic relativism is that "Alf's being ... justified in believing β does not imply that others are openly justified in believing β".[233] In fact, "Alf may continue holding β and Betty $\sim\beta$ despite their both being committed to objectivity".[234]

Now although they are related, the two objections Gaus hints at can be rephrased as two independent theses. The first seems to imply that, on a discourse-theoretical view, Andy's being openly justified in holding β is not a *necessary* condition for β to be a belief of his (1). Since the notion of intersubjective agreement raises the level of idealization, Andy can be said to have a reason to hold β despite the fact that he is not openly justified in doing so. Call (1) the Unnecessary Open Justification Thesis:

Unnecessary Open Justification Thesis: On a discourse-theoretical view, *R* may be a reason of Andy's even if *R* is not openly justified to him.

On the other hand, the second objection suggested by Gaus can be seen as rely-

231 G. Gaus 1996: 119.
232 Ibid.
233 Ibid.: 119.
234 Ibid.: 120.

ing on a weaker thesis: although on a discourse-theoretical view Andy's being openly justified in holding β is a *necessary* condition for β to be a belief of his, this is not *sufficient*, because if β is not freestanding it is not actually a reason (2). Gaus thus seems to imply that, according to Habermas, Andy has a reason to endorse β if, and only if, everyone, including him, is openly justified in holding β. Call this the Insufficient Open Justification Thesis:

Insufficient Open Justification Thesis: On a discourse-theoretical view, *R* is a reason of Andy's if, and only if, *R* is openly justified to all.

Now I want to show that the Unnecessary Open Justification Thesis is mistaken and that the Insufficient Open Justification Thesis is only partially correct.

2.5.4 Ethical discourses and open justification

Let me begin with the Unnecessary Open Justification Thesis and with some general considerations about the role of idealizations within discourse theory. I think Gaus's worries about an excessively idealized conception of rational agreement ultimately rest upon a common misunderstanding of Habermas's position. Gaus claims that, contrary to Habermas's assumption, "discourse does not necessarily aim a rationally motivated consensus".[235] Indeed, we learn from daily experience that the more we talk about certain issues, the more we disagree. So it seems that if the idea of discourse is to be of any avail, we must surreptitiously employ an idealized notion of discourse – one according to which people are moved "solely by the force of the better argument"[236] and eventually reach unanimous agreements. Thus actual discourse (what we deliberate here and now) and ideal discourse (what we *would* deliberate under certain unspecified ideal conditions) dangerously come apart, whereby the latter takes over the justificatory role that the former is meant to play. It is a common oversight to think that Habermas ends up committing this sort of error, taking some sort of ideal rationality as an "invisible hand" that guides and ultimately overrules actual discourse. Ironically, and to the surprise of many deliberative democrats, Habermas has always been strongly skeptical about the feasibility of a rationally motivated consensus.[237] Since "[m]ore discourse means more contradiction and difference",[238]

235 Ibid.: 118.
236 J. Habermas 1994: 31.
237 Habermas emphasizes, for instance, that the bulk of the political process depends on compromise and on the outcome of fair procedures. See J. Habermas 1996: 282.

we must always take consensus as a *counterfactual regulative standard*, which only serves the role of reconciling our implicit communicative presuppositions with the fact of disagreement. We must presuppose that, although we disagree, agreement is possible, since without the prospect of an intersubjective agreement our deeply rooted understanding of ourselves as communicatively oriented agents would fall apart.

Yet precisely because of its strongly counterfactual nature, consensus should not be misinterpreted as a substantive outcome that we can anticipate by assuming away disagreement. What we need to posit is rather the purely regulative prospect of an intersubjective agreement, which emerges as a precondition of possibility for the realization of those expectations that arise out of our inescapable understanding of communication. As Habermas has been at pains to insist, "the ideal presuppositions of communicative action must not be hypostatized into the ideal of a future condition".[239] Although justificatory discourse gestures toward transcendent *validity* (*Geltung*), it is always bound to the *facticity* (*Faktizität*) of the limited cognitive horizon of the speakers. When we engage in justification we always start from "within", and transcendence is always "transcendence from within".[240] The idealizations we necessarily make in everyday communication rather serve as a critical standpoint, which, just as the objectivity to which it tends, is always heuristically postulated but never realized in actual discourse. Counterfactuals are first and foremost "*standards* for a self-correcting learning process".[241] But actual discourse always starts from a bundle of taken-for-granted beliefs and values; moreover, it is always bound to the background cognitive resources provided by the "form-of-life" within which justification occurs.[242]

Now we have to refine this point and show that, on Habermas's view, Andy's being openly justified in holding β is indeed a *necessary* condition for β to be a belief of his. This is an easy task, since Habermas maintains that the only idealizations we are allowed to inject into the discursive model have to do with considerations of *consistency* and *authenticity*. Speech consistency is purely formal: "No speaker can contradict himself".[243] If Andy utters A, he cannot utter ~A; nor can he utter both A and B if A contradicts B. Speech authenticity is more interesting. Recall that, for Habermas, in everyday interaction we always raise validity claims, at least implicitly. We take it for granted that what we say can be

238 J. Habermas 1992: 140.
239 Ibid.: 144.
240 J. Habermas 1998.
241 J. Habermas 2008: 84.
242 See J. Habermas 1994, chapter 6; 1998 chapter 4.
243 J. Habermas 1990: 87.

accepted by all as objectively valid. But in doing so we also raise parallel *authenticity claims*, which refer to our internal world of subjective needs, feelings and beliefs. By raising authenticity claims we want to assure the hearers that our utterances, arguments and demands are sincere or truthful. They are sincere not only in the straightforward sense of non-deceptiveness toward the hearers, but also in the deeper sense that they follow from what we believe. As speakers, we must take a self-critical stance toward our own beliefs, which implies some sort of "hermeneutic self-understanding".[244] We must assert only what we have *reason* to believe given our present set of convictions, beliefs and needs.

It is easy to spot a substantial overlap between the demand for authenticity and Gaus's idea of open justification. After all, what open justifications requires of Andy is that he be authentic – that he only endorse claims which in some way follow from what he already believes. To put it the other way round, discourse theory requires that speakers only raise claims that are openly justified to them. But apart from this weak requirement of internal coherence, discourse theory introduces no further idealizations to determine which reasons speakers have. Hence to say that $R \rightarrow \beta$ is (provisionally) objective is to say that $R \rightarrow \beta$ is *openly justified to all*. The Unnecessary Open Justification Thesis is therefore wrong because it mistakenly presupposes that discourse theory raises the bar of idealization, and hence that, on Habermas's view, Andy can be said to have a reason to hold β despite the fact that he is not openly justified in doing so. I argued that this view should be resisted. Unless Andy is openly justified in raising or endorsing a validity claim, no "external" reasons for endorsing that claim can be attributed to him.

But what about the Insufficient Open Justification Thesis? Remember that, according to this second thesis, on a discourse-theoretical view Andy's being openly justified in holding β is a necessary yet not sufficient condition for β to be a belief of his. Given his commitment to objectivity, Andy must drop any openly justified beliefs of his that are not openly justified to all. Now on the one hand the Insufficient Open Justification Thesis certainly captures a crucial element of Habermas's conception of rationality. To be rational is to hold beliefs and perform actions that can be discursively validated as provisionally objective. Let us make a distinction between reasons as inputs and reasons as outputs. When considered as inputs, reasons are necessarily private, since they always stem from the personal perspective of a speaker, whose validity claims have not been discursively scrutinized yet. Still, a speaker can present her private views in the form of universal validity claims only under the reasonable expectation that the

244 J. Habermas 1994: 5.

reasons she intends to advance in their support will gain unanimous assent. She must presuppose, that is, that her private inputs will yield public outputs cast in the form of freestanding inferences. The discourse-theoretical argument for consensus, then, only applies to reasons as outputs. Here the Insufficient Open Justification Thesis seems correct: if a private reason introduced as a justificatory input cannot be turned into a freestanding viz. provisionally objective output, it is not a proper justificatory reason.

On the other hand, however, the Insufficient Open Justification Thesis is too strong. The fact that $R \rightarrow \beta$ is not openly justified to all does not mean that Andy does not have a reason to hold β. His being openly justified in holding $R \rightarrow \beta$ is indeed a sufficient condition for R to be a reason of Andy's. The point, however, is that R would not be a proper justificatory reason, in the sense that it would be unable to justify sensible beliefs in a context where an "objective" justification is required. Recall that radical arguments for consensus hold that private reasons, qua subjective, cannot warrant rational belief in the law's legitimacy – they are actually defeated by the very fact that they are not freestanding. It is true that for Habermas "there is only one criterion by which beliefs can be judged valid, and that is that they are based on agreement reached by argumentation".[245] But there is little reason to believe that by endorsing this view Habermas commits himself to rejecting open justification as such.[246] I take rather Habermas to imply that "private" reasons would boil down to mere personally endorsable views, which, being discursively downgraded to subjective beliefs, cannot count as proper justificatory reasons.

Moreover, it is interesting to notice that, in Habermas's view, some beliefs can be discursively validated despite the fact that they are deliberately subjective. Recall that according to (I) only "unrestricted" discourses are in pursuit of objectivity. As we will see, "moral", "pragmatic" and "empirical discourses" are unrestricted. Their ultimate aim is to show that validity claims can be (provisionally) seen as objective because they could be unanimously accepted by an unrestricted audience of competent speakers. "Ethical" (or "ethical-existential", or "ethical-political") discourses, by contrast, are restricted. Here a limited number of speakers sharing a common cultural background engage in a strongly evaluative process of self-understanding. What matters in ethical discourses is personal authenticity, rather than objective validity. As such, ethical discourses bear strong resemblance to the idea of open justification, in that they seek to determine which reasons and beliefs we should endorse in the light of our deepest convictions. But because ethical discourses yield inherently "subjective" results,

245 J. Habermas 1990: 14.
246 G. Gaus 1996: 117.

discourse theory by no means endorses the view that only provisionally objective beliefs are justified. What discourse theory holds is that "ethical" beliefs, though openly justified to some, cannot serve as proper justificatory reasons. In the end, the "outputs" of restricted ethical discourses are merely private "inputs", which, in order to gain justificatory strength, should be turned into freestanding "outputs" of unrestricted moral discourses. Although Andy's being openly justified in holding $R \rightarrow \beta$ is a necessary and sufficient condition for R to be a reason of Andy's, R would be devoid of any significant justificatory strength if it remained an essentially private or ethical reason.

To put the point somewhat more precisely, we should distinguish between a "restricted" context of justification, in which the question is "What is justified to us as members of a given community" from an "unrestricted" context of justification, in which participants aspire to achieve an impartial, objective justification.[247] The Insufficient Open Justification Thesis is wrong because in the former context subjective reasons do qualify as reasons. However, such reasons are inadequate in the latter context – to use our terminology, they are by definition defeated within the unrestricted context of justification.

Now Gaus would of course reject this view, too. Contrary to Habermas's intuition, he would insist that Andy's being openly justified in holding $R \rightarrow \beta$ is a sufficient condition for R to be a proper justificatory reason even in the unrestricted context of justification, though only from Andy's personal perspective. As I shall argue in the next section, this objection points to a valuable insight. Yet it is unclear why Gaus takes this to be an objection against (I), which holds that objectivity should be understood in terms of intersubjective agreement. His objection seems rather to press Habermas on (II), which holds that only provisionally objective reasons are proper justificatory reasons – subjective reasons are by definition defeated within the "unrestricted" context of justification. It is therefore (II) on which our critique of the (radical) discourse-theoretical argument for consensus must turn.

2.6. Public reason and post-metaphysical rationality

2.6.1 Are private reasons necessarily defeated?

The first premise of the (radical) discourse-theoretical argument (I) essentially holds that freestanding ness should be understood in terms of discursive agree-

247 I borrow the idea of different contexts of justification from Forst (2002).

ment aiming at (provisional) objectivity. For Habermas, (I) builds on the fact that communicative action is an inherently consensual form of social coordination in which actors inevitably mobilize the potential for rationality implicit in ordinary language Thus far, I have argued that (I) is not implausible. But the second premise of the radical discourse-theoretical argument (II) is more problematic. Why should only provisionally objective reasons be proper justificatory reasons, as (II) states? Observe that (II) does not follow from (I). The fact that provisional objectivity is tantamount to intersubjective agreement does imply that we should regard only provisionally objective reasons as properly justificatory (in the unrestricted context of justification). To be sure, if Bea is openly justified in rejecting R as a reason for β, Andy is committed to regarding $R \rightarrow \beta$ as a "subjective" belief of his, which has proven unable to withstand unrestricted discursive scrutiny. Moreover, if post-metaphysical reason strives for objectivity, as implied by (I), then we have a strong case for believing that only provisionally objective reasons are truly freestanding. The question, however, must be raised as to whether post-metaphysical reason exhausts the idea of public justification. The question, in other words, must be raised as to whether objectivity and public reasoning are as interwoven as discourse theory seems to suggest.

To affirm (II), defenders of the discourse theoretical argument for consensus must establish a convincing case for an "objectivist" post-metaphysical conception of public reason, according to which public reason aspires to provide an impartial, universal justification of rightness claims based on truth-tracking objective reasons. If this is the function of public reason, then (II) is warranted: all subjective/non-freestanding reasons are defeated because they are by definition unable to warrant truth-analogous rightness claims to an unrestricted "community of investigators". To get clearer on this passage from (I) to (II), it is necessary to say more about Habermas's distinction between "truth-claims" and "truth-analogous rightness claims".

2.6.2 Validity claims

From a Habermasian perspective, to say that β is justifiable is to say that someone who asserts or utters β raises a justifiable "validity claim" (*Geltungsanspruch*). But validity claims can take mainly two forms: they can be either claims to *truth* or claims to *rightness*. By raising a truth-claim, the speaker advances an empirical claim concerning the objective world of states of affairs. He or she invokes the external world as a truth-maker supporting claims such as "The door is locked", "Frankfurt is rainy", "$E=mc^2$" etc. By raising a rightness claim, instead, the speaker refers to the world of normatively regulated social interactions. He or she thus claims that the norms of action he/she considers valid deserve "universal recognition among the circle of addressees".[248] Let us consider the first category of claims.

Suppose Andy is openly justified in holding a scientific theory *T* on the basis of a given set of empirical data *S1*. He thus raises a truth-claim, with the strong expectation that every competent speaker will accept that *S1* →*T*. But now imagine Bea is openly justified in rejecting his discursive "input". It turns out that she is openly justified in holding a slightly different set of empirical claims, *S2*, which rebuts *T*. Now could we say that *S1*, being openly justified to Andy, may provide him with a proper justificatory reason for holding *T?* Could we say that, things being equal, *S1* may be strong enough to warrant Andy's rational belief in *T*? The answer seems to be no. Unless every competent speaker agrees with him, Andy must recognize that something is amiss. If competent speakers are justified in rejecting his scientific theory, he must conclude that perhaps he was wrong all along. This is not to deny, of course, that *T* can still make sense to him. The point, however, is that he would have a strong reason to doubt whether *T* is really true after all.

To be sure, many followers of Kuhn dismiss this as a naïve view of scientific inquiry, probably with good reasons. Kuhn's fundamental claim is that even when scientific inquiry is largely dominated by conflicting paradigms, which revolve around unchallenged substantive assumptions and are often insensitive to each other.[249] Still, the naïve view of scientific inquiry has much intuitive appeal. Scientific inquiry and truth-oriented deliberation in general, seem inherently "objective", at least in principle. If two groups of scientists disagree, it may seem odd to insist that each group is rationally justified in looking at the empirical world through the prism of their own "subjective" belief system. Some may thus insist that disagreement over scientific matters must be provisional. When it comes to truth-claims, then, Habermas might be right: unless *R* is freestanding or objective, *R* is not a proper justificatory reason.

Now there are two important kinds of "discourses" that revolve around truth-claims. The first encompasses the broad family of "empirical-theoretical discourses". Here speakers assert, in a descriptive manner, the existence of some objective state of affairs relating to the external world. Participants are thus understood as members of what C. S. Peirce called a "community of investigators".[250] Like scientists, they gather, exchange and process information in order to assess the reliability of empirical claims. "Pragmatic discourses" also hinge

248 J. Habermas 2008: 86

249 T. Kuhn 1962.

250 See K. O. Apel: 1981; J. Habermas 1992: 88-111.

upon truth-claims. Here speakers are conceived of as rational calculators presented with a limited set of means for the achievement of some given goal, whose validity is taken for granted and not discursively thematized. According to Habermas, "pragmatic questions" arise from the point of view of someone who looks for the best means to reach certain ends and to bring about some desired states of affairs. Thus, although pragmatic discourses, unlike "empirical-theoretical discourses", deal with norms of action, they are not concerned with rightness-claims, since they are limited to questions of purposive rationality. Pragmatic discourses do not verify whether the goals we may wish to achieve deserve to be achieved; they simply assume them as conditionally given. Pragmatic discourses are led by the conditional question: "*If* we want to bring about some state of affairs X, what means must we choose?" This is a purely empirical question. What is, objectively speaking, the best set of means for the achievement of a given goal? The primary aim of pragmatic discourses is thus to "relate causes to effects in accordance with value preferences and prior goal determinations".[251] Hence even in pragmatic discourses "the core empirical issue is the redemption of truth claims".[252]

Yet empirical-theoretical discourses and pragmatic discourses, however important, by no means exhaust the idea of public justification. For here the core normative issue is the redemption of rightness-claims. We achieve public justification when we show that all those subjected to a political regime have reason to accept it as legitimate. Here we are no longer concerned with the empirical (and normatively conditional) question: "What are the best means to achieve X?", but rather with the purely normative question: "Why should we accept a norm that compels us to achieve X?" We should therefore ask ourselves whether the redemption of rightness-claims must be as objective as that of truth-claims. Suppose, then, that Andy is openly justified in holding $R \rightarrow \beta$. He then raises a rightness-claim and expects every hearer to respond with a rationally motivated "yes". But what if Bea is openly justified in rejecting his discursive "input"? Could we say that *R*, being openly justified to Andy, may commit him to *β?* Could we say that, other things being equal, *R* may be strong enough to warrant Andy's rational belief that *β* is right? Now Habermas seems to imply that even in this case the answer must be no. He is adamant that rightness claims are "truth-analogous claims".[253] Although they cannot qualify as "true", but only as "justifiable", rightness claims do call for an objective and discursively mediated verification, just as truth-claims do.

251 J. Habermas 1994: 3.
252 J. Habermas 2008: 85.
253 Ibid.: 86.

But is practical objectivity required of public reason? Most theorists of public reason think it is. Immanuel Kant, Charles Larmore, Thomas Nagel, Christine Korsgaard and David Estlund, to name just some, have been deeply attracted to the idea that public justification must be conducted on objective grounds. In particular, Estlund understands public justification as something akin to scientific inquiry.[254] In his view, democracy works essentially like science. It contributes to public justification by presenting itself as an epistemic procedure seeking to uncover some given truths about normatively regulated social relations. Estlund's comparison between science and public justification is interesting precisely because it deliberately overlooks the fundamental asymmetry between truth-claims and rightness claims that I want to highlight.

2.6.3 The asymmetry between rightness claims and truth claims

To illustrate this asymmetry, let us make a distinction between theoretical and practical rationality. Let us stipulate that "theoretical rationality" has to do with reasons for beliefs about empirical states of affairs and "truth-claims" in general, while "practical rationality" deals with reasons for beliefs about courses of actions, normative/prescriptive statements and "rightness-claims" in general.[255] Now consider how theoretical rationality is normally thought to work when it comes to the validation of "truth-claims". Suppose Bea and Andy are justified in holding two different scientific theories *T1* and *T2*. It turns out, however, that these two theories converge in support of a given truth-claim *P*. Would it make sense to say that *P* is rationally justified on the basis of an "overlapping consensus" of scientific theories? Those who are impressed by what I have called the naïve view of scientific inquiry (§2.6.2) seem bound to insist that the answer is no, for the same reason why Andy is not rationally justified in holding *T* unless Bea agrees. The naïve view of scientific inquiry holds that given its aspiration to objectivity, scientific inquiry demands that descriptive statements about the world be grounded in objective reasoning.

When it comes to the validation of rightness claims, however, things look differently. If public reason shows that Andy and Bea have two different convergent reasons *R1* and *R2* for endorsing a rightness claim *N*, there is nothing odd in

254 D. Estlund 1997.

255 I use the qualifications "practical" and "theoretical" to simplify my subsequent discussion about the validation of rightness-claims and truth-claims, respectively. This definition is unusual. It holds that both theoretical and practical rationality are concerned with reasons for beliefs, while in traditional philosophical jargon the term "practical rationality" refers to the assessment of reasons for action.

saying that they are rationally justified in endorsing *N*. Of course, if Andy and Bea regarded *N* as truth-analogous, they would be bothered by the lack of a common ground for endorsing *N*, just as they would be bothered by an overlapping consensus of scientific theories. If valid claims are truth-analogous, and if we endorse the naïve view of scientific progress, then it is inevitable to concur with Habermas that "valid statements deserve the acceptance of everyone for the same reasons".[256] Just as scientific inquiry aims to discover objective truths by uncovering objectively justificatory reasons, moral reasoning aspires to justify impartial norms that all could endorse for the same objective, truth-tracking reasons. But my point is precisely that public justification does not require that the law be seen as truth-analogous.[257] In fact, public justification and theoretical rationality differ in both a) *function* and *scope* b).

a) Public reason and theoretical rationality have different functions. Public justification is first and foremost justification *to somebody*. By contrast, theoretical justification is first and foremost justification *of something*. As a result, while the former focuses primarily on the *addressees* of justification, the latter places greater emphasis on the *justificandum*. According to the naïve view of scientific inquiry, what matters in science is that theories be objectively validated. Scientists are not interested in reasoned agreements as such, at least on the naïve view. They want to agree for the same reasons, for only in this case can their theories live up to the standard of objectivity that the naïve view expects from science. Who cares whether or not a scientific theory is justified *to all* scientists if we cannot provide an objective justification *of* that theory? Public justification points to the opposite direction. To the members of the public committed to the ideal of public reason, what matters is that the law be justified *to its addressees*. Unlike scientists, they are indeed interested in reasoned agreements as such. Once we show that law *L* is justified to all those subjected to it, why should it matter if acceptance of *L* is based on an overlapping consensus of non-public reasons? Hasn't public reason already served its function? Habermas objects that such an overlapping consensus would make public justification rest on the contingent, shaky grounds of a "lucky convergence".[258] He claims that that it is "counter-intuitive" to ground a conception of justice in non-freestanding non-universalistic reasons.[259] I disagree. In fact, it is Habermas's view that may have

256 J. Habermas 1998: 86.

257 As Gaus says, public reasoning must not be seen as a "collaborative" scientific enterprise. See G. Gaus 2008.

258 J. Habermas 1998: 84.

259 Ibid.: 86.

counter-intuitive implications. To see this, we must get clearer on the *scope* of public reason.

b) Theoretical reasoning is universal in scope, in that it presupposes an enlarged, unlimited "community of investigators". All competent speakers must have a say. Public reason, by contrast, is local in scope. Unless Andy is subjected to a political regime, he is not entitled to demand that that regime be justified to him. Now suppose Andy is a fierce supporter of the death penalty. But one day he discovers, to his puzzlement, that in some foreign country *C*, a thick overlapping consensus of comprehensive doctrines resolutely supports a criminal law *L* which under no circumstances allows for the death penalty. Though for different convergent reasons, the citizens of *C* agree on *L*. Would it be reasonable for Andy to complain about the fact that his private views are not encompassed by this overlapping consensus? Certainly not: since he is not subjected to *L*, *L* need not be justified to him. Yet Habermas seems committed to a counter-intuitive view of this kind. In fact, although for the time being nobody in *C* accepts the death penalty, someone like Andy could, and this makes the legitimacy of *L* fundamentally contingent. But to say that those who are actually subjected to *L* should see this as a problem is to say that they should take Andy's views into account as a potential source of criticism, despite the fact that, ex hypothesi, none of those who share Andy's views are entitled to have a say. But Andy has indeed a say: for *L* is *not* justified unless it can be acceptable to people like him. His potential dissent must be vicariously accounted for, *as if* Andy were part of that polity. Indeed, any possible source of criticism should be taken into account, for only in this case could *L* be justified on firm, objective grounds. Again, *L* must be taken to be a truth-analogous rightness-claim. Consequently, although the law must be justified to a limited polity, the reasons supporting it should be acceptable to a much larger, and potentially unrestricted, "community of investigators".

This strikes me as implausible. Given the local scope of the law, public reason should itself be understood as local in scope. Notice, moreover, that this assumption is already built in the Principle of Public Justification, which is a constitutive element of the general Concept of Public Reason. In chapter 1 (§1.2.5), we saw that the Principle of Public Justification combines two leading ideas. The first is *generality*: in order to be justified, *L* must present itself as a law which could gain the assent of all those subjected to it. The second requirement is *non-universality*: the addressees of public justification are the members of given society, for the laws and rules of social cooperation are binding only on them. The rationale of these two views is, of course, implicit in the Principle of Political Liberty. We must focus on the addressees of coercive laws, because *they* are subjected to political authority. Again, public reason is limited in scope.

The alleged analogy between truth-claims and rightness-claims seems therefore to overlook both the specific function of public reason and its limited scope. In a way, function and scope of public reason are two sides of the same coin. By conflating the function of public reason with that of theoretical reasoning, Habermas ends up neglecting the limited scope of the former. He says that on a convergence view "citizens simply observe that their fellow citizens accept the political conception for their own reasons but they cannot judge whether this acceptance has a genuine *rational basis*".[260] To rescue the political conception from an undesirable lack of "rational basis", Habermas suggests regarding it as a bulk of truth-analogous rightness-claims. As a result, he sees public justification primarily as an objective justification *of* rightness-claims. Thus the main target of public reason is the presumed objectivity of the justificandum. But this mischaracterizes the *function* of public justification. Its function is first and foremost to justify rightness claims *to* its addressees. As a result, the scope of public justification is also unduly widened. If the law must be justified on (provisionally) objective grounds, it must be backed by universal freestanding reasons which all possible speakers could accept. The counter-intuitive upshot of this view is that the members of a given polity end up owing a justification to a potentially unlimited "community of investigators".[261]

2.6.4 A discourse-theoretical approach to universalization

These considerations speak in favor of at least a prima facie asymmetry between public reason and theoretical reason. And this prima facie asymmetry, in turn, warrants a prima facie presumption against the thesis that the law should be seen as truth-analogous. The onus of justification is now on discourse theory. It must come up with some arguments able to rebut the presumption in favor of asymmetry. To do so, discourse theory could resort to the "argument from universalization", which we have hitherto ignored. According to that argument, it will be recalled, proper justificatory reasons must pass some threshold of universalization. Unless each and every similarly situated moral agent is committed to ϕ-ing, Andy is not rationally justified in ϕ-ing. Extending this argument to the level of public justification, one could argue that proper justificatory reasons must be public not because the law is truth-analogous, but because the law must be im-

260 Ibid.: xix.
261 For a different criticism of Habermas's position see T. McCarthy 1996; for an attempt at reconciliation between Rawls's doctrine of the "overlapping consensus" and discourse theory see K. Baynes 2010.

partially justified. And because impartial reasons are by definition freestanding, Andy does not have a proper justificatory reason to accept L unless that reason is impartial.

Generally speaking, the argument from universalization is in tune with a discourse theoretical approach to discourse-theory. After all, the argument from universalization is largely employed by Kantian constructivists, who, like discourse-theorists, typically favor a "bottom-up" defense of the Shareability Requirement. Kantian constructivism starts from the assumption that apart from a "procedure of constructing the principles of justice there are no moral facts".[262] Kantian constructivism rejects the view that "statements about good reasons" are "true or false in virtue of a moral order of values that is prior to and independent of our conceptions of person and society and of the public and social role of moral doctrines".[263] No antecedently given "criterion of justice" can be taken to have the sort of unrestricted authority which would entitle us to view it as the source of normativity.[264]

To be sure, Habermas has repeatedly criticized "Rawlsian" versions of Kantian constructivism. While for Habermas impartiality is embodied by discursive procedures receptive to actual reasons, Rawls undertakes the substantive task of determining, "monologically", which moral or impartial reasons would be seen as objectively sound under idealized conditions of fairness.[265] "Moral discourses" are built around the Kantian principle of universalization, which is clearly in tune with the rationale of the argument from universalization. For Kantians, moral reasons are essentially impartial. As such, they are essentially freestanding, or, as Rainer Forst says, "*reciprocally* and *generally* justifiable".[266] But in Habermas's formulation, universalization should not be understood as an "*imaginary* – because counterfactually extended and virtually enacted – process of argumentation".[267] Whereas Kant and Rawls are still held captive by a *monological* approach to morality, which seriously risks lapsing into a hypostatized metaphysical conception of moral reasons, Habermas is adamant that "the fact of plurality of agents"[268] should be taken seriously. We start from the reasons that we have and we verify, by means of actual moral discourses, which reasons we can share.

262 J. Rawls 1980: 307.
263 J. Rawls 1989: 511.
264 See O. O'Neill 2003.
265 J. Habermas 1990: 51-4; 1995: 117.
266 R. Forst 2001: 362.
267 J. Habermas 1994: 15.
268 Ibid.: 16.

In any event, the argument from universalization (however "detranscendentalized") is of little avail to discourse theory. Far from showing that impartiality speaks in favor of a fundamental symmetry between truth-claims and rightness-claims, the argument from universalization works only under the *presupposition* that practical and theoretical rationality are symmetrical. To see why, consider the fundamental assumption on which the argument from universalization relies: since morality demands impartiality, moral reasons must be impartial; in other words, the (impartial) shareability of norms must reflect the deeper (impartial) shareability of the reasons justifying those norms. Despite its intuitive plausibility, this view is question-begging. The intuition of convergence theorists is precisely that an "overlapping consensus" of comprehensive doctrines, though based on non-impartial reasons, exhausts the idea of impartiality that lies at the heart of the ideal of public reason. Notice that we implicitly introduced this idea when we distinguished three different levels of publicness (chapter 1, §1.3.4). All public reason requires is Publicness as a Property of the Commitment to Justify Coercion to All, which essentially holds that Andy's reasoning justifying coercive law *L* is public when Andy is committed to justifying *L* to all his fellow citizens. Unless Andy accepts this view, he is not engaging in public justification. But this kind of commitment to public justification is independent of Publicness as a Property of the use of Reason and of Publicness as a Property of Reasons, which essentially introduce a Shareability Requirement on the reasons citizens can advance.

Publicness as a Property of the Commitment to Justify Coercion to All entails that to be impartial is to refrain from issuing demands that favor some groups of people over others. Public reason is certainly impartial in this sense, since it seeks to show that the law can be *equally* acceptable to all those subjected to it. But from this it does not follow that the reasons given in support of the law must be themselves impartial or shared. Of course, Rainer Forst is entirely right in stressing that, both on a Kantian and a discourse-theoretical understanding of morality, moral demands should be justified by appeal to "shared reasons" (i.e., freestanding reasons which are by definition shareable and conclusive).[269] But this is due to the fact that Kant, Habermas and Forst presuppose a *universalistic* conception of morality. And universalism is inextricably intertwined with a truth-analogous conception of objectivity. For Kant, it is not enough to show all existing conceptions of the good can overlap in support of some maxim. In order for a maxim to be rational, one must believe that every possible self-legislating agent could will it as a universal law. Hence moral maxims must be backed by

269 R. Forst 2002.

impartial reasons, to wit, by reasons that could be endorsed by all. But to say that morality is universalistic and objectivistic in this sense is tantamount to saying that moral claims should be seen as truth-analogous. But this begs the crucial question that discourse-theory needs to address: *why* should we take the law to be truth-analogous?

2.6.5 Discourse theory and epistemic pluralism

In order to avoid terminological confusion I shall maintain, along with the Habermasian tradition, that moral reasons aspire to be impartial, universal, and objective. By contrast, ethical reasons typically offer contextual grounds for endorsing rightness-claims. So the question now is: Given a prima facie asymmetry between public reason and theoretical reasoning, why should we take ethical reasons to be intrinsically non-justificatory? To put it differently: why should we interpret every relevant area of practical reason in terms post-metaphysical rationality? David Couzens Hoy rightly contends that "Habermas's philosophy … is driven by a … Kantian (and perhaps even German idealist) paradigm of *systematic* philosophy whereby a stance on theoretical reason entails a similar stance on practical reason".[270] Post-metaphysical rationality, albeit fragmented, porous and linguistically mediated, is always in pursuit of objectivity, both in the practical and in the theoretical domain – with the exception of ethical discourses. Perhaps we need not jettison this alleged convergence between theoretical and practical reason as such. What we need to stress is that there is a clear presumption against the thesis that public reason, which is inherently practical, demands the same amount of objectivity required of theoretical reason. For only under this assumption can we downgrade ethical arguments to mere subjectively endorsable beliefs devoid of any significant justificatory strength.

The law always comes down to a bulk of rightness-claims, which must be impartially justified. But public justification is not primarily justification *of* the law. It is justification of the law *to* its addressees. Hence, public justification does not in itself require that the law be *objectively* justified by appeal to freestanding or impartial reasons. But because the discourse-theoretical rendition of the argument from universalization begs the question as to why the law should be seen as truth-analogous, the presumption in favor of asymmetry is still in place. I think there is no need to press this point any farther. For however weak that presumption may be, discourse theory seems to have no arguments to rebut it.

270 T. McCarthy / D. C. Hoy 1994: 178. I take it that D. C. Hoy relies on the peculiar definition of "practical" and "theoretical" rationality I gave above (note 255).

This establishes a strong case for rejecting the second premise of the discourse theoretical argument for consensus (II), which holds that when it comes to public justification, non-freestanding reasons are necessarily defeated. Bear in mind that the discourse-theoretical argument for consensus I have been considering so far is radical. It purports to show that private reasons are as such (i.e., simply because they are private) unable to warrant rational belief. To drive this point home, advocates of discourse theoretical argument for consensus must defend an "objectivist" post-metaphysical conception of public reason, according to which public reason aspires to provide an impartial, universal justification of rightness claims based on truth-tracking objective reasons. If this is the function of public reason (and if we endorse the naïve view of scientific inquiry, which understands scientific inquiry as aiming to uncover objective truths for objective reasons that all could endorse), then (II) is warranted: subjective/non-freestanding reasons are defeated because they are unable to warrant truth-analogous rightness claims to an unrestricted "community of investigators". Yet we have seen that legally binding rightness-claims need not be objectively justified because as public reason liberals we are not committed to viewing them as truth-analogous. Consequently, we should resist the claim that only provisionally objective reasons are properly justificatory. In other words, we should reject (II). But if (II) is rejected, then the discourse-theoretical argument for consensus fails.

2.7 Some provisional results

2.7.1 Rejecting some major arguments for consensus

We can draw three important conclusions from my critique of the (radical) discourse-theoretical argument for consensus. The first is that the argument from universalization should be resisted. Given the local scope of public reason and given Publicness as a Property of the Commitment to Justify Coercion to All, there is no compelling rationale behind the idea that impartial laws should be necessarily justified by impartial reasons. Insofar as those subjected to *L* have sufficient grounds for endorsing *L*, *L* is publicly justified, regardless of whether or not the reasons supporting it are objective or universal.

Secondly, it follows from what I have said thus far that discourse theory seems committed to endorsing some kind of epistemic pluralism such as Gaus's, at least with respect to the domain of public justification. Habermas's thesis that discursive agreement is the only "criterion by which beliefs can be judged valid" may be right. But we should dissent from the view that if beliefs are judged valid by "ethical" discourses, they cannot serve as proper justificatory reasons for accepting the law. Also, we may endorse Habermas's overall discourse-theoretical view but not his claim that ethical reasons are not proper justificatory reasons. Similarly, we may endorse Habermas's epistemic approach, according to which only reasons that could be discursively shared are epistemically justified. But we should dissent from the view that if *R* is shared only by participants in ethical discourses, then *R* is by definition unable to serve as a justificatory ground.

Thirdly, my critique of the radical discourse-theoretical argument for consensus enables us to reject the last strength-based argument left, which I called the "social argument for consensus". As Korsgaard says, reasons are like rules. They are normative concepts, which presuppose a legislator to lay them down and a citizen to obey. But since normative concepts are open to countless interpretations, any citizen could make up her own rationality in the absence of socially sanctioned guidelines determining what counts as a sound reason. To rephrase this point in discourse-theoretical terms, we can say that in order for $R \rightarrow L$ to qualify as a sound inference, it must be shared by all participants in justificatory discourses, whose rationally motivated assent assumes the role of socially recognized guideline. Still, the fact that $R \rightarrow L$ must be shared by all participants does not mean that it must be shared by *all* rational agents. In fact, it is sufficient that $R \rightarrow L$ be shared by the "restricted" community of participants in *ethical* discourses. By saying "this is a private reason of mine for accepting *L*", Andy does not necessarily engage in a solipsistic process, where "individual words … are to refer to what can only be known to the person speaking", that is, "to his immediate private sensations".[271] Quite the contrary, Andy points to the fact that *R* gains the unanimous assent of his "ethical" community. In short, the discourse-theoretical argument for consensus and the social argument for consensus founder on the same point: they mistakenly assume that since justificatory reasons must be shared by somebody else than the speaker, then they must be shared by all.

In sum, the radical discourse-theoretical argument, the social argument and the argument from universalization (in its radical version) fail to show what radical strength-based arguments are supposed to show, namely, that subjective, non-freestanding reasons are defeated by the very fact that they are private. The same applies to the top-down argument for consensus. But if freestanding objective reasons may be defeated by private reasons, as the failure of radical strength-based arguments allows us to maintain, then freestanding reasons may be neither conclusive nor shareable. The twofold presumption in favor of convergence I described in chapter 1 (§1.5.6) has not been rebutted yet.

271 L. Wittgenstein 2001: 243.

2.7.2 A more moderate defense of consensus?

Let us draw some more general conclusions from what we have said thus far. To begin with, our defense of weak externalism enables us to refine the definition of "shareability" we gave in chapter 1 (§1.3.3). That is to say, we can turn the Justificatory View of Shareability, which is purely formal and hence neutral on the externalism/internalism distinction, into a Weakly Externalist View of Shareability:

Weakly Externalist View of Shareability: If *R* is a reason for law *L*, *R* is a public/shareable reasons if, and only if, every reasonable citizen would be openly justified in believing that *R* is a reason justifying *L* (or in believing that *R* is a reason in the sense expressed by the Expanded View of Reasons).[272]

The Weakly Externalist View of Shareability is to be contrasted with a radically internalist or, as I shall say, "populist" conception of shareability:

Populist View of Shareability: If *R* is a reason for law *L*, *R* is a public/shareable reason if, and only if, it is affirmed by all.

As Christopher Eberle says, on "populist" views of this kind "a rationale R counts as a public justification only if the members of the public find R acceptable in light of their existing [subjective motivational sets], irrespective of their epistemic pockmarks and doxastic defects".[273] Of course, both consensus and convergence conceptions can be populist. A populist consensus view would hold that a given law is justified if and only if citizens actually share some reasons for accepting it, while a populist convergence model would maintain that a given law is justified if and only if the private beliefs people actually hold converge in its support. But justificatory populism is clearly an extreme and clearly implausible position, which rests on a radical internalist conception of reasons – a conception from which even declared internalists such as Williams shy away. As Gaus says, "[p]eople can withhold their assent because of obstinacy, selfishness, laziness, perversity, or confusion. That an obstinate Betty simply refuses to assent to any of Alf's moral demands cannot demonstrate that Alf has failed to publicly justify them".[274]

272 See chapter 1, §1.5.4.
273 C. Eberle 2002: 200.
274 G. Gaus 2006: 121. For other arguments against populism see B. Barry 1995b: 167, C. Eberle 200-07 and D. Estlund 2008: 184-206.

Furthermore, we stressed that weak externalism is an epistemic thesis concerning the reasons that moral agents have. It is freestanding from metaphysical conceptions of reasons which affirm or deny the existence of reasons understood as external facts. Interestingly, this lends some more plausibility to the definition of conclusive justification (CJ) we defended in chapter 1 (§1.4.5). Recall that according to CJ, belief β is conclusively justified to Bea if, and only if, the set of reasons Bea has for accepting β defeats the set of reasons she has for rejecting β. The plausibility of CJ lies in the fact that it presents itself as an *epistemic* definition of shareability, which focuses on the reasons Bea *has*.

As a result, CJ differs from Raz's canonical definition of conclusiveness, according to which "p is a conclusive reason for x to ϕ if, and only if, p is a reason to ϕ, which has not been cancelled, and there is no q such that q overrides p".[275] Unlike CJ, Raz's account is *metaphysical*, in that it ties conclusiveness to the reasons that there are. To be sure, given his strongly externalist conception of justification he sees no relevant distinction between the conclusive reasons that there are and the conclusive reasons that rational agents have. But because strong externalism should be resisted, we have to maintain that L is conclusively justified to Bea if and only if the reasons that she can be said to *have* under open justification conclusively support L. In order to determine which reasons can be attributed to Bea, according to weak externalism, one must start from her initial set of beliefs and verify to what extent a "sound deliberative route" conducted under moderate idealizing conditions could commit her to partially revising her overall belief system.

These remarks are important also because they help dispel a worry about the very notion of "conclusive justification": Isn't "conclusive justification" synonymous with "final" or "irrefutable" justification, to which only a fully rational Hercules with unlimited cognitive faculties could have access? No, at least not on a weakly externalist view. Although I have been critical of Habermas's radical argument for consensus, discourse theory points to a valuable insight, in that it stresses that justificatory discourse is an open-ended process which always plays out within a bounded cognitive horizon. Justification is thus always "provisional" and "all-things-considered", rather than "fully conclusive", as it were, because deliberation must be constantly open to, and if possible vicariously bring forward, potential future objections. The idea behind CJ is that if minimally idealized participants in actual discourses have more reason for accepting L than for rejecting it, then L is conclusively justified to them; but of course, conclusive

275 J. Raz 1975: 27.

justification is only reached on the proviso that someone may, in the future, raise valid objections.

Talk about conclusiveness takes us back to the core problem faced by consensus models. In chapter 1 (§1.4.6) I argued that conclusiveness is a requirement of public reason. According to the Conclusiveness Thesis (CT), it is illegitimate to impose defeated proposals upon the public. Again, though, the question must be raised as to whether the exclusion of private reasons does not make consensus vulnerable of the charge of falling foul of CT. Moreover, I have stressed that if private reasons can defeat freestanding reasons, the latter may be not only "non-conclusive", but also "non-shareable" (§1.5). Now of course this twofold problem would be of little concern for defenders of the Shareability Requirement if they could advance some sound radical strength-based argument for consensus. Recall that these arguments are essentially built around the following pattern:

(I) There is some procedure of abstraction Ω for identifying the set of freestanding reasons *U* (where freestanding reasons are objective reasons)
(II) If *R* is not objective, it is defeated by definition (i.e., by the fact that it is private)
Therefore,
(T1) If *R* is freestanding, it cannot be defeated by non-freestanding reasons
Therefore,
(T2) Freestanding reasons are both shareable and conclusive.

However, I have argued that arguments of this kind fail, mainly because the top-down argument, the (radical) discourse-theoretical argument, the social argument and the (radical) argument from universalization offer unconvincing justifications of (II). Even if we assume that freestandingness should be understood in terms of objectivity, as (I) claims, those arguments fail to explain why subjective reasons are by definition defeated. At this point, advocates of strength-based consensus models could resort to a "moderate" strategy, arguing that although private reasons can in principle warrant rational belief, they are always defeated by freestanding reasons. As I said above, the pattern on which moderate strength-based arguments for consensus are based is the following:

(I) There is some procedure of abstraction Ω for identifying the set of freestanding reasons *U* (where freestanding reasons are objective reasons).
(II) If a) *R* is a freestanding reason while *R** is a private reason and b) *R* and *R** conflict, then *R* defeats *R**.
Therefore,
(T1) If *R* is freestanding, it cannot be defeated by non-freestanding reasons

Therefore,
(T2) Freestanding reasons are both shareable and conclusive.

Both the discourse-theoretical argument for consensus and the argument from universalization can be reinterpreted in this weaker form.

2.8 The discourse-theoretical argument: a moderate version

2.8.1 The (alleged) priority of freestanding reasons

So far I have assumed that the discourse-theoretical argument for consensus is a radical strength-based argument: unless *R* is a freestanding reason, it is by definition defeated. But while this interpretation captures, I think, the kernel of Habermas's own view, the discourse-theoretical argument may well present itself as a moderate strength-based argument for consensus.

As defenders of the social argument for consensus and Habermas himself point out, reasoning cannot be conducted in a purely "monological" or "solipsistic" way. But of course, ethical or private reasons pass the minimal discursive threshold, in the sense that they gain the assent of a restricted audience of discussants committed to some "thick" conception of the good. The upshot is that shareability is ultimately a matter of degree, which is determined by the width of the audience sharing a given reason. In short, both ethical and moral reasons are shareable, but ethical reasons are "less shareable". But since discourse theory sees an intimate connection between epistemic strength and discursive shareability, discourse theory does not commit us to downgrading ethical reasons to non-justificatory reasons. From the perspective of participants in ethical discourses, their private reasons are justificatory, at least pro tanto, though of course they are not shared by all citizens. This interpretation suggests that it may be inaccurate to attribute to Habermas a radical strength-based defense of consensus. Rather, his argument seems moderate: although people are indeed justified in regarding their private reasons as justificatory other things being equal, rational agents are committed to the view that freestanding reasons, being "more sharable", always defeat private reasons.

This weaker reading of the discourse-theoretical argument for consensus is suggested by Habermas's claim that juridical discourse should be understood as a three-stage process, whereby discussants turn pragmatic questions into ethical questions first, and eventually into moral questions.[276] Suppose participants in political deliberation set out to verify the legitimacy of a given law *L*. At a first stage discussant typically ask themselves whether *L* is likely to bring about some desired state of affairs, whose desirability would however be taken for granted and not discursively thematized. But once participants have considered the pragmatic benefits of a given proposal, according to Habermas, they ought to ask themselves whether its implementation fits within their "ethical-political" evaluative standards. Finally, they ought to assess its moral permissibility, discussing whether *L* deserves to be accepted by an unrestricted community of moral agents who reason from a universalistic viewpoint.

As a general rule, then, public justification cannot stop until moral considerations have been brought into play. Moral reasons, then, have the final say in the sense that ethical and pragmatic discourses must be "at least compatible with moral principles".[277] As Rainer Forst puts it:

> In political discourses, ethical, pragmatic and moral points of view … do not constitute discourses in their own right but present different aspects of practical problems that have to be weighed … These aspects are connected in complex but not inexplicable ways. Particularly with problems where moral questions play a role … the moral points of view must take precedence; they must not be sacrificed to ethical or, even worse, pragmatic considerations.[278]

276 See J. Habermas 1996, chapter 4.

277 Ibid.

278 R. Forst 2002: 126. Forst also describes moral arguments as having the power to put a "veto" on politically binding decisions, *ibid.* I should like to stress, however, that while Habermas and Forst concur on the priority of moral over pragmatic and ethical reasons, they suggest different routes from moral discourses to legal rights, and offer two slightly different accounts of how discourse theory should establish a conclusive case for an extensive system of rights. For Habermas, rights protecting both private and political autonomy are primarily *presupposed* by the justificatory procedure. Discourse theory starts from the assumption (which Habermas terms "principle D") that "just those actions are valid, to which each possibly affected person could agree as participant in rational discourses" (J. Habermas 1996: 138). Now as I stressed above (§2.5.2), Habermas's thesis is that principle D, in conjunction with the legal form, *implies* a wide-ranging set of basic rights. This is the core of his *Verschränkungsthese*: political rights protecting both private and political autonomy spring immediately from the application of the ideal of discursive justification to the domain of law and politics. If these rights we not recognized and upheld, free and equal citizens would not be able to engage in public reasoning in the first place. Forst, on the other hand, is skeptical about this sort of justification of basic rights. He claims that private and public autonomy should not be *primarily* seen as functional implications of the institutionalization of principle D because this would risk neglecting their moral content. In other words, Habermas places too much emphasis on the fact that rights are a *precondition* of a legal system modeled after principle D, thereby obscuring

In other words, if *L* gains the assent of participants in moral discourses, the fact that *L* might be open to ethical or pragmatic objections does not impugn the legitimacy of *L*. Thus, discourse theory holds that whenever *L* is backed by moral reasons, these can never be trumped by any pragmatic or ethical reasons that might speak against it.

2.8.2 What defeats what?

To get clearer on Habermas's and Forst's critique, we need to distinguish two interrelated issues. The first is whether moral reasons are understood as liberty-preserving or as liberty-constraining. That is, it is important to distinguish cases where participants in moral discourses would agree on a rationale *R* that justifies a coercive law *L* from cases where participants share a moral reason *R* to reject coercive interference. The second issue concerns the kinds of reasons purporting to defeat moral reasons: that is, we have to make a distinction between cases where moral reasons are trumped by ethical considerations from cases where moral reasons conflict with pragmatic considerations. By crossing these two variables, we obtain four different cases:

Case a) *R* is a liberty-preserving moral reason against *L*; *R** is a pragmatic reason for *L* (where *R** defeats *R*).
Case b) *R* is a liberty-constraining moral reason for *L*; *R** is a pragmatic reason against *L*. (where *R** defeats *R*).
Case c) *R* is a liberty-preserving moral reason against *L*; *R** is an ethical reason for *L*. (where *R** defeats *R*).
Case d) *R* is a liberty-constraining moral reason for *L*; *R** is an ethical reason against *L*. (where *R** defeats *R*).

Habermas and Forst would insist, I take it, that in all these cases *R* should take precedence over *R**. Assuming this is the case, let us consider cases a) to d) one by one.

To use Ronald Dworkin's terminology, case a) represents a conflict between matters of "principle" and matters of "policy". For Dworkin, a "policy" is a "kind of standard that sets out a goal to be reached, generally an improvement in some economic, political, or social feature of the community", whereas a "principle" is "a standard that is to be observed, not because it will advance or secure

the fact that they could be themselves agreed upon *within* political discourses led by the Kantian principle of universalization or "principle U" (see R. Forst 2012, chapter 4).

an economic, political, or social situation deemed desirable, but because it is a requirement of justice or fairness or some other dimension of morality".[279] Justificatory liberals would agree, I think, that in case a) *R* should indeed take precedence over *R**, at least as a general rule. In many cases liberty can be curbed on pragmatic grounds, especially under non-ideal circumstances, but this is certainly undesirable when the deontic value of liberty is strengthened by moral discourses, as in case a). It is important to see that in case a) participants in moral discourses do not tackle the abstract question concerning the absolute value of liberty. Rather, they address a specific question: Is liberty preferable to coercion with respect to the specific issue that *L* would regulate? Or to put it differently: do we have moral reasons for ranking *L* over no law at all? Now in case a) participants do not simply *lack* moral reasons for *L*; that is, they do not simply "confirm" the presumption in favor of liberty, which already assumes by default that coercion is worse than liberty. Rather, they strengthen the presumption in favor of liberty, in that they add further moral reasons against *L*.

Arguably, discussants would agree that the moral case for liberty trumps pragmatic considerations purporting to limit what Rawls has called the "central range" of liberties. In defending the "priority of liberties", Rawls describes them as having a core set of applications or "central range", which we ought to "preserve intact" when adjusting rights and liberties to one another.[280] For example, Rawls suggests that the central range of the liberty of conscience includes at least "the freedom and integrity of the internal life of religious associations and the liberty of persons to determine their religious affiliations".[281] To take other cases, the "central range of the freedom of political speech" must include full protection of subversive doctrines from charges of "seditious libel".[282] Few would deny, I think, that a liberal state cannot seize upon the central range of liberty on pragmatic grounds. In any event, this is not an objection against convergence, since pragmatic reasons may well be seen as freestanding: they identify states of affairs that benefit the community at large, though bringing them about might require limiting the liberty of many. To say that moral reasons ought to take precedence over pragmatic considerations, then, is to defend the priority of *some* freestanding reasons over others, a priority which both consensus and convergence theorists would probably accept.

For pretty much the same reason, case b) does not pose any particular threat to convergence. Here citizens endorse a moral reason for endorsing a coercive law

279 R. Dworkin 1978: 22.
280 J. Rawls 1993: 364.
281 Ibid.: 341.
282 Ibid.: 343.

L, but are also aware that the implementation of *L* would incur pragmatic problems. I would conjecture that even in this case many would resist the view that a morally justified coercive norm should not be implemented because it endangers political stability or thwarts strategic economic assets. Again, though, the problem here is to establish a priority between freestanding moral reasons and freestanding pragmatic concerns, and not a priority of freestanding over private reasons.

Case c) is more interesting. Here Habermas's insistence on the priority of moral discourses takes him down a safe alley, for in case c) the priority of *R* over *R** rests on what is normally refereed to the "priority of the right over the good". While the right has to do with universally justifiable obligations, which we owe to each other as moral agents, the good reflects our particular conceptions of the "good life". What is problematic in case c) is precisely that *R**, a private ethical reason based on some non-public conception of the good, alleges to overturn a morally justified scheme of liberties, which participants in moral discourses would recognize as right.

Now while this is a powerful argument against the use of private reasons, it does not undermine the convergence view of public justification. If we dismiss the unlikely prospect of an "overlapping consensus" of ethical reasons that converge against a morally justified liberty, we should certainly maintain that in case c) liberty is publicly justified over coercion. Obviously, convergence does not correspond to the view that Andy can coerce Bea on the basis of his own "ethical" reasons. Unless Andy can show that *all* have their own private reasons to accept his demands, he is committed to withdrawing them. This fundamental justificatory requirement is embodied in the idea of the priority of the right over the good, but more fundamentally, it is the upshot of what Gaus calls the fundamental "liberal principle": "Impositions on others require justification; unjustified impositions are unjust".[283]

Suppose that Bea has her own private reason *R* to oppose Andy's freedom of religion (call this basic liberty *N*, and assume there are moral reasons for ranking *N* over *L*, as case c) suggests). Bea finds it intolerable that people like Andy can worship "false" gods. She therefore proposes enacting some coercive law that prevents him from freely exercising his own religion. But this means that her proposal must be justified to him. And because Andy is obviously justified in rejecting *R*, *N* is not publicly defeated. One might contend that *N* would still be unjustified to Bea. But this is an idle claim from a justificatory perspective. Since *N* does not coerce Bea, Andy's freedom of religion need not be justified to her. If

283 G. Gaus 1996: 165.

Bea argues for restrictions on Andy's freedom, Bea alone must shoulder the task of justifying her claim. The onus of justification, as Stanley Benn reminds us, is always on the would-be interferer.[284]

2.8.3 Back to post-metaphysical rationality

But one might ask: if private reasons cannot justify coercion, what is the point of convergence? Shouldn't we simply conclude that private reasons should be expunged from public justification? Of course not. First, private reasons can justify coercion if they converge. Moreover, private reasons can serve as defeaters against coercion. It is in this twofold sense that convergence allows "doctrines that are not publicly justified [to] play a crucial role in public justification".[285] Again, the key idea behind convergence models of public reason is that unless coercive laws can be accepted by all citizens in the light of their private evaluative standards, public justification cannot be achieved.

Of course, Habermas and Forst would reject this view as well, insisting that ethical reasons cannot be used as defeaters against coercion, provided coercion is justified on freestanding moral grounds. This means that the moderate discourse-theoretical argument for consensus presses convergence on case d), where moral reasons justify coercion while *some* citizens have private ethical objections to it. So the crucial question must be raised as to whether Habermas's thesis that R defeats R^* should apply to case d). This is *the* core issue we need to explore. Recall that I intend to defend a two-stage convergence conception (see introduction, II.c and chapter 1, §1.5.2). First, we have to identify general principles, which, we take it, all have (freestanding) reason to endorse. Then we need set out to verify whether citizens' private reasons can *confirm* the outcome of "pro tanto" justification. To put it in Habermasian terms, the question is whether or not citizens' "ethical" doctrines will align with "moral reasons" expressing "generalizable interests". Thus, the fundamental problem is to understand whether or not in case d) Habermas's priority rule should apply.

Now there are many different reasons why we may wish to accord priority to moral reasons in cases of this kind, but it is important not to lose sight of the specific question Habermas needs to address. Recall that the discourse-theoretical argument for consensus is *strength-based*, and not *appropriateness-based*. It does not merely aim to explain why it is *morally inappropriate* to use ethical reasons as defeaters against morally justifiable coercive norms. Rather, it

284 S. Benn 1988: 103-121. See Introduction, §I.b.
285 G. Gaus 1996: 171.

purports to show that ethical reasons cannot defeat moral reasons because private reasons lack epistemic strength compared to freestanding reasons. To be sure, discourse theory is compatible with many appropriateness-based objections to convergence, which I shall review in the next chapter. But insofar as it attacks convergence on epistemic grounds, the (moderate) discourse-theoretical argument for consensus must uncover an epistemic flaw in the claim "Andy is justified in believing that *R** defeats *R* even if *R* is freestanding while *R** is not".

What is wrong with this claim, epistemically speaking? Well, Habermas's answer to this question would probably draw on the thesis we hinted at in section §2.8.1: *R** cannot defeat *R* because the epistemic strength of a reason is directly dependent on its shareability. The problem with this reply, however, is that it runs up against the same sort of problem faced by the discourse-theoretical rendition of the argument from universalization. Notice that, essentially, the moderate discourse-theoretical argument presupposes a moderate argument from universalization. If *R* is universalizable while *R** is not, then *R* defeats *R**. But even in this case, everything hinges upon the assumption that moral agents should be concerned with the discursive redemption of truth-analogous rightness claims. Surely if Andy's problem were to convince Bea that *L* is "objectively" false, he could not appeal to *R**, for by stipulation *R** is acceptable to him and his fellow participants in ethical discourses, and not to an unrestricted "community of investigators". But the point is precisely that *R** is not meant to substantiate the truth-analogous claim that *L* is objectively worse than no law at all. All Andy would point out by invoking *R** is that *L* is not justified to him. To say that Andy would discard *R** if he soared into a detached universalistic perspective is to beg the crucial question that moderate strength-based arguments need to answer: If the fundamental aim of public reason is to justify coercion *to* its addressees, including Andy, why should we expect Andy to advocate only reasons which all rational agents have reason to regard as defeaters against coercion?

Again, Habermas's insistence on the priority of moral reasons over ethical considerations is heavily indebted to his post-metaphysical conception of practical reason. Particularistic theories of morality fall short of what post-metaphysical rationality ultimately requires, since they rest on unchallenged substantive assumptions: they cannot go beyond the model of ethical discourses, as they take the situated perspective of a given group of individuals as the fundamental justificatory yardstick. Of course, Habermas stresses that ethical discourses serve important functions. After all, we often need to engage in a "clinical" process of self-understanding relating to our ethical identity. But this is not the fundamental aim of practical reason, according to Habermas. Rather, post-metaphysical rationality tries to get at the bottom of all normatively regulated social relations, challenging taken-for-granted ethical convictions. Practical rationality is therefore naturally oriented toward *moral* argumentation, in that it turns the particularistic question "What is good for us?" into the universalistic question "What is good for all?" This chapter was largely devoted to showing that this conception of rationality ends up distorting the commitment to publicly justify coercion to its addressees.

I conclude that both the moderate and the radical discourse-theoretical argument for consensus fail for the same reason: they presuppose a truth-redeeming post-metaphysical conception of rationality which has proven inadequate for the doctrine of public reason. Carrying the problem to a higher level of abstraction, the failure of radical strength-based arguments in general leads to the failure of moderate strength-based arguments in general. Above (§2.7.2) I stressed that radical arguments should be resisted because they cannot explain why subjective reasons are defeated by definition. Now moderate strength-based argument face a similar problem: they cannot explain why freestanding reasons necessarily defeated private reasons. Of course, citizens will often be openly justified in believing that freestanding reasons have greater epistemic weight than their "ethical" views. However, epistemic questions of this kind need to be assessed on a case-by-case basis. Sometimes Andy's belief system will provide him with sufficient defeaters for freestanding reasons, sometimes it will not. And of course, in many cases Bea's belief system could yield different results than Andy's with respect to the same issue. The crucial point, however, is that there is no compelling rationale behind the claim that private reasons always defeat private reasons in every belief system, as moderate strength-based arguments for consensus would instead imply.

2.8.4 The scope of private defeaters

Before concluding, an important remark is in order. In discussing the moderate discourse-theoretical argument, I have assumed that the members of the public are presented with a binary choice: either they accept *L*, or they reject it. However, things could be more complicated than this, as *L* may be one interpretation of a more general principle or general law *L*. This is an important point. In fact, private defeaters against coercion should not be necessarily understood as reasons for rejecting general coercive principles and general laws altogether. In fact, private defeaters may well attack specific interpretations of general laws and principles. Consider the following situation:

Andy (ΣA)	Freestanding rationale (ΣF)
L_2	L
L_1	No law at all
No law at all	
L_5	
L_3	
L_4	

Display 1

The higher the position occupied by a law in display 1, the higher its desirability. So for instance Andy believes that L_5 is better than L_3 but worse than no law at all. The symbol "ΣA" indicates the set of private reasons used by Andy to rank proposals. The last column indicates the ordering of options justified by a freestanding rationale ΣF. Here I rely on the following definition of "freestanding rationale":

R is a freestanding rationale for *L* if, and only if, on the balance, all freestanding reasons available warrant $R \rightarrow L$.

A "freestanding rationale" is not just one freestanding reason, but rather the outcome of freestanding reasoning, whereby all single freestanding reasons are accounted for and factored in. If all participants in justificatory discourses, weighing and balancing all freestanding reasons available, conclude that *L* is justified, then they have a freestanding rationale for *L*. Now a freestanding rationale is nothing but a "pro tanto" justification in Rawls's sense: taking all freestanding reasons into account, we conclude that we have reason for endorsing *L*.

Now in display 1 the freestanding rationale justifies *L* over no law at all; however, *L* is open to five different interpretations, L_1, L_2, L_3, L_4 and L_5. In our example, Andy's private ranking would lead him to reject not *L* as a whole, but only the interpretations of it which ΣA ranks below liberty, namely L_3, L_4 and L_5. As a result, on a convergence view some version of *L* might still be publicly justified, though to the eligible set of proposals could not comprise anything more than L_1 and L_2. I shall come back to this important point in the next chapter (§3.5.1, §3.6.5 and §3.7.6).

2.9 Summary

I started by highlighting the twofold problem faced by the Consensus View of Public Reason (§2.1, see also §1.5.6). First, justificatory reasons must be conclusive: if they are to justify coercive laws, they must be stronger than citizens' objection to coercion. But how can the Conclusiveness Thesis (CT) be made consistent with consensus models which exclude a priori some potentially decisive reasons for (and especially against) coercion? Second, if private reasons may defeat freestanding reasons identified by the correct abstraction procedure Ω, the latter may be not only non-conclusive, but also non-shareable. In this chapter, I reviewed an intriguing response to this puzzle: it is an error to believe that private reasons can defeat freestanding reasons because the former lack epistemic strength, and are therefore unable to tip the balance of justificatory reasons (§2.2.1). In one way or another, the top-down argument for consensus, the argument from universalization, the discourse theoretical argument for consensus and the social argument for consensus seek to show that only freestanding reasons can contribute, epistemically speaking, to the full justification of coercive laws. If some of these arguments were sound, then the twofold presumption in favor of convergence would be rebutted, and in a very elegant way indeed.

Unfortunately, though, strength-based arguments for consensus fail. In criticizing the attempt to defend consensus on epistemic grounds, I stressed that strength-based arguments for consensus rest on two core premises. The first premise is that freestanding reasons are objective reasons – though of course the arguments I reviewed rely on quite different conceptions of objectivity (§2.2.2). The second premise is that objective reasons are defeated either by freestanding reasons (as moderate strength-based arguments claim) or by the very fact that they are private (as radical strength-based arguments insist). In this chapter I did not generally challenge the first premise. Rather, I argued that even if we assume that freestanding reasons are objective reasons, as the first premise maintains, strength-based arguments fail because the second premise is unwarranted. That is to say, no strength-based argument for consensus (be it radical or moderate) convincingly shows that private reasons are defeated.

To begin with, the top-down argument for consensus assumes that because *there are* some objective reasons, then every rational agent *has* conclusive reason to act and believe as those objective reasons instruct them to act and believe – which means, again, that private reasons are necessarily defeated (§2.3.1). This claim, however, is warranted only if we endorse either a strongly externalist (§2.3.2) or a moderately externalist (§2.3.3) conception of reasons. Following Gaus, I argued that both views should in fact be resisted, whereas weak externalism (§2.4.1 – 2.4.2), as opposed to sheer internalism (§2.3.4), is the correct conception of reasons. As a result, the top-down argument for consensus fails (§2.4.3).

The radical discourse-theoretical argument for consensus (§2.5.1 – 2.5.2) understands *U* as the set of provisionally objective reasons by means of some discursive procedure Ω. While I conceded that freestandingness may well be interpreted in this way (§2.5.3 – 2.5.4), I argued that there is little reason to believe that every subjective reason is by definition undermined. Essentially, the problem is that while (on the naïve view of scientific inquiry) truth-claims can be redeemed only by objective, truth-seeking reasons, rightness claims are not truth-analogous and can therefore be justified by "overlapping" private reasons (§2.6.1 – 2.6.3). For this reason, the radical discourse-theoretical argument fails (§2.6.5). Building on my critique of the radical discourse-theoretical argument, I have argued that even the argument from universalization (§2.6.4) and the social argument for consensus (§2.7.1) should be resisted: the former wrongly assumes that since laws must be justified to all, they must be justified to all with the same reasons; the latter errs by assuming that because ought-claims must have some social, linguistically mediated backing, they must be affirmed by all members of a given society. Finally, I sought to see whether moderate strength-based arguments for consensus (especially in a discourse-theoretical fashion) can do the job (§2.7.2 – 2.8.3). However, I argued that even this line of reasoning is unpersuasive because, again, there is little reason to believe that private reasons are necessarily defeated. I closed by emphasizing that private defeaters may defeat specific interpretations of "pro tanto" justified laws, rather than general laws and principles altogether (§2.8.4).

It seems therefore safe to assume that the twofold presumption in favor of convergence cannot be rebutted on epistemic grounds. Epistemically speaking, freestanding reasons may be neither conclusive nor shareable, as private reasons might on occasion defeat them. At this point, consensus theorists could resort to a completely different strategy. They could argue that although private reasons are "good reasons" epistemically speaking, they are morally inappropriate justificatory grounds. Consensus, according to these critics, is preferable to convergence because reliance on freestanding reasons is necessary to protect and do justice to a number of important values, which convergence neglects or downplays. The next chapter analyzes this alternative defense of consensus.

3. Appropriateness-based arguments for consensus

3.1. Overview of the argument

Defenders of the Consensus View of Public Reason insist that we should "[limit] arguments to shared reasons in political contexts".[286] But why such a constraint? As Jeffrey Stout says, "why limit oneself ... to the quest for a common basis?"[287] Consensus theorists answer: because private reasons are bad reasons. We saw, however, that the term "bad reasons" is open to two competing interpretations. It can either mean "epistemically weak (or flawed) reasons" or "morally inappropriate justificatory grounds". If the criticism of strength-based arguments for consensus I developed in the previous chapter is sound, advocates of the Shareability Requirement can only go for the second interpretation.

Appropriateness-based arguments for consensus do not view freestanding reasons as "objective" epistemic trumps. Rather, they view freestanding reasons as more appropriate justificatory grounds than private reasons. On an appropriateness-based consensus view, reasonable citizens should ignore the fact that freestanding reasons might be non-shareable and defeasible, as allegiance to freestanding reasons is required of reasonable citizens. In other words, appropriateness-based arguments for consensus suggest that the constituency of public reason should only comprise members who content themselves with a freestanding justification. Those who view freestanding reasons as defeasible may not commit any epistemic mistake, and yet in an important sense freestanding reasons are indeed indefeasible: for those who believe otherwise, being excluded by the constituency of public reason, are not supposed to share those reasons in the first place.

Yet those who insist that citizens should put aside potentially decisive reasons (or, which is the same, that only citizens who are actually willing to do so should be part of our constituency of public reason) have a high price to pay: they end up ignoring the potential objections of some citizens on the grounds that these citizens should not be given a say, without however showing that freestanding reasons are conclusive and shareable, epistemically speaking, in the eyes of those citizens (see chapter 1, §1.6.4). Of course, this would be a tolerable price to pay should consensus fare much better than convergence with respect to other desiderata of public reason. But the fact that under consensus citizens might be required to accept coercive impositions that are unjustified to them creates a very

286 S. Freeman 2007: 382.
287 J. Stout 2004: 73.

strong presumption against the Shareability Requirement. To rebut it, defenders of consensus must come up with some very strong appropriateness-based objections to convergence. In this chapter I shall argue that none of the appropriateness-based arguments for consensus that have appeared in the literature on public reason live up to this task.

This chapter has the following structure. Sections §3.2 and §3.3 refute "the argument from sincerity", according to which convergence skews the ideal of public reason by permitting or even encouraging citizens to be insincere with one another. I shall consider the argument from sincerity at great length because this will give me the opportunity to clarify some important concepts that we have already come across, such as the nature of reasonable disagreement, the notion of shareability and the role of epistemic pluralism. Section §3.4 turns to the "argument from publicity", which holds that without a civic guarantee that reasoning will be conducted on the basis of shared commitments, "full publicity" cannot be achieved. I shall argue that even this argument fails. Section §3.5 rejects two other appropriateness-based objections to convergence, which I will call the "argument from normative stability" and the "argument from reasonable compliance".

Section §3.6 critically reviews another appropriateness-based argument for consensus, which builds upon a line of criticism pursued by Rainer Forst and Steve Wall. I shall call it the "argument from symmetry" because it contends that convergence neglects the inherently symmetrical character of public reason, placing asymmetrical justificatory burdens on proponents and opponents of coercive legislation. Although the argument from symmetry is unconvincing, in section §3.7 we will see that a more narrow version rightly suggests making some adjustments to Gaus's convergence conception. I shall call this revised convergence model "symmetrical convergence". Section §3.8 concludes.

3.2. Sincerity and public reason

3.2.1 The argument from sincerity

Jonathan Quong has recently argued that convergence should be resisted because it allows citizens to violate a commonly adopted sincerity requirement. Sincerity is necessary to ensure that attempts at public justification do not lapse into rhetorical manipulation. Only when we are sincere with others, Quong argues, do we respect them as free and equal fellow citizens, in that "... we acknowledge that every citizen is to be treated as someone ... who is the source of moral claims ... someone over whom power cannot be exercised without appropriate justification".[288] Drawing on Micah Schwartzman's comprehensive account of sincerity,[289] Quong argues that public reason's sincerity requirement compels us to endorse consensus.[290] Quong's argument is clearly appropriateness-based, as it does not claim that freestanding reasons are epistemically indefeasible. Rather, it insists that reasonable citizens should eschew all appeals to private defeaters because this is what the sincerity requirement demands. Thus, freestanding reasons are shareable and conclusive in the sense that they are viewed as shareable and conclusive within our constituency of public reason. In fact, our constituency will comprise only members who endorse and abide by the principle of sincerity, thereby relying exclusively on freestanding reasons in public political debate.

Quong's argument rests on four core premises. The first premise is that sincerity is an important value. The second premise is that honoring public reason's ideal of sincerity means respecting what Quong calls the "principle of justificatory sincerity" (hereafter: PJS):

Principle of Justificatory Sincerity (PJS): Andy can support proposal X only if he reasonably believes that (a) he himself is justified in endorsing X, that (b) Bea is/could reasonably be justified in endorsing X and that (c) Bea is/could reasonably be justified in accepting the arguments he has offered in support of X (and vice versa for Bea's proposals).[291]

To see how PJS could help select conceptions of public reason, we need to bear in mind that under a given conception of public reason *C*, participants in justificatory discourse will be allowed to invoke only the reasons that qualify as "good reasons" according to *C*. So for instance convergence conceptions permit citizens to argue from comprehensive premises, while consensus conceptions do not. Still, PJS might prevent citizens from appealing to some of the reasons that a conception of public reason labels as justificatory. This takes us to the third core premise of Quong's argument: if a given conception *C* allows citizens to rely on

288 J. Quong 2011: 266.

289 Both Schwartzman and Quong reject convergence on the grounds that it permits insincerity. However, Schwartzman appears to see the sincerity requirement more as a means for the achievement of "actual" or "full publicity", rather than as a fundamental justificatory principle in Quong's and Rawls's sense. In this respect, Schwartzman's argument for consensus seems closer to Stephen Macedo's thesis that convergence fails to justify shared principles on the basis of common knowledge, thereby leading to a "privatized" conception of politics. See section §3.4 below.

290 Gerald J. Postema defends consensus on similar grounds, arguing that participants in political deliberation are "bound by a principle of *sincerity* to present evidence, arguments and interpretations that they can fully endorse" (G. J. Postema 2005b: 369).

291 J. Quong 2011: 266. I have slightly simplified Quong's original formulation of PJS.

reasons that PJS deems impermissible, defenders of PJS are committed to discarding *C*, provided some better alternative is available. In other words, taking PJS seriously involves accepting what we could call the "sincerity-promoting principle" (hereafter: SPP):

Sincerity-Promoting Principle (SPP): Things being equal, a conception of public reason C_2 is preferable to a conception of public reason C_1 if 1) C_1 holds that reasons of type R_X are good reasons while C_2 does not and 2) PJS prevents some citizens from justifying proposals by appeal to reasons of type R_X.

Finally, Quong claims that, if properly understood, PJS prevents citizens from appealing to private reasons. His argument from sincerity, then, can be formulated in the following way:

(I) Sincerity is a prima facie desideratum.
(II) If we cherish the value of sincerity, we ought to accept PJS.
(III) If PJS prevents citizens from appealing to private reasons, we ought to endorse consensus (SPP).
(IV) PJS prevents citizens from appealing to private reasons.
Therefore,
(T) We ought to endorse consensus.

I take it for granted that (I) is true. It seems uncontroversial that an adequate theory of public reason should to some extent be concerned with the way in which citizens deliberate. And it would be recommendable if the members of the public respected some sincerity requirement while discussing political issues with one another. After all, public reasoning aims at *bona fide* justification. Hence, the arguments citizens put forward in support of their political proposals should not lapse into rhetorical attempts at persuasion.

Let us also assume, for the sake of the argument, that (II) is correct, too. After all, PJS seems to fully capture the ideal of justificatory sincerity on which many justificatory liberals place primary emphasis. To begin with, condition (a) of PJS seems necessary to any tenable account of justificatory sincerity. Unless Andy thinks he is justified in endorsing X, his arguments for X are obviously insincere. Requirement (b) is implicit in Rawls's principle of legitimacy, according to which "our exercise of political power is proper only when we sincerely believe that the reasons we would offer for our political actions are sufficient .... and we also reasonably think that other citizens might reasonably accept those reasons".[292] For to believe that X is justified to others simply *is* to believe that they have sufficient reason to accept it. Finally, requirement (c) restates what Rawls's principle of legitimacy says about the importance of giving others reasons that they could reasonably accept. Thomas Nagel concurs, arguing that "the sense of justice should lead us to try, in good faith, to offer to our fellow citizens grounds for the exercise of collective power that we believe they ... have reason to accept".[293] In a similar vein, Gaus stresses, very plausibly, that "justifying your ... principles to others does not simply involve *giving others reasons that they will accept*, but in some way advancing reasons that you think are good reasons for them to accept".[294]

In addition, there are other important considerations that seem to lend plausibility to PJS. We should in fact note that PJS rests on three crucial theses which most justificatory liberals would find compelling. First, PJS resists the radical and highly controversial claim that Andy's meeting conditions (a) to (c) is a sufficient condition for X to be legitimately imposed upon Bea. Important though it may be, sincerity is not the only relevant element of an adequate theory of public reason. It thus follows that

(T1) Andy might be required not to support X despite his sincere and reasonable belief that X is justified to all.

PJS makes room for this possibility, in that it holds that Andy's sincere and reasonable belief that X is publicly justified is only a necessary condition. Second, Quong's formulation of PJS is tune with justificatory liberalism's core commitment to justify coercion. In fact, as Nagel, Rawls, Gaus and Quong point out, it is first and foremost the use of "collective" and "political" power that requires a sincere justification. It follows from PJS, then, that

(T2) Bea is not subject to PJS insofar as she does not propose/support X.

Third, PJS is promising because it stresses that Andy must "reasonably" hold his beliefs. Unreasonable people, however sincere, should be of no concern to the public reason liberal. For instance, a religious fundamentalist might well be sincerely convinced that a theocracy modeled after her indisputably true religion would be justified to all, but this hardly entitles her to reasonably support such a view in public political debate. Hence,

292 J. Rawls 1997: 578.
293 T. Nagel 2003: 66.
294 G. Gaus 1996: 139.

(T3) Andy's sincere belief that X is publicly justified is relevant if and only if Andy is reasonable.

3.2.2 Intelligibility and relevance

It might seem that once (II) is granted, (III) and SPP follow smoothly from (I) and (II). But this is not quite right. (I) simply states that sincerity is an important desideratum, whereas (III) turns sincerity into a strict requirement, which, in turn, serves as a principle (SPP) for selecting eligible conceptions of public reason. For the time being, however, we can set this issue aside and focus on (IV), according to which under convergence citizens are allowed or even encouraged to violate PJS. According to Quong, the problem with convergence becomes apparent in cases like the following:

Case 1) Andy, an atheist socialist, proposes X. Bea rejects Andy's comprehensive doctrine on religious grounds. Andy argues that Bea's religious beliefs about social justice, which he rejects, provide her with a private reason R_B for endorsing X, while his socialist doctrine provides him with a convergent reason R_A. Andy and Bea know that the freestanding reasons available do not justify X over alternative options.

In case 1), Andy puts forward what Gaus calls a "convergence argument", which seeks "to show that we have different reasons for endorsing X, though we all have some reasons for endorsing it."[295]

Rawls himself admits of this kind of reasoning, which he terms "reasoning from conjecture". If we reason "from conjecture" we "argue from what we believe, or conjecture, are other people's basic doctrines, religious or secular, and try to show them that, despite what they might think, they can still endorse a reasonable political conception".[296] By reasoning from conjecture we attempt to show that our interlocutors can see the reasonable political conception affirmed in our society as acceptable on their own terms and for their own comprehensive reasons.

In Quong's view, however, Andy's convergence argument in case 1) would be a clear example of insincere justification. By stipulation, Andy "does not believe that R_B justifies X"[297], so how could he sincerely say to Bea "R_B is a reason for

295 G. Gaus 2003: 190-91.
296 J. Rawls 1997: 594.
297 J. Quong 2011: 267.

you to accept X"? Robert Audi makes a similar point when he asks: "Why should others be moved if I am not?. . . [I]f the reason is adequate, why does it not move me?"[298] It thus seems that Andy's convergence argument falls foul of requirements (b) and (c) of PJS. He does not believe that X is justified to Bea because he does not think that she has any good reasons for accepting it. But there is more. Recall that according to (T2), Bea is not subject to PJS as long as she rejects X. If, however, she accepts it, then she assumes the role of would-be coercer with respect to Andy. She must thus believe that X is justified to him, as requirement (b) states. But since Bea rejects his non-public doctrine, she can hardly believe that.

Of course, convergence theorists could protest that this reading of case 1) is too narrow. Quong seems to imply that if Andy "conjectures" based on beliefs he rejects, he simply tries to get Bea to believe what he wants her to believe, without however providing her with reasons that he sincerely believes are good reasons for her to accept. Surely it is hard to disagree with Bryan Garsten when he says that reasoning from conjecture "sounds strikingly like a sympathetic portrayal of a rhetorical argument, in that it recommends beginning with a particular audience's opinions and trying to use those opinions as a basis of persuasion".[299] But we should make a crucial distinction between arguing from premises that we believe to be plainly *crazy or irrational* a) and arguing from premises that we deem *wrong yet not unreasonable* b). What sets apart b) from a) is that in case b) we can believe that, in the light of their reasonable belief systems, our interlocutors are *justified* in holding the premises from which we argue, although we reasonably reject such premises.[300]

298 R. Audi 1991: 74.

299 B. Garsten 2006: 186.

300 D'Agostino points out that if a) were a likely scenario, then convergence would lead to an unstable social order. Suppose, he writes, that "[t]here are A and Rb such that, were A to come to realize that B finds the regime reasonable on account of Rb, A would not be able himself to find it reasonable, whatever other grounds he might have for doing so. For instance, if Rb was that B would be able to fulfill her conception of the good in that regime and if A believed B's conception of the good was depraved, then A might not be able any longer to support the implementation of such a regime, perhaps even despite the fact that in it his conception of the good might also be realizable" (F. D'Agostino 1996: 76). Surely in cases of this kind convergence does not seem an appropriate approach to justification, but it is questionable whether consensus would fare any better. For if citizens viewed others' doctrines as "crazy" or "depraved", such that no social order at all is better than a system of social cooperation under which "depraved" doctrines are permitted to thrive, it is difficult to see how they could still conceive of each other as minimally decent free and equal reasoners. A diffuse and intractable hostility among bad-willed citizens would make the project of public reason impossible. Justificatory liberals must

We can therefore stipulate that Andy thinks that R_B is a good reason *from Bea's* perspective (and vice versa). In fact, Gaus argues that Andy would not be "objectionably insincere" if he could see R_B as an "intelligible and relevant" consideration which Bea could endorse from her perspective after engaging in a sufficient degree of deliberation.[301] There are, however, two very different ways is which Andy could deem R_B "intelligible and relevant":

(x) Andy believes that R_B is a *reasonably endorsable* reason for accepting X, in that it is consistent with the non-public doctrine that Bea reasonably adheres to. However, he does not think that her doctrine is epistemically justified.

(y) Andy believes that R_B is a *justificatory* reason supporting X. He thinks not only that R_B is consistent with the non-public doctrine that Bea reasonably adheres to, but also that her doctrine is epistemically justified, though he does not endorse it.

Now if *(x)* is the correct interpretation of what Andy believes in case 1), then Quong's objection is still in place. Andy recognizes that it is not unreasonable for Bea to hold a religious doctrine, and yet he resists the view that religion can warrant rational belief. Still, Andy insists that R_B *justifies* X to Bea. So in order to sincerely make this sort of claim, Andy must believe that R_B is not merely a tolerable mistake, but rather a proper *justificatory* reason, as *(y)* suggests.

Quong aptly notes that in order to accept *(y)* as a plausible interpretation of Andy's stance toward X in case 1), we need to assume that Andy endorses some moderately relativistic epistemology such as Gaus's. As we saw in the previous chapter, Gaus rests on the assumption that "a rational belief system is to be analyzed in terms of the relations among its members (reasons and beliefs) and not with reference to the idea of truth".[302] But since reasoners typically start with different sets of beliefs and inferential norms, they may be epistemically justified in holding different and largely conflicting belief systems. Reasonable pluralism thus turns into "relativism of reasons": it becomes possible that "people can have systems of beliefs that contain different norms of inference and belief acceptance and still be able to recognize each other's systems as rational".[303] Therefore, if Bea's belief system commits her to acknowledging that R_B is a reason for en-

therefore presuppose that while a) may (regrettably) eventuate in some sporadic cases, b) should be the norm.

301 G. Gaus 2011b: 289.

302 G. Gaus 1996: 42

303 Ibid.: 40.

dorsing X, then Andy should see the inference from R_B to X as epistemically warranted from her perspective (and vice versa for Andy's private reason R_A). In effect, Gaus explicitly stresses that "intelligibility" does not merely involve "observing" that others affirm a given reason, but rather regarding other people's reasons as justificatory: "Not only must reasons be intelligible [in the sense presupposed by *(x)*], they must be relevant to the *justification* of the social practice of morality".[304]

3.2.3 Why the sincerity requirement undermines convergence

Now according to Quong, the reason why we should prefer *(x)* to *(y)* is that *(y)* depicts an unlikely scenario. In fact, "many reasonable citizens … *do not* think that doctrines that conflict with their own are *justifiable.* They view those other doctrines as both false *and* unjustifiable".[305] Consider again the example of religious doctrines, which is particularly germane to the point Quong wants to make. As an atheist socialist, Andy will probably believe that religion is an irrational illusion, so how could he take it to be a source of justification? Conversely, religious people often regard religious and secular doctrines that differ from their own as unjustifiable, though of course "intelligible and relevant". For instance, many Catholics do not believe that – say – skeptical, utilitarian and Muslim doctrines are anything more than reasonably endorsable errors. Also, perfectionists (both religious and secular) typically deny that people who fail to grasp the evident truth about human flourishing can be seen as rational in Gaus's sense. In sum, *(x)* seems to better reflect what many people believe in good faith about the epistemic status of other people's non-public doctrines.

To see the force of Quong's point, it is important to see that, in an important respect, sincerity is not a deontic or normative notion. On the one hand, sincerity is obviously normative in the sense that, according to PJS, citizens ought to be sincere. On the other hand, however, sincerity is not a normative notion in the sense that what people (sincerely) believe does not depend on what they ought to believe. As Schwartzman aptly puts it, "[i]f *A* says that *p*, *A* is sincere if and only if (i) *A* intends to say that *p* and (ii) *A* believes that *p*".[306] To avoid unnecessary complications, let us assume that condition (i) will always obtain in the context of public justification. By stipulation, the members of our constituency will never utter "unintentional" statements. Still, they might say things that they do not

304 G. Gaus 2011b: 280, emphasis mine.
305 J. Quong 2011: 270.
306 M. Schwartzman 2008: 992.

actually believe, in which case they would be obviously insincere, as condition (ii) suggests. This is important. Openly (and intentionally) stating what you actually happen to believe is a necessary and sufficient condition for you to be sincere.

On this view, then, sincerity is not a deontic notion, in that it does not refer to what people ought to believe, or to what they would believe if they took the trouble to carefully think things through. Of course, on Quong's view it is not enough to state that *p* in order to be sincere, if *p* stands for "I believe that X is legitimate". For Quong, being a sincere proponent of X entails being moved by the reasons which one believes justify X. But if *p* means "I believe that X is legitimate because I believe that all, including myself, have reason to endorse it", then Schwartzman's non-deontic account of sincerity can be smoothly embedded into Quong's.

To be sure, not all kinds of beliefs deserve to be taken seriously. As (T3) states, sincerely held yet unreasonable beliefs are irrelevant. In modeling the members of our constituency of public reason, then, we need to introduce at least some minimal degree of idealization. Still, those who cherish the value of sincerity should be wary of pushing this point too far. The more we idealize the members of our constituency, the more we demand that their real counterparts in flesh and blood accept reasons and proposals which they sincerely reject. Since we should avoid raising the bar of idealization too much, it is sufficient that Andy be "reasonable". It is sufficient, that is, that he recognizes the fact of reasonable pluralism and that he refrains from coercing Bea on sheer "comprehensive" grounds which she rejects.

Still, the "reasonable beliefs" clause of PJS is open to two different interpretations. Gaus seems to imply that being reasonable means in some way recognizing that others have "justified beliefs" which we do not share.[307] If we accept this interpretation of the reasonable, then we have little reason to worry about Quong's empirical claim that many citizens do not view other citizens' doctrines as justified. Quite simply, we could dismiss this common view as not fully reasonable. As a result, we could invoke the reasonableness clause to reject (IV) while at the same time accepting (II) and hence PJS. That is, we could grant that PJS is an important principle (II) and yet deny that convergence permits insincerity (IV) because fully reasonable persons view other citizens' doctrines as justified in Gaus's sense. Quong, however, resists this "epistemic" account of the reasonable. In fact, he sides with Rawls in refusing to tie the ideal of public reason to anything more demanding than a "deliberately loose" conception of the

307 G. Gaus 2011b: 292.

reasonable:[308] as Rawls says, reasonable doctrines and views need not be "open to rational appraisal or evidentially supportable".[309] Reasonable persons, for Rawls, accept the burdens of judgment and the correspondent fact of reasonable disagreement. In particular, according to Rawls, the "burdens of judgment" are due to six permanent sources of disagreement, which reasonable people recognize:

> "a. The evidence – empirical and scientific – bearing on the case is conflicting and complex, and thus hard to assess and evaluate. b. Even where we agree fully about the kinds of considerations that are relevant, we may disagree about their weight, and so arrive at different judgments. c. To some extent all our concepts, and not only moral and political concepts, are vague and subject to hard cases; and this indeterminacy means that we must rely on judgment and interpretation (and on judgments about interpretations) within some range (not sharply specifiable) where reasonable persons may differ. d. To some extent ... the way we assess evidence and weigh moral and political values is shaped by our total experience, our whole course of life up to now; and our total experiences must always differ. Thus, in a modern society with its numerous offices and positions, its various divisions of labor, its many social groups and their ethnic variety, citizens' total experiences are disparate enough for their judgments to diverge, at least to some degree, on many if not most cases of any significant complexity. e. Often there are different kinds of normative considerations both sides of an issue and it is difficult to make an overall assessment. f. Finally, ... any system of social institutions is limited in the values it can admit so that some selection must be made from the full range of moral and political values that might be realized. This is because any system of institutions has, as it were, a limited social space. In being forced to select among cherished values, or when we hold to several and must restrict each in view of the requirements of the others, we face great difficulties in setting priorities and making adjustments. Many hard decisions may seem to have no clear answer".[310]

Now apparently items a) to f) would suggest an "epistemic" interpretation of the fact of reasonable pluralism, which is in tune with Gaus's worries about exaggerated degrees of idealization presupposed by strong and moderate externalist conceptions of reasons. Reasonable pluralism, it might seem, is the upshot of our limited cognitive capacities, which lead us to hold different yet *equally justified* belief systems. Rawls, however, resists this epistemic rendition of the burdens of judgment. Reasonable people view reasonable disagreement as a bare "fact" about liberal democracies: they recognize that over certain issues pervasive disagreement is "the inevitable long-run result of the powers of human reason at

308 J. Rawls 1993: 59.
309 J. Rawls 1997: 592.
310 J. Rawls 1993: 56-7.

work within the background of enduring free institutions".[311] Rawls thus maintains that although the doctrine of the "burdens of judgment" has "epistemological elements", being reasonable "is not an epistemological idea".[312] And this is so because epistemology is itself a controversial branch of philosophy, over which reasonable disagreement reigns. We *can* see others' doctrines as epistemically justified, but it is not unreasonable to simply tolerate others' views as innocuous mistakes. All Andy must do in order to qualify as reasonable is accept disagreement as an unavoidable consequence of the free exercise of reason under liberal principles.

Now the Rawlsian account of the reasonable seems more in tune with PJS because, again, in an important respect sincerity is not a deontic notion. Therefore, we should favor conceptions of public reason that exclude as few actually (i.e., sincerely) held beliefs as possible. If the members of our idealized constituency of public reason endorsed some fully-fledged epistemic theory such as Gaus's, our model would barely reflect what most actual citizens sincerely believe. And yet sincerity *is* about actually held beliefs. The upshot is that we have to assume that the members of our constituency are reasonable in Rawls's sense simply because relatively few citizens are reasonable in Gaus's sense. Relatively few citizens, that is, would sincerely believe that norms backed by overlapping private reasons only are justified to all. This explains, by the way, why the argument from sincerity is appropriateness-based. The case for consensus is independent of any claim about the epistemic status of private reasons and doctrines. Regardless of whether or not Gaus's epistemology is correct, it would be inappropriate for citizens to rely on reasons they do not sincerely affirm. But if this is the case, then we must take *(x)* to be the proper interpretation of what Andy believes in case 1). As a result, (IV) seems correct: convergence permits citizens to violate PJS.

Moreover, Gaus himself seems sometimes to grant that citizens cannot be actually expected to endorse his epistemic theory, and hence to view other citizens' doctrines as justified. Gaus has in fact distinguished between the "perspective of philosophical reflection" and the "perspective of real moral agents".[313] Epistemic pluralism, in his view, is necessary to formulate a model of public justification from the perspective of one theorizing about justice. But if we employ this epistemic theory as political theorists we do not thereby assume, far less demand, that the agents modeled by the theorist actually endorse it. We simply lay out the epistemic framework within which public justification can occur. We can, to be

311 Ibid.: 4.
312 Ibid.: 62; see also ibid.: 44.
313 G. Gaus 2011b: 264.

sure, hope that a large number of reasonable citizens will endorse our epistemic theory. Moreover, as Habermas stresses, some rough but important epistemic concepts are already implicit in our everyday communicative practice.[314] However, it is implausible to assume that citizens largely endorse a fully-fledged epistemic theory such as epistemic pluralism. But if we admit that epistemic pluralism need not itself be agreed upon, we have little reason to reject (IV). It is not unreasonable for citizens to reject epistemic pluralism. And since many citizens actually reject it, PJS compels us to maintain that convergence allows citizens to engage in insincere public reasoning.

3.2.4 Why the sincerity requirement does not justify consensus

Should we conclude that we have reason to reject converge models of public reason, as (T) implies? No. To see why, let us begin by considering a modified version of case 1):

Case 2) Andy proposes X. Andy and Bea think that R_F is a freestanding reason for endorsing X. Andy thinks that R_S is strong enough to justify X over any other alternative options, while Bea does not. Andy argues that Bea's religious beliefs about social justice, which he rejects, provide her with a further reason R_B for conclusively endorsing X. Andy does not think that Bea's religious doctrine is epistemically justified.

In case 2), Andy fulfills requirement (b) of PJS, as he sincerely believes that X is justified to Bea. To be sure, he partially contravenes requirement (c) of PJS, in that he seeks to "strengthen" the freestanding justification of X by appealing to Bea's private doctrine, which, we take it, he sincerely deems both false and unjustified. A public reason liberal, however, might wonder to what extent this counts as an objection against the use of convergence arguments. In case 2) Andy may well be in some sense insincere, one could argue, but what is important is his sincere belief that X is conclusively justified to all.

Of course, Quong could reply that Andy's course of action is less problematic in case 2) only because he believes that R_S is strong enough to justify X. At the end of the day, Andy's further claim that R_B backs R_F up is superfluous. With this move, though, Quong would indirectly open up a line of reasoning that we have not explored yet. Couldn't we simply say that if Andy is to ignore Bea's

314 Speakers are committed, for instance, to regarding intersubjective agreement as the paramount standard of objectivity (see chapter 2, §2.5.3).

private reasons for *accepting* X, as PJS ultimately demands, then Bea may use her private reasons to *reject* X? To get clearer on this point, consider a different case:

Case 3): Andy proposes X. Andy and Bea think that R_F is a freestanding reason for endorsing X. Also, they agree that R_S is sufficiently stronger than all public reasons against X. However, X is radically incompatible with Bea's religious views about social justice. Bea takes this to be a powerful private reason R_B for rejecting X. She thus insists that, all things considered, X is not justified to her. Andy does not think that Bea's religious doctrine is epistemically justified. However, Andy caves in to Bea's objection and withdraws his proposal.

Notice that according to (T2) Bea does not violate PJS in this case, since she simply rejects a coercive proposal. It does not follow, of course, that Bea's claim in case 3) is *eo ipso* unproblematic. Indeed, one of the main reasons why consensus theorists are skeptical about convergence conceptions is that under convergence citizens are allowed to reject norms for which there is a freestanding justification. We already hinted at this point in the previous chapter, when we discussed Habermas's moderate strength-based argument for consensus (§2.8.3). Specifically, case 3) is akin to case d), in which a private (ethical) reason against coercion trumps a moral (freestanding) reason for coercion. Consensus theorists obviously concur with Habermas that there is something wrong with this. Yet Quong's principle of sincerity cannot explain *what* is wrong with this, since (T2) relieves the opponent of coercive legislation of the duty to justify her liberty to the would-be coercer.[315]

Perhaps, though, one could retort that in case 3) it is Andy, and not Bea, who defies the ideal of justificatory sincerity. In fact, Andy is convinced that R_S conclusively justifies X to all, including Bea, as in his view R_B rests on an epistemically flawed comprehensive doctrine. So wouldn't he be hypocritical if he said to Bea "You are right, X is not justified after all?" But this would be a mistake. In case 3), Andy does not change his mind about X. He rather concedes that his sincere and reasonable belief that X is publicly justified may not entitle him to insist that Bea should endorse it. As we stressed above, PJS permits Andy to hold this sort of view, at least in principle. In fact, (T1) states that justificatory sincerity is not a sufficient condition for the legitimacy of political proposals, but only a necessary one. There is therefore nothing contradictory in the view that, if Bea

315 Although Quong repeatedly insists that PJS justifies consensus, sometimes he seems to admit that an independent argument is needed to explain why private reasons should not be allowed to defeat coercion. See J. Quong 2011: 265n.

has reasons to reject X, then Andy may have to withdraw it, even if his arguments justifying X fully respect PJS.

We have arrived at a key point. Quong is right when he stresses that a conception of public reason tailored to PJS should prevent citizens from justifying coercion by appeal to private reasons. However, PJS allows citizens to use private reasons as defeaters against coercive proposals. The upshot is that SPP cannot discard the mixed conception of public reason which we called "negative convergence":[316]

Negative convergence: (A) Liberty should be the norm; coercion stands in need of justification. (B) Coercive law *L* is publicly justified if, and only if, every reasonable citizen, taking all good reasons into account, would endorse *L*. (C) Public reasons are good reasons. Private reasons are good reasons unless they justify coercion.

Now since under negative convergence private reasons cannot serve as justificatory grounds for coercive proposals, this mixed conception is immune to Quong's sincerity objection. Consequently, we have reason to resist Quong's claim that SPP leads to endorse a consensus model of public justification, as consensus and negative convergence fare equally well with respect to PJS.

It is important to emphasize that these two models are *equally compatible* with PJS. For observe that in case 3) Andy would not violate PJS if he did not withdraw X after all. In fact, as we stressed above, Andy sincerely believes that X is justified to all, since he regards Bea's private objections as unjustified. Indeed, as Quong rightly points out, this is what many reasonable citizens believe in good faith about other citizens' comprehensive doctrines. Once again, consensus is in tune with PJS because it requires ignoring reasons which most proponents of coercive legislation would actually believe to be irrelevant. We have seen, however, that negative convergence should look equally permissible to defenders of PJS. Hence, although SPP leads us to reject convergence, it permits us to endorse both consensus and negative convergence.

Indeed, one could defend negative convergence by raising an independent sincerity objection against consensus, along the following lines. One of the main reasons why PJS applies only to the proponent of coercive legislation is that for public reason liberals coercion calls for special justification. The opponent of coercive legislation need not be sincere according to PJS, since she does not raise any claims that stand in need of justification. But precisely because public reason

316 See chapter 1, §1.5.6.

liberals are concerned with the justification of coercion, one could argue, they should also be truly worried by the fact that some citizens might *sincerely* object to proposals backed by public reasons. Another way of putting this point consists in making a distinction between *personal* and *civic* sincerity.[317] We are civically sincere when we justify our proposals to others in accordance with PJS. We are personally sincere when we openly state what we believe is justified to us. Now in case 3) Andy is no doubt civically sincere in proposing X; still, we should also heed Bea's "personally sincere" belief that Andy's coercive demand is not justified to her. Therefore, although consensus honors the ideal of civic sincerity on which PJS relies, the importance of personal sincerity should lead us to favor negative convergence over consensus. In any event, defenders of PJS are committed to the view that negative convergence is, at the very least, as compatible with PJS as consensus. Therefore, even if we accepted premises (I) to (IV) of Quong's argument, we would not be committed to consensus.[318]

3.3. Public reason: epistemological and not political

3.3.1 The role of moral epistemology

More, however, needs to be said. In fact, we have hitherto taken for granted that (III) is correct, and yet I think there is good reason to resist it. Specifically, we should resist the sincerity-promoting principle (SPP), on which (III) relies. According to SPP, it will be recalled, we should favor conceptions of public reason that do not permit (let alone require) citizens to neglect PJS. To see why we should resist SPP, we need to keep in mind two things we stressed above. First, sincerity is not a deontic notion, in the sense that it has nothing to do with what people ought to believe. Hence, the more our justificatory model departs from what most citizens actually believe, the more we permit or even demand insincerity. Second, most citizens disagree over epistemology. The upshot is that if we endorse SPP, we ought to favor conceptions of public reason that do not presuppose any kind of epistemology.

Importantly, these two questions are inextricably intertwined. In fact, if a consensus model presupposed some controversial epistemological doctrine, then it would score almost as poorly as convergence with respect to SPP. In other words, SPP does not rank convergence below consensus in general, but only be-

317 I owe this distinction to David Owen.

318 I am not saying that Quong should endorse negative convergence, which seems in fact vulnerable to a further objection he raises against convergence models. See §3.5.1 below.

low "political" consensus conceptions such as Rawls's, which are typically committed to epistemic restraint. Since reasonable people disagree over epistemology, political liberals such as Quong, Rawls, Larmore and Macedo insist that a suitable conception of public reason must be neutral on controversial epistemic doctrines. Quong thus claims that "[p]olitical liberalism cannot affirm or deny the truth of Gaus's epistemic theory because that theory conflicts with what some reasonable citizens believe about the epistemic status of other people's non-public doctrines".[319] Following Rawls, Quong alleges to seize upon justificatory accounts such as Gaus's and Habermas's, which rely on tethering public justification to controversial epistemic theories. Again, though, SPP requires political liberals to reject *any* kind of epistemology, not just Gaus's.

However, it is hard to see how any doctrine of public reason can be freestanding with respect to epistemology in general, since key concepts such as "reason", "justification" and "shareability" are deeply epistemological. This is not to deny, of course, that justificatory reasons are primarily moral, in the sense that they speak for or against ought-statements regulating behavior. But moral reasons, qua reasons, have also an epistemic dimension: they can be more or less able to support the belief for which they are reasons. So for instance if Andy says to Bea "Please lend me some money because I have none", he may well have given a moral reason to her. But to conclude that Bea should be convinced by that reason, we need to assess its epistemic weight. We need to verify, that is, whether or not that moral reason rationally commits her to believing that she should actually help him out. Again, all this is a roundabout way of saying that (moral) reasons for or against ought-statements (in our case: pieces of coercive legislation) need to be justified. Thus the moral and epistemological aspects of reasons cannot come apart. Rather, we need a *moral epistemology* in order to make sense of the idea of public justification.

To say that X is publicly *justified* is to say that all members of the public have some reason *R* to accept X. And this, in turn, is tantamount to saying that Andy's affirming X on the basis of *R* is not epistemically flawed. By the same token, to say that *R* is a shareable reason justifying X is to say that all citizens are committed to regarding $R \rightarrow X$ as justificatory. So how can political liberals do away with epistemology? One response could consist in equating shareability which unanimous actual endorsement. If people reasonable disagree over epistemology, we cannot admit of any gap between people's actually shared beliefs and justificatory public reasons. For it we did admit that these two categories come apart, we should inevitably employ an epistemic theory to bridge the gap between the rea-

319 J. Quong 2011: 270.

sons we actually affirm and the reasons that we ought to share. Apparently, Quong seems committed to resorting to such a populist conception of public reason. That is, he seems committed to the view that

1) Reasonable citizen Andy actually rejects $R \rightarrow X$

is incompatible with

2) *R* publicly justifies X.

As a matter of fact, 1) and 2) could be made consistent only under the assumption that

3) There are some publicly available epistemic tools to detect flawed forms of reasoning.

Yet Quong seems unable to affirm 3). Political liberalism cannot afford to make any distinction between shared reasons and shareable reasons. However, we already rejected this radical conception of shareability, which we called the "Populist View of Shareability" (see chapter 2, §2.7.2). Clearly the fact that Andy stubbornly insists on rejecting a reason that is openly justified to all cannot show that that reason is not shareable. Moreover, it is questionable whether there really are such things as "actually shared" reasons, to wit, reasons that are actually affirmed by all, ranging from Nazis to Maoists. Of course, Rawlsians could retort that political liberalism is not committed to the Populist View of Shareability, but only to a populist conception that is concerned with the beliefs of reasonable people. Call this the "Moderately Populist View of Shareability":

Moderately Populist View of Shareability: *R* is a public reason for *L* if and only if it is affirmed by all reasonable citizens (if properly conducted, Ω would lead to a set of freestanding considerations *U* whose elements are affirmed by all reasonable citizens).

But this revised populist view accomplishes little, for the simple fact that "reasonableness" is not an epistemic property of beliefs, but a moral attitude of persons, which means that reasonable people might hold flawed beliefs. In any event, Rawls rejects populism. In his view, we can certainly advocate reasons and values that are not actually shared as long as we reasonably believe that they *could be* shared by others. He claims, for example, that public reason asks us to "conduct our fundamental discussions in terms of what we regard as a political conception … based on political values everyone can reasonably be expected to endorse…".[320] Quong agrees. Rather than drawing on actually shared reasons we should appeal to reasons that we *can* share: "In a large and diverse liberal society, public reason … requires that the reasons we offer to one another in political debate be reasons that we *can* all share".[321] But this raises an obvious question: "Reasons we can all share" *under which conditions*? This is a purely epistemic question. If shareability and actual unanimous acceptance come apart, as Rawls and Quong rightly believe, we must explain which epistemic standards a reason must live up to in order to deserve the assent of all. Therefore, we must in some way show that 1) and 2) are not incompatible in principle, since Andy may fail to see that $R \rightarrow X$ is a sound inference which everyone, including himself, should accept. But how can 1) square with 2) if we deny 3)?

Quong could reply in two ways. First, he could grant that shareability is an epistemic concept and yet contend that a "loose" political epistemology can reconcile 1) with 2) (§3.3.2 – 3.3.3). Second, he could insist that 1) can be made consistent with 2) even in the absence of an epistemic theory because the concept of shareability need not be spelled out in epistemic terms (§3.3.4). In both cases he would eschew a controversial definition of shareability to retain a good deal of actual consensus about the nature of the concept.

3.3.2 The Commonsense View of Shareability

Let us consider the first strategy. Quong could retort that political liberals are not committed to rejecting 3) because political liberalism must be neutral on *controversial* epistemological doctrines, and not on epistemology as such. The members of the public, he could claim, can and should obviously master some basic epistemic tools. As Rawls stresses, reasonable people accept both commonsense reasoning and the non-controversial conclusions of science.[322] With this move, the political liberal apparently catches two birds with one stone. On the one hand, he can resist the radically populist view that the reasons we can share come down to the reasons we actually share: 1) and 2) can be made consistent whenever Andy's actual rejection of $R \rightarrow X$ goes against common sense. On the other

320 J. Rawls 1993: 241. Moreover, in his later works Rawls argued for the so called "wide view" of public reason, which allows citizens to introduce their comprehensive views into debate at any time, provided supporting public reasons are offered in due course (J. Rawls 1997: 591-94). Here the link between shareability and actual unanimous endorsement is even more tenuous.

321 J. Quong 2011: 273, emphasis mine.

322 See J. Rawls 1993: 139.

hand, the political liberal can avoid the charge of relying on a controversial epistemology, since commonsense epistemology is implicitly shared by all reasonable citizens. This leads to:

Commonsense View of Shareability: *R* is a public reason for *L* if and only if the belief that *R* is a shareable reason does not violate relevant standards of commonsense reasoning (if properly conducted, Ω would lead to a set of freestanding considerations *U* whose elements do not violate relevant standards of commonsense reasoning).

Still, there are three major problems with the Commonsense View of Shareability. Firstly, significant evidence shows that commonsense reasoning is typically flawed by shortcuts, fallacies, pitfalls and heuristics.[323] This comes as no surprise. If our epistemology must conform to what citizens actually believe, then it is hard to see how it could yield results that differ much from a sheer populist view. In a way, political liberalism can avoid populism only by resorting to a populist epistemology. Secondly, the claim that commonsense reasoning is an adequate epistemic theory because people are likely to accept it is weirdly counterintuitive. Overwhelming evidence shows that commonsense reasoning is often flawed, but now we are told that the mere fact that many average reasoners are likely to commit errors or reasoning shows that commonsense reasoning is in fact sound. Finally, there is a more subtle problem with the view that the content of moral epistemology must in some way reflect people's beliefs about epistemology. Let *T* be an epistemic theory assessing the epistemic status of reasons and beliefs. Now if we accept the view that commonsense reasoning is a sound epistemic theory because it is widely acceptable, we are committed to the "Political View of Epistemology":

Political View of Epistemology: *T* is a sound epistemic theory (if and) only if, all reasonable citizens have a justified belief that *T* is a sound epistemic theory.

Now claiming that justification in general should depend on citizens' beliefs may be a legitimate position, but to defend it one must already presuppose that citizens' beliefs are grounded in good reasons. In fact, insofar as it purports to justify *T* in terms of intersubjective agreement, the Political View of Epistemology leads to infinite regress. In order to determine whether citizens are justified in endorsing *T*, we would need a further epistemic theory *T** that explains whether

323 For more on this see T. Gilovic / D. Griffin / D. Kahneman (eds.) 2002 and G. Gaus 1996: 131-36.

their endorsing *T* is justified. But of course, the Political View of Epistemology implies that only an agreement on *T** among (reasonable) citizens could justify *T**. But how can we know if they have good reasons for endorsing *T**? Again, we need a further point of reference cast in the form of a deeper epistemic theory *T***, and so on ad infinitum. To stop this infinite regress, one must assume that citizens' deliberation is bound by an epistemological theory whose validity is not itself dependent upon the outcome of deliberation.

It is not accidental that all attempts to publicly justify the very idea of public justification (as well as its constitutive elements, such as *T*) typically lead to skeptical results: the ideal of public reason turns out to be either "self-defeating"[324] or "essentially contestable".[325] How can we publicly justify *T* if *T* is necessary to determine what can be publicly justified? To be sure, Habermas's discourse theoretical approach lends plausibility to the view that justification should be understood in terms of intersubjective agreement. But this is a viable option only if the object of agreement is *L*, and not *T*, for *T* must be already at work as a constraint on deliberation. Habermas is, of course, aware of this. It is only because he first fixes a discourse-theoretical epistemic theory of justified belief that Habermas can maintain that the justification of substantive norms is dependent on the agreement of participants in justificatory discourses. We should, then, replace the Political View of Epistemology with

Shareability as Agreement among Good Reasoners: *R* is shareable if, and only if, all citizens deliberating under conditions specified by *T* would share *R*.

But Shareability as Agreement among Good Reasoners takes us back to square one. We need an epistemic theory *T* to determine which reasons count as justificatory, and this theory must be independent of what reasonable citizens believe about epistemology. But since we already established that epistemic pluralism is the epistemic theory we are after, then we are committed to the Weakly Externalist View of Shareability (see chapter 2, §2.7.2), which stitches the concept of shareability into the broader category of "openly justified beliefs": a shareable reason is a reason that is openly justified to all.

This establishes a strong case against SPP. Let C1 be a consensus model based on the Commonsense View of Shareability, C2 be a consensus model based on the Weakly Externalist View of Shareability and C3 be a convergence model based on the Weakly Externalist View of Shareability. Now SPP would certainly rank C1 over both C2 and C3, since C1, unlike C2 and C3, does not

324 S. Wall 2002.
325 F. D'Agostino 1995, 1996.

presuppose a controversial epistemology over which citizens reasonably disagree. But because the Commonsense View of Shareability should be resisted, SPP cannot be a reliable principle for selecting eligible conceptions of public reason. An interesting question is how well C2 and C3 would fare with respect to PJS and SPP. I would conjecture that SPP would favor C2 over C3, but not by much. On the one hand, C2 would still be preferable from the standpoint of sincerity because it would not permit citizens to advance convergence arguments. But on the other hand, C3 would be only marginally worse than C2 with respect to PJS, for both conceptions would employ the *same* (controversial) epistemic theory to identify the reasons citizens have. Even in this case, though, SPP looks hardly reliable. It is mysterious why citizens should be barred from using reasons which a sound epistemic theory suitable for public justification deems justificatory. The whole point of public reason is to lay out a justificatory procedure whose results are justified to all members of the public. To do so, the theorist of public reason must favor the epistemic theory that is better able to track the reasons that "real moral agents" can be said to *have*. Epistemic pluralism states that even private reasons are justificatory. Hence, whether or not citizens in flesh and blood actually and sincerely believe that other people's "ethical" views are justified amounts to little. For epistemic pluralism has already established that they are.

3.3.3 The Meta-Convergence View of Shareability

Political liberals could insist that epistemic pluralism is only one epistemic theory among others, a theory over which it is possible to disagree. So why not endorse the following view of shareability?

Meta-Convergence View of Shareability: R is a shareable/public reason for L if, and only if, all reasonable epistemic doctrines hold that R is a shareable/public reason for L.

The Meta-Convergence View of Shareability does not deny that shareability is an epistemic concept, as it does not deny that one needs some epistemic account of justified belief to determine whether a given reason is public. However, the Meta-Convergence View of Shareability need not be seen as an epistemic thesis; in fact, it actually looks more like a thesis that accounts for different, conflicting epistemic theories: if R is public according to all epistemic theories, then political liberals can assume that R is shareable, without however having to endorse any such theory; that is to say, they can argue that R is public because, regardless of the epistemic theory one happens to affirm, one is committed to endorsing *R*. Let us distinguish between three groups of epistemic theories:

Group A): Those that claim that R is public if and only if it is freestanding.
Group B): Those that claim that R is public only if it is freestanding.
Group C): Those that claim that R is public if and only if it is undefeated by private reasons.

Group A) comprises all theories that affirm the Freestandingness Thesis (see §1.5.1 above); group B) includes epistemic doctrines that endorse something akin to the Weak Freestandingness Thesis (see §1.5.6 above); finally, epistemic theories such as Gaus's (which are consistent with the Undefeated Public Reasons Thesis, see §1.5.6 above) fall into group C). Now political liberals could claim that since epistemology is the subject of reasonable disagreement, all three groups express equally reasonable epistemic theories. The Meta-Convergence View of Shareability has the virtue of giving an account of shareability that is sensitive to the fact of reasonable disagreement over epistemology. As long as all epistemic theories converge in defining *R* as public, then *R* is the object of a "meta-convergence", so to speak. If this meta-convergence on *R* occurs, then political liberals can maintain that *R* is shareable without having to affirm any controversial epistemology. Political liberals could both give an epistemic definition of shareability and refrain from affirming or denying any of the epistemic theories which, by means of meta-convergence, jointly define what counts as a shareable reason.[326]

There are, however, two obvious problems with the Meta-Convergence View of Shareability. The first problem is that it would essentially us back to a populist conception of public reason. Recall that reasonable citizens may affirm implausible views of epistemology such as commonsense-theories. But of course, political liberals could hardly discriminate against flawed views and beliefs, as to do so they should take sides in the thorny issue (on which, again, they wish to remain agnostic) of what constitutes a justified belief. Given their commitment to epistemic neutrality, political liberals who may be attracted to the Meta-Convergence View of Shareability should give a say to implausible epistemic theories. This is a populist approach in disguise: *R* is shareable if and all if all epistemic theories (including, alas, implausible ones) would regard *R* as public. The Meta-Convergence View of Shareability should therefore be resisted.

326 Elsewhere, I argued that this view is the best option for "political liberals" committed to "epistemic neutrality" (Zoffoli 2012).

The second problem with the Meta-Convergence View of Shareability is that is inconsistent with consensus, as those who affirm theories that fall into groups B) and C) may reasonably regard some of the reasons comprised by *U* as non-public. To these citizens, then, consensus models are self-defeating for the reasons I mentioned in §1.5.7: they overlook the fact that private reasons are necessary to determine what counts as a public reason. In other words, a meta-convergence on the set of shareable reasons would inevitably lead to a convergence model of public reason. The upshot is that political liberals may indeed live up to their commitment to epistemic neutrality, provided they accept the Meta-Convergence View of Shareability (and are willing to lapse into some populist approach to public justification). But if they do, they are committed to rejecting consensus models of public reason.

3.3.4 The Political View of Shareability

Thus far, I have taken for granted that shareability is an epistemic concept, but now Quong could try denying this assumption. Above (§3.3.1) I argued that "reasonableness" is not an epistemic property of beliefs but a moral characteristic of persons. Now in some places Quong steers a middle way between these two views, arguing that reasonableness is indeed (also) a quality of beliefs, but not an epistemic property of *justified* beliefs. That is, beliefs (and not only persons) are reasonable, and yet reasonable beliefs need not be epistemically justified. On Quong's definition, a "reasonable belief" is "any belief held by a reasonable person that is arrived at through an exercise of theoretical reason, which is to say that it is arrived at 'in a more or less consistent and coherent fashion'".[327] However, reasonable beliefs may fall short of full epistemic warrant because "[y]ou do not have to be subjectively justified in holding a belief in order for that belief to be a reasonable one".[328] Now according to Quong, political liberals can only demand that beliefs be "reasonable". Consequently, Quong seems attracted to the following conception of shareability:

Political View of Shareability: *R* is a public reason for *L* if and only if the belief that *R* is a shareable reason is not unreasonable (if properly conducted, Ω would lead to a set of freestanding considerations *U* whose elements represent reasonable beliefs, though not necessarily epistemically justified ones).

327 J. Quong 2011: 231.
328 Ibid.: 232.

If we start from the assumption that the vast majority of actual citizens are in fact reasonable, SPP ranks consensus models based on the Political View of Shareability over convergence. But once again, this seems a reason to reject SPP, rather than a reason to reject convergence. Since Quong explicitly concedes that reasonable beliefs may have poor epistemic credentials or be altogether unjustified, political liberalism permits epistemically flawed reasons to shape the outcome of public reasoning. But if this is so, then, political liberalism hardly counts as a justificatory conception. How can we achieve public *justification* if we start from the assumption that justificatory reasons may fail to warrant rational belief?

Political liberals would be probably dissatisfied with this conclusion, arguing that to place too much emphasis on the epistemic dimension of justification is to downplay other relevant aspects of an adequate theory of liberalism. Since it is desirable to work out a theory of public reason whose results can be widely seen to be reasonable, we should be wary of expunging too much actually held beliefs from the justificatory process. This is certainly one of political liberals' main concerns, so it is not implausible to interpret along these lines their reluctance to inject too much epistemic substance into the justificatory model.

I do not mean to belittle this urge. My point is simply that if we reject epistemology, we cannot plausibly defend a theory of public justification. Consider what Macedo says about the importance of appealing to widely shared reasons: "[A]t its most basic level, public justification has dual aims". On the one hand, "it seeks reflective justification (good reasons)"; but on the other hand, "it also seeks reasons that can be widely seen to be good by persons such as they are".[329] This claim strikes me as admitting that for political liberals justification is just a desideratum, which, however important, may be traded off against other values, such as the achievement of a good deal of actual consensus on political principles. Of course, as we stressed in the previous chapter, epistemic pluralism presupposes a low level of idealization. Indeed, Gaus and Habermas reject strongly and moderately externalist approaches to justification on these grounds: justification is about the reasons that average reasoners have, and not about the reasons that there are. Still, we also saw that endorsing this view means willy-nilly endorsing epistemic pluralism. Insofar as we reject this sort of pluralistic epistemology, we lower the bar of idealization too much, thus losing sight of the reasons that the members of the public have.

I conclude that although Quong's argument from sincerity is prima facie appealing, it fails to justify the standard consensus view. Recall that his argument rests on four core premises: First, sincerity is a prima facie desideratum (I); sec-

329 S. Macedo 1990: 281.

ond, if we cherish the value of sincerity, then we ought to accept PJS (II); third, if PJS prevents citizens from appealing to private reasons, then we ought to endorse consensus, as SPP implies (III); finally, PJS prevents citizens from appealing to private reasons (IV). I sought to show that there are two main problems with this argument. First, even if we accepted premises (I) to (IV), (T) would not be warranted. In fact, SPP would not rank convergence over negative convergence, though it would rank consensus over convergence. Thus, consensus theorists cannot content themselves with the argument from sincerity. Second, (III) is false because SPP would lead to both endorse populist conceptions of public reason and downplay the inherently epistemological character of justification.

To come back to our taxonomy of arguments for consensus, Quong puts forward an appropriateness-based argument for consensus in that he argues that failure to comply with PJS would be morally inappropriate. As a result, according to Quong, our constituency of public reason should comprise only members who refrain from advocating their private reasons. We have seen, however, that this line of reasoning is both unable to justify consensus (as opposed to negative convergence) and based on the misguided assumption that SPP should be able to rank conceptions of public reason. As far as sincerity is concerned, then, consensus can hardly be justified on grounds of moral appropriateness.

3.4. The argument from publicity

3.4.1 The value of full publicity

Let us now consider another appropriateness-based argument for consensus, which has been recently advanced by Stephen Macedo and others. I call it the "argument from publicity" because Macedo seems to imply, among other things, that on a convergence view it would be very hard to reach what Rawls dubs "full publicity". Recall that in chapter 1 (§1.3.3) we distinguished three levels of publicness. Publicness as a Property of the Use of Reason and Publicness as a Property of Reasons link publicity to the shareability of reason(s), while Publicness as a Property of the Commitment to Justify Coercion to All stresses that public justification must be addressed to all members of the public. But now we can introduce a fourth dimension of publicness, which equates publicness with full common knowledge or "publicity" in Rawls's sense:

Publicness as Full Publicity: *R* is a public reason for *L* (where *L* is a law binding on society *S*) only if $R \rightarrow L$ is or can realistically be the object of common knowledge in society *S*.

For Rawls, "full publicity" can be achieved through a three-step procedure. With a first step we ensure that citizens understand that "society is effectively regulated by public principles of justice: citizens accept and know that others likewise accept those principles, and this in turn is publicly recognized".[330] With a second step we show that all free and equal citizens have some shared beliefs "in the light of which first principles of justice themselves can be accepted, that is, the general beliefs about human nature and the way political social institutions generally work, and indeed all such beliefs relevant to political justice".[331] Finally, we arrive at "full publicity" when "the public concept of justice ... presented in its own terms" becomes "publicly known or at least publicly available".[332] Thus "full publicity" is achieved when all citizens can see the conception of justice as the object of common knowledge. Rawls thinks full publicity is important because it will render citizens "confident that this avowed reckoning itself will strengthen and not weaken public understanding".[333]

Now Macedo argues that by rejecting the necessity of shared commitments convergence damages common knowledge, thereby hampering the achievement of full publicity. Convergence, according to Macedo, departs from public reason's traditional ideal of a shared commitment to justice, whereas public reasoning is meant to "empower a common point of view"[334] by encouraging the exchange of accessible reasons and information. Common knowledge "helps people coordinate their actions in service of mutual advantage" and aids "cooperation on the basis of shared values".[335] For Macedo common knowledge and full publicity are much easier to achieve under a consensus conception of public justification. When we reason in shared terms, our interlocutors can better appreciate and evaluate our arguments. Convergence theorists fail to see that common knowledge and mutually intelligible shared commitments provide valuable benefits. They "downgrade or reject the ways in which liberal public reason is concerned to justify shared principles on the basis of *common knowledge*"[336], thereby embracing "privatism" or "partialism". This leads to an incongruously loose conception of politics, which encourages citizens to find their sense of community only in "the partial associations of civil society, and the bosom of family and

330 J. Rawls 1993: 66.
331 Ibid.: 67.
332 Ibid.
333 Ibid.: 68.
334 S. Macedo 2010: 1.
335 Ibid.: 19.
336 Ibid.: 3.

friends".[337] Therefore, convergence justification is of little avail to "the constitution of the public sphere".[338]

Macedo's argument is appropriateness-based: it does not claim that freestanding reasons are epistemically indefeasible, and hence both shareable and conclusive. Rather, it claims that reasonable citizens should rely on freestanding reasons because reliance on private reasons is inappropriate qua detrimental to the achievement of full publicity. Thus, the members of our constituency of public reason will only advocate freestanding reasons, and will in fact believe that those reasons are indefeasible. As far as *these* members are concerned, then, freestanding reasons are indeed shareable and conclusive.

Before reviewing this objection against convergence I should like to stress that there are other versions of the argument from publicity other than Macedo's. For instance, Micah Schwartzman and Samuel Freeman have also defended consensus on the grounds that it safeguards the value of "full" or "actual" publicity, while Paul Weithman concurs with Macedo that reliance on some "common logics" can help reassure each other of our allegiance to rules of conduct.[339] Charles Larmore has gone so far as to argue that, although Rawls did not seem to see this at first, publicity is necessary to make sense of the very idea of justice as fairness:

> In *A Theory of Justice*, the "publicity condition" generally enters the discussion from the side, as though merely a further desideratum that principles of justice should possess. … Rawls's statements about publicity in this book generally equate it with public knowledge, as though it entailed only that citizens know the operative principles of justice and one another's reasons for accepting them. The work he expects from it shows, however, that he has something more ambitious in mind. Publicity really amounts to the demand that the reasons each person has to endorse the principles be reasons the person sees others to have to endorse them as well. It requires that the principles of justice be grounded in a shared point of view. In several essays published after *A Theory of Justice*, the notion of publicity receives more systematic attention, and not by accident. Its greater prominence reflects the new direction in Rawls's thinking that leads to *Political Liberalism*. In the course of this transformation the ideal of publicity grows into his doctrine of "public reason."[340]

Unlike *A Theory of Justice*, then, *Political Liberalism* brought to light a latent intuition which already lurked beneath the surface of Rawls's original idea of justice as fairness: being a truly fair principle of justice amounts to being *publicly* known to be supported by *public* reasons which all citizens could "affirm togeth-

337 Ibid.: 16.
338 Ibid.: 3.
339 See M. Schwartzman 2011, S. Freeman 2007: 315-18 and P. Weithman 2010: 54-9.
340 C. Larmore 2003: 371-75.

er".[341]

I shall focus especially on Macedo's version of this argument, however, because this will enable us to highlight a crucial ambiguity hidden in the argument from publicity in general. The ambiguity is that it is not clear whether according to these critics the value of full publicity is part of the ideal of public reason or something that the public sphere is meant to promote. In effect, Macedo uses the terms "public reason" and "public sphere" interchangeably, and yet these are two distinct concepts. "Public reason" is a justificatory ideal that explains which reasons citizens can advocate when they put forward political proposals or defend some existing laws. The "public sphere", by contrast, is normally seen as something akin to what Rawls calls the "background culture" or the "culture of civil society". For Rawls, "in a democracy this culture is not ... guided by any one central principle or idea ... Its many and diverse agencies and associations with the internal life reside within a framework of law that ensures the familiar liberties of thought and speech, and the right of free association".[342] Similarly, Habermas regards the "public sphere" (*Öffentlichkeit*) as a site of free exchange of reasons and information which is neither governed by the mechanisms of the market nor constrained by the authority of the state.[343]

Now although many, including Habermas, have emphasized the cognitive and emancipative potential of an enlightened public sphere, the "background culture" is not meant to justify the law, at least not directly. It is meant first and foremost to safeguard and foster a multifaceted and inclusive political dialogue. To be sure, public sphere and public reason overlap in many important respects, especially on a Habermasian understanding of politics and deliberation. Still, public reason and public sphere are conceptually distinct. While the former justifies the law, the latter compels a publicly justified system of norms to undergo some further critical inspection. The public sphere presents publicly justified laws as the object of a fully-informed "common knowledge". Macedo's argument is therefore open to two different interpretations. It can be taken to claim both/either that (a) convergence damages the constitution of the public sphere (§3.4.2) and/or that (b) convergence is not an appropriate paradigm for public reason or public justification (§3.4.3).

341 Ibid.

342 J. Rawls 1997: 576.

343 See J. Habermas 1989. For a critical overview see C. Calhoun (ed.) 1992.

3.4.2 The role of the public sphere

Interpretation (a) seems much more in tune with Macedo's concern with the generation of "common knowledge". In fact it is the public sphere, and not public reason, which serves the function of enhancing "common knowledge" and "full publicity", espousing the reasons employed in public justification. But (a) has unacceptable implications. While public reason may well rule out some kinds of reasons as inadequate justificatory grounds, there can be no comparable constraints on the reasons and arguments that people can advance within the public sphere. It would be grotesque to say that newspapers, television and other communicative media should be gutted by some sort of principle of "restraint" that only allows for freestanding arguments being circulated within the background culture.

Furthermore, (a) is off-target. It alleges that convergence does not do justice to the idea of a "public sphere" devoted to generating "shared rationales", but the consensus/convergence distinction does not apply to the "public sphere". Dialogue among "private" doctrines is the essence of the public sphere. Yet it would be inappropriate to say that the public sphere must be understood as aiming at "convergence". Since the public sphere has no direct justificatory function, there is nothing to converge upon. Again, it is true that the public sphere significantly contributes to the generation of "common knowledge" and to the pursuit of "full publicity" through openness, exchange of information and disclosure – indeed, this is its main function. But making a justified political conception the object of "common knowledge" in this sense is not the same as publicly justifying it. Consequently, there is no need to assume that the arguments put forward within the public sphere should measure up to the justificatory standards employed by public reason.

Macedo and Schwartzman could reply that I am selling short the justificatory potential of the public sphere. Public knowledge does serve a crucial justificatory function, they could argue, for a number of reasons. To begin with, full publicity makes the justificatory reasons advocated by public reason fully available, so that they can be evaluated and examined in greater detail. Additionally, as Schwartzman stresses, full publicity is both "necessary for democratic accountability" and able to "enhance the quality of political decisions".[344] Indeed, for Schwartzman the main virtue of "actual publicity" understood as reliance on "shared reason" is that it fosters a transparent commitment to "public sincerity" and "democratic accountability".[345] So it seems appropriate to say that the public

344 M. Schwartzman 2010: 7-8.
345 Ibid.

sphere should strongly favor the exchange of freestanding reasons and arguments. Again, though, this is an incredibly demanding claim. Judges, congressmen and other public officials can be required to avoid justifying the law by appeal to certain considerations, but it is very hard to see how constraints of this kind could be extended to the public at large. To defend this view, one should provide some compelling proof that an excess of private reasons is in effect a threat to the creation of "common knowledge".

Macedo seems to take it for granted that this is the case. Relevant information is more easily understood and exchanged when we speak in shared terms, avoiding reliance on our private values and beliefs. But this seems a questionable claim. Observe, first, that private reasons are a superset of public reasons – just like convergence is a superset of consensus. Convergence does not rule out common reasoning; it only allows diverse reasoning. It allows citizens to advocate *both* freestanding *and* private views. Similarly, to state that the public sphere must permit the use private reason is not to state that *only* private reasons can circulate within it. That said, it is unclear why openness toward private reasons should enervate the public sphere's ability to generate common knowledge. One could argue that by letting private reasons in we may in fact increase the opportunities to develop shared commitments and values. We will no doubt increase the amount of information available to the members of the public. And with more reasons on the table, citizens can become aware of a broader range of reasonable considerations and have more cognitive resources to generate common knowledge. This is, to be sure, a highly conjectural claim; but it is not more conjectural than Macedo's.[346]

3.4.3 Full publicity as a justificatory device

But perhaps interpretation (b) can help us better grasp Macedo's point. On this second interpretation, "full publicity" means something like "effective justifica-

346 Recently, Macedo has tried to strengthen this point by arguing that successful coordination requires public "common logics", which would allow us to anticipate possible reactions to violations to commonly accepted rules of conduct (S. Macedo 2010: 16; for a similar view see Weithmann 2010: 54-9). The problem here is not simply the lack of shared rationales, but rather the lack of successful coordination which those rationales make possible. Even in this case, however, Macedo's (and Weithmann's) claim seems dubious, since we can certainly conceive of a number of cases in which two or more agents act cooperatively while having different reasons for doing so. As Gaus says, "Fred Astaire and Ginger Rogers need not have had common reasons for dancing together" (G. Gaus 2011a: 317).

tion" of the law. What is at stake here is no longer a pervasive critical examination, empowered by the mass-media, of a publicly justified system of legal norms. Rather, the point is that by introducing their private reasons into debate, participants in justificatory discourse would endanger the very justification of political principles.

Macedo argues, for instance, that without a civic guarantee that reasoning will be carried out on the basis of shared reasons and beliefs, common knowledge will fracture into a variety of privatistic viewpoints, which would render the justification of political principles too thin:

> Without the common rationale or shared reasons, we would be like a group of mathematicians who agreed on a certain result, but differed widely on how to arrive at the result. But our capacity to assure one another of our shared commitment would seem more solidly grounded and stable, and also more mutually intelligible, if we share a rationale, or agree on a widely convincing proof. Then we not only agree each for our own reasons, but share a powerful rationale in common.[347]

Macedo equates public practical rationality with scientific knowledge. In the previous chapter I argued, however, that this is a crucial error.[348] Public reason is not concerned with the objective justification of the law, but rather with the justification of the law *to* its addressees. Therefore, the law need not and should be seen as "truth-analogous", as Macedo (here apparently following Habermas) seems to imply.

But Macedo appears also to have something else in mind when he claims that convergence damages the publicity of shared rationales. In many places he criticizes convergence by appealing to a "thick" and Rousseauvian-flavored conception of politics, according to which justification is first and foremost about partaking of a collective self-legislating body driven by a common republican ethos:

> If people defect and free ride with respect to our political association and its aims, it is unlikely to be the powerful who suffer most. .... So if we ask for whose sake we seek to make our commitment to shared principles of justice, including distributive justice, a matter of common knowledge and shared understanding, the obvious answer is: for all our sakes, so that we can all enjoy the good of shared intelligible commitment to fair cooperation for its own sake, but most especially for the least well-off who are most liable to be rendered vulnerable to exploitation or oppression by the breakdown of public commitments or the threat thereof..

347 S. Macedo 2010: 16.
348 See §2.6.3.

A fragmented and "privatistic" justification of collective principles will leave citizens with no shared rationales, thus making it harder to "pin-point" exactly the reasons why free riders are blameworthy. By contrast, a "republican" justification based on common rationales will be much better able to condemn free riders on political-moral grounds. With a thin conception of public reason, the relatively powerful will have relatively few problems, but the powerless and the marginalized will fare poorly: for "who will have the resources to engage in private self-help and defense when others act unfairly?"[349]

I find Macedo's argument unpersuasive. Bear in mind that we are discussing an appropriateness-based argument from consensus: regardless of the epistemic status of private reasons, reliance on them would be inappropriate because it would endanger full publicity. As I stressed above, however, appropriateness-based arguments for consensus are acceptable only if they are very powerful, as they are supposed to compensate for fact that consensus may uphold defeated proposals. But I take it that even if it were sound, Macedo's argument would not meet this burden, because it presupposes a radically republican and arguably controversial conception of politics, which justificatory liberals are not committed to accepting.

In any event, Macedo's argument is *not* sound. Macedo seems to take it for granted that under convergence publicly justified laws will be backed *exclusively* by private rationales. But this is clearly not the case, especially if we follow Gaus and Rawls in understanding public justification as a two-step procedure. I have repeatedly stressed that on my account public justification does indeed proceed in two steps. First, we identify a set of "pro tanto" justified principles backed by sharable reasons; at the second stage we verify whether citizens' private reasons confirm the outcome of pro tanto justification. But because justification always starts with the first step, laws are always "pro tanto" justified by freestanding rationales expressing core or "generalizable" interests. It is therefore a mistake to think that an "overlapping consensus" of private rationales supporting the law overshadows (let alone: nullifies) the freestanding rationales on which Macedo places so much emphasis. In conclusion, there is little reason to believe that the argument from publicity poses any serious threat to convergence.

349 See S. Macedo / K. Hatfield 2011.

3.5. Other appropriateness-based objections to convergence

3.5.1 The argument from normative stability

Another common worry about convergence is that it risks leading to illiberal results. On the face of it, this concern is by no means unwarranted. Under convergence, defeaters against coercion proliferate, as citizens are allowed to reject any coercive proposal which they rank below liberty. We could call this the "argument from normative stability": consensus is preferable to convergence because an excess of private defeaters would make it extraordinarily difficult to identify principles on which all evaluative standards can realistically converge. In a recent paper, Christopher Eberle has criticized convergence on similar grounds. Although Eberle sees convergence as an enticing alternative to the standard consensus view, which is guilty of leaving little if any room for religious beliefs, he also argues that under convergence the degree of coercion required for a minimally stable liberal democracy may be defeated by private objections.[350] Brian Barry, Samuel Scheffler, J. Quong and S. Macedo have raised similar objections to convergence.[351]

We should first note that this appears to be a serious objection to *negative* convergence, according to which private reasons can defeat coercion but not justify it. Negative convergence really looks like a terribly libertarian view, in that it narrows down the set of reasons justifying coercion to a small pool of freestanding values but permits citizens to advocate private reasons to defeat coercion. Indeed, negative convergence may lead not only to libertarian result, but also to pretty odd ones. In chapter 1 (§1.5.3-1.5.5-1.56) discussed three different cases in which a citizen may have private defeaters for freestanding reasons but be nonetheless committed to accepting coercion all things considered. [352] The common pattern on which those cases relied was: *R* is a freestanding reason for *L*; Andy has a private defeater *R** for *R*; yet Andy is committed by some other

350 C. Eberle 2010.

351 See J. Quong 2011, 165-68, S. Scheffler 1994, B. Barry 1995a and S. Macedo 2008. Barry and Scheffler are worried about utilitarian objections to liberalism. Although utilitarianism may be consistent with liberalism, under certain circumstances "it can lead to the rejection of both liberty and democracy" (Barry 1995: 907). S. Macedo (2008), instead, is worried about "libertarian" comprehensive doctrines which could reject the welfare rights protected by the third principle of the generic liberal conception (see section 4 above). More generally, Quong (2011: 167) argues that the comprehensive stage is problematic because it would permit illiberal people to "veto the liberal conception of justice by claiming that it isn't congruent with their illiberal comprehensive views".

352 I am referring to cases B), E) and F).

private reasons of his to endorsing *L* all things considered. Oddly enough, negative convergence implies that in cases of this kind Andy could not accept *L* despite the fact that he has reason to do so; in fact, he should reject *L* on the basis of his private reasons, as he could not advocate the further private reason he would need (and have) to accept *L*. Unlike negative convergence, the Convergence View of Public Reason would not allow odd libertarian results of this kind.

Of course, none of this rescues convergence from the more general charge of relying on a potentially libertarian justificatory standard. For what if some citizens conclude that, taking all their private reasons into account, their comprehensive doctrines instruct them to reject a good deal of coercion? To verify to what extent this is a real problem for convergence models, we need to distinguish different cases in which private doctrines might turn out to be incompatible with a law justified by freestanding reasons. Let *P* be a freestanding principle and *C* be Andy's private doctrine. Suppose further that *P* is open to two different interpretations, which would correspond to two different laws, L_1 and L_2. Here are four possible instances of incompatibility between *C* and *P*:

Case I) *C* offers no grounds for endorsing *P*.
Case II) *C* ranks L_1 over L_2 and L_2 over liberty.
Case III) *C* ranks L_1 over liberty and L_2 below liberty.
Case IV) *C* ranks *P* below liberty.

Case I) is not particularly problematic. Andy's private doctrine does not "confirm" the freestanding justification of *P*, but this does not necessarily entail that *C* provides him with reasons for rejecting *P*. In fact, case I) is entirely consistent with Andy's having no private defeaters against *P*. To begin with, Andy may have neither rebutting nor undermining defeaters for the freestanding reasons supporting *P*. Also, importantly, *C* may not provide him with any "suspending defeaters" against *P*, which would make *P* presumptively unjustified: that is, Andy may have no reason to assume that the freestanding case for *P* falls short of the required burden of justification set by his comprehensive doctrine.[353] In this case, Andy would take the freestanding justification for *P* to be provisionally conclusive: unless he has some strong private reasons against *P*, *P* is justified to him on account of the freestanding justification. This point is not irrelevant. Critics of the overlapping consensus such as Barry and Quong have suggested that

353 See chapter 1, §1.5.5. Here I assume, for simplicity, that *P* is arrived at through the right freestanding procedure Ω (whatever it is), and hence that, by stipulation, Andy is committed to endorsing *P* as "pro tanto" justified (in the sense specified in §1.5.7).

Rawls's second justificatory stage is highly unstable because it is hard to see how we could infer directly from certain comprehensive doctrines to particular principles of justice, such as Rawls's two principles of justice.[354] But direct support from comprehensive doctrines may not be necessary to the justification of principles of justice. If *C* is not as radically incompatible with *P* as to provide Andy with strong private defeaters, then the outcome of the first justificatory stage is not overturned in Andy's view, even if *C* does not explicitly sustain *P*.

Case II) is not worrisome at all. Because *C* ranks both interpretations of *P* over coercion, L_1 and L_2 are permissible options from Andy's perspective. It is important to stress that in case II) Andy *cannot* claim that because L_1 is better than L_2, then no law other than L_1 is justified to him. As Gaus says, in this case Andy would act like a "libertarian dictator", insisting that the only alternative to coercion must be his favorite option.[355] This would be definitely unreasonable. The commitment to publicly justify is a commitment to justify coercion, which involves showing that coercion is preferable to liberty. Whenever this condition is met, coercion is justified. But because more options can be preferable to coercion, "free and equal persons can freely act on nonoptimal options (including those that employ more coercion than one thinks optimal) so long as the gains (in terms of one's evaluative standards) exceed the costs". [356]

Case III) is more problematic, for here *C* narrows down the list of eligible options. While L_1 is justified to Andy, L_2 is not. Of course, Andy and Bea could converge on L_1, but only if L_1 were not excluded from Bea's personal ranking. An obvious problem, then, arises in the following case:

Case III*): Andy's private doctrine ranks L_1 over liberty and L_2 below liberty; Bea's private doctrine ranks L_2 over liberty and L_1 below liberty.

Here convergence short-circuits. Andy and Bea have reason to endorse some law, but they cannot coordinate on any proposal. The optimal set is therefore null and no law on this matter can be publicly justified. [357] The same problem arises in case IV). Since no law on this matter is justified to Andy, no law can be publicly justified according to the Convergence View of Public Reason. Notice that

354 See J. Quong 2011, 165-68, and B. Barry 1995a.

355 G. Gaus 2011b: 501.

356 Ibid.: 502.

357 However, there is strong reason to believe that Andy and Bea would try to avoid situations of this king. After all, both prefer some law to no law at all. Yet if they both stick to their rankings, they both end up with no law at all, as neither is willing to accept the other's favorite proposal. To avoid this impasse, Andy and Bea should find some alternative interpretation(s) of *P*, which they both have reason to rank over no law at all.

in case IV) Bea's ranking is irrelevant. If no proposal on this matter is justified to Andy, then *C* "vetoes" *P*: regardless of what Bea believes, *P* is publicly defeated because it fails to gain an "overlapping consensus".

Of course, things would be much easier if we accepted the Shareability Requirement, for *P* would be obviously justified also in cases III*) and IV). But this is not in itself a reason to prefer consensus. Convergence will reduce opportunities for coercion with respect to some matters but, without the ability to defeat unjustified coercion, laws and policies passed might fail to meet the conclusiveness requirement. Still, the argument from normative stability would provide a strong (appropriateness-based) case for consensus if, as Eberle and others fundamentally suggest, cases like III*) and IV) were likely to undermine the justification of the basic structure of society. Surely if convergence led to quasi-anarchical results, we would have little reason to abandon the dominant consensus view.

Gaus is, of course, aware of this potential danger. He grants that, in principle, some members of the public might "deem every proposal ineligible because in *their* eyes it fails to meet constraints on moral rules or its costs exceed the benefits for *them*".[358] But Gaus responds that although "sometimes the optimal set will certainly be null", this will not be the case "in relation to many rules", especially in relation to those "concerning the most basic matters".[359] In fact,

> [s]ocial morality is fundamental to social life, and each person has strong commitment to moral practices sustaining her moral emotions and, indeed, her own moral dignity, as well as protecting her basic good… [T]his does not ensure that they will do so in the eyes of all, but we should not imagine that Members of the Public are sorting through a variety of palpably self-interested bargaining ploys. Denying moral authority to basic moral rules is a grave matter indeed. Members of the Public would do so only when confronted by rules that, in their view, palpably fail to adequately perform their tasks.[360]

Gaus then argues extensively that convergence will justify some important right and duties, such as free speech, privacy and other civil rights, some rights to private property, positive duties of assistance and some (perhaps minimal) redistributive or welfare rights. Of course, all this supposes that radical libertarians do not figure among the members of the public. But libertarians, according to Gaus, are unreasonable because "they err by leaping from a well-founded worry about state coercion to a rejection of almost all (or perhaps even all) state authority", whereas state coercion performs the "core function of articulating and protecting

358 Ibid.: 323.
359 Ibid.
360 Ibid.

our fundamental moral rights".[361] If we exclude arch-libertarians and anarchists from our constituency of public reason, it seems plausible to assume that all reasonable "comprehensive doctrines" would converge on fundamental rules of cooperation. Moreover, as I stressed toward the end of the previous chapter (§2.8.4), private defeaters are better understood as reasons for rejecting permissible interpretations of pro tanto justified principles, rather than as reasons for rejecting those principles altogether. This is certainly the case if we ignore objections from radical libertarians. In the introduction I stressed that these (hopefully small) minority of people should indeed be excluded from our constituency of public reason, since the ideal of public reason requires the willingness to cooperate and agree on some principles governing society. Those who go so far as to reject even the basic tenets of social cooperation should not be allowed to impugn their legitimacy.[362] Insofar as these people are excluded from our constituency, the argument from normative stability does not seem to pose a serious threat to convergence.

3.5.2 The argument from reasonable compliance

I now want to consider another interesting argument for consensus, which fundamentally holds that convergence would encourage citizens to be unreasonable. Insofar as reasonableness is taken to be primarily a property of persons, and not an epistemic property of justified beliefs,[363] this argument is appropriateness-based: some private defeaters could be epistemically justified and yet reasonable citizens should nonetheless put them aside on grounds of inappropriateness. If sound, such an argument would provide a powerful case against convergence, as reasonableness is a crucial requirement, which no tenable conception of public reason can afford to ignore. After all, this requirement is part of the Principle of Public Justification, which states that coercion is justified if and only if all *reasonable* citizens (taking all good reasons into account) could endorse it. Because the Convergence View of Public Reason embodies the Principle of Public Justi-

361 Ibid.: 544.

362 On my account, this exclusion is justified on grounds of inappropriateness (though I believe that a strength-based exclusion might also be a viable and, indeed, preferable option, cfr. Zoffoli 2012). That is to say, I do not claim that all are committed to believing that some minimal principles of social cooperation are necessary to social life. I simply claim that it would be inappropriate to advocate radically libertarian views of this kind because they conflict with the ideal of public justification as I have described it.

363 As Quong argues, even beliefs that are not epistemically justified may be reasonable (see §3.3.4 above).

fication, it is imperative for convergence theorists to show that reliance on private defeaters is reasonable.

Now justificatory liberals normally assume that being reasonable simply *means* reasoning in freestanding terms, so the link between the Consensus View of Public Reason and reasonableness may look like a taken-for-granted assumption. However, if we stick to the Rawlsian definition of the reasonable, it is not immediately clear why this should be so. Surely convergence does not downplay the first feature of the reasonable, which requires acknowledging the fact of reasonable pluralism. Indeed, one of the main virtues of convergence is that it less open to the charge of shrinking reasonable pluralism. As Gaus and Vallier stress,

> [b]y recognizing that reasonable citizens have different reasons to accept a proposal, public recognition of convergence justification reinforces the public awareness of reasonable pluralism. Convergence reasoning, then, expresses a commitment to pluralism of values in public justification … [T]he aim of consensus tends to be frustrated by the very reasonable pluralism upon which justificatory liberalism is based.[364]

But reasonable persons are also willing to propose and abide by fair terms of cooperation, provided others are as well. Many deliberative democrats would be tempted to claim that reliance on private reasons undermines this second feature of the reasonable because on these accounts fairness should be understood in terms of "reciprocity". To honor the ideal of fairness, for many deliberative democrats, simply *is* to rely exclusively on reciprocally endorsable or freestanding reasons.[365] But this widespread view is either an appropriateness-based restatement of the argument from universalization or an analytical claim about the justificatory ideal underpinning the Consensus View of Public Reason. In the first case, appeal to fairness is not an objection against convergence because we already rejected the argument from universalization.[366] In the second case, consensus theorists would simply affirm what convergence theorists deny, namely, that principles justified in isolation from private reasons are fair. For justificatory liberals, fairness is a property of justified principles. Convergence theorists claim that coercive laws are fair (i.e., justified) only if they gain an overlapping consensus, while consensus theorists deny this. The concept of fairness cannot cater to a critique of a conception of fairness.

364 G. Gaus / K. Vallier 2009: 70.

365 This sort of "reciprocity" requirement is defended by (among many others) J. Rawls (1999), A. Gutmann and D. Thompson (1996) and especially R. Forst (2002, 2012).

366 See chapter 2, §2.6.4 and §2.8.3.

There is, however, a more interesting aspect of the reasonable that some convergence models might fail to preserve. For Rawls, reasonable people are not simply willing to propose fair terms of cooperation, but also to *abide by them provided others are as well.* In short, reasonable persons do not free ride. Now if we interpret the notion of "private reason" in a sheer instrumentalist fashion, then convergence becomes vulnerable to a well-known objection: insofar as people accept terms of cooperation simply because these are effective means for promoting the good of each, then the very concept of instrumental rationality that leads people to cooperate invites them to cheat. Although all benefit from cooperation, all are tempted to cheat because this will maximize their personal benefits. But if *all* cheat, then all will be worse off. This famous problem is typically referred to as the "prisoner's dilemma":

	Bea does not attack (cooperate)	Bea attacks (defect)
Andy does not attack (cooperate)	Peace	Bea queen Andy slave
Andy attacks (defect)	Andy king Bea slave	War

Display 2: Prisoner's dilemma

In this display, Andy and Bea find themselves in the situation Hobbes was deeply worried about. Andy and Bea know that peace will secure their interests, so as instrumentally rational agents they have strong reason to escape from the state of nature dominated by intractable conflict. Instrumental rationality instructs them to converge on mutually acceptable terms of cooperation. But of course, Andy would be even better off if he could become King and enslave Bea. So why not cheat and attack, exploiting the fact that Bea abides by the terms of cooperation and will be thus caught off guard? But the obvious problem is that the trick works only under the assumption that Bea is in fact willing to cooperate. If Bea is instrumentally rational, however, she will be attracted to exactly the same line of reasoning that leads Andy to defect. The bottom-line is that following instrumental rationality, Andy and Bea would fall back into the original state of war, which was a suboptimal option for both all along.

Situations of this kind seem bound to occur as long as Andy and Bea rely exclusively on their own private judgment, taking the satisfaction of their own ends and values as the only relevant yardstick. The political upshot is straightforward. Convergence undermines the project of public reason because it renders citizens prone to free ride. Let us call this the "argument from reasonable compliance": since the Shareability Requirement demands that people reason from a "detached" universalistic perspective, assigning less weight to their private ends and value, consensus is necessary to free public reason from the instrumental conception of rationality of which convergence is held captive.[367]

This potentially decisive argument rests on two core assumptions. The first (1) is that reliance on sheer instrumental rationality necessarily leads to situations like the prisoner's dilemma. The second (2) is that convergence models of public reason conflate the notion of private reason with that of individual purposive rationality. Instrumentalists such as David Gauthier believe that (1) is false. Gauthier's Hobbesian conception of public reason ultimately seeks to show that "private reasoners" can both converge on a mutually beneficial scheme of cooperation out of private self-interest *and* nonetheless regularly obey its rules of conduct.[368] Gauthier's conception is thus a convergence conception which takes citizens' own goals and interests, in a Hobbesian fashion, as the only relevant evaluative standards. Rawls objects that attempt to derive the reasonable from the (instrumentally) rational conclusively fails.[369] In a similar vein, Kurt Baier argues that the justification of social morality must draw first and foremost on "society-anchored reasons", and not merely on "self-anchored reasons".[370] The idea behind Baier's notion of "society-anchored reasons", which Gaus takes up, is that individuals committed to the ideal of public reason must take a "deontic" stance toward social rules:[371] they must switch from a "self-anchored" instrumental perspective driven by goal-promoting reasoning to deontic, rule-based reasoning. Very roughly, on this deontic view the question is not "What's my

367 It might be objected that the argument form reasonable compliance is moot because theorists of public reason are concerned exclusively with reasonable citizens: if Andy defects is unreasonable and should be excluded from the constituency of public reason, both on a consensus and a convergence view. But the problem is precisely that, according to the argument from reasonable compliance, convergence would in some way encourage citizens to act unreasonably.

368 See D. Gauthier 1986; 1995.

369 Cf. J. Rawls 1993, chapter 2.

370 See K. Baier 1975, chapters 4 and 5.

371 G. Gaus 2011b: 122-30.

payoff if others cooperate?", but rather "Do I have reason to endorse this rule of conduct as generally binding?"

If critics of instrumentalism are right, convergence theorists must resist (2) because (1) is false. But of course, denying (2) is not a problem at all. As Gaus and Rawls stress, the idea of an "overlapping consensus" need not and should not be confused with that of a "coordination of sheer private interests", on which convergence models such as Gauthier's rely. Citizens' private reasons will reflect their different "conceptions of the good", systems of values and commitments, and "ethical" beliefs in general (in Habermas's sense). The point is to verify whether these different evaluative standards can overlap in support of a collectively binding system of laws. But of course, this plurality of evaluative standards need not undermine citizens' deontic attitude. While it is true that instrumentalist approaches lead to "privatistic" conceptions of reasoning, citizens who care about their non-shareable conceptions of the good may well engage in deontic reasoning: they will regard political norms as deontological prescriptions which are worth obeying, provided these are justified in the light of their reasonable "comprehensive doctrines". Therefore (assuming the failure of instrumentalism is real), we can conclude that the argument from reasonable compliance undermines Gauthier's peculiar convergence conception, but not convergence in general.

3.6 The argument from symmetry

3.6.1 Framing the issue

A further appropriateness-based argument for consensus is implicitly suggested by Rainer Forst's and Steve Wall's sweeping criticism of the presumption in favor of liberty. The presumption in favor of liberty gives voice to the key liberal intuition that, as long as I mind my own business without coercively interfering with others, I have no case to answer.[372] In other words, that presumption assumes that (would-be) coercer and (prospective) coercee stands in an *asymmetrical* relation of justification. While the former is committed to justifying his demands to the latter, the latter is not required to justify his liberty to the former. Yet it seems that, at least in some relevant cases, my freedom to act as I see fit may itself be something that stands in need of justification. And this, in turn, seems to speak in favor of what Steven Wall has called a normative "symmetry"

372 See introduction, §I,b and chapter 1, §1.2.1.

between coercion and freedom: both liberty-preserving demands and liberty-constraining proposals may equally call for justification.[373] Drawing on Samuel Scheffler's thesis that morality is "pervasive" [374], Wall contends that, in principle,

> any voluntary action or voluntary decision to refrain from acting can be subject to moral assessment. Take the most trivial action. Suppose I am ironing my socks in my apartment. Depending on context, this action may require justification. For example, if someone desperately needs my help next door and I continue to iron my socks, then my action plausibly requires justification. So, in principle, any type of voluntary human conduct, whether that of private individuals or individuals serving as state officials, can require moral justification. Whether it does will depend on, in a given context, whether it is an instance of salient voluntary conduct. [375]

On the face of our moral intuitions, Wall's point seems all the more warranted. There is, to be sure, much intuitive plausibility to the view that, as a general rule, restrictions on someone else's freedom call for justification. Typically, though, we also take it for granted that moral agents are under some prima facie moral duties, which can be both negative ("One should not harm innocent people"; "One should not lie" etc.) and positive ("One should assist people in pain"; "One should honor promises" etc.). Such prima facie duties are implicitly taken to constitute a solid normative background, against which liberty-claims (i.e., claims advocating one's liberty not to act in accordance with a prima facie duty) ought to be justified. Similarly, in his critique of Gaus's liberal principle, Forst claims that "there is a standing duty to justify morally relevant actions".[376] Once some kinds of actions have been identified as morally relevant, one may be under a duty of justification even if one does not interfere, or propose to interfere, with others' freedom.

Thus, Wall and Forst seem to imply that the liberal presumption in favor of liberty is misguided because it mistakenly assumes that the (prospective) coercee is never committed to justifying her liberty to the (would-be) coercer, whereas both may in fact have a "symmetrical" case to answer. [377] In chapter 1 (§1.2.2) I

373 S. Wall 2010: 129-133.

374 See S. Scheffler 1992, chapter 2.

375 S. Wall 2010: 130.

376 R. Forst 2005: 240n.

377 To be sure, Forst and Wall defend symmetry from two very different perspectives. Forst's works fall within the tradition of the so-called "Critical Theory", according to which one of the main tasks of political philosophy is to engage in a thorough emancipative critique of existing institution and practices, endeavoring to uncover and expose socially reified relations of power or, in Horkheimer's words, "to liberate human beings

already refuted this objection to the presumption in favor of liberty. In fact, we saw that the presumption in favor of liberty is entirely consistent with the view that even the (prospective) coercee might have to justify his liberty. Specifically, I stressed that, in its general formulation, the presumption in favor of liberty holds that unless a law L regulating ϕ-ing is publicly justified, Andy should be free to ϕ. However, I also argued that this basic claim does *not* entail the further claim Andy is never committed to publicly justifying his liberty to ϕ. The presumption in favor liberty holds that liberty is the default position, deviation from which requires justification. So if Bea proposes a coercive norm L regulating ϕ-ing, the justificatory burden is on her. She must kick off the justificatory process by providing Andy with reasons he can accept. But if Bea's reasons for L rebut the presumption in favor of liberty, the onus is now on Andy, the prospective coercee. So it is not true that Andy is never committed to justifying his liberty. If Andy wants to reject a law L regulating ϕ-ing for which Bea has provided a convincing case, he is committed to advancing counterarguments defeating L. If he cannot do that, L is justified to him on account of Bea's arguments.

Therefore, the presumption in favor of liberty is by no means inconsistent with Forst's and Wall's claim that something else than coercion may call for justification. However, their criticism of the presumption in favor of liberty in general, though misguided, does cater to a more specific criticism of convergence models of public reason, which, being interpretations of the general Concept of Public Reason, rely on the presumption in favor of liberty.[378] That is, one could argue that although the presumption in favor of liberty as such is not objectiona-

from the circumstances that enslave them" (1982: 224). In a way, Forst's critique of the presumption in favor of liberty is indebted to, and builds upon, this fundamental commitment to a critical analysis of relations of power. Liberals seem to take it for granted that if Andy rejects Bea's coercive proposals, he owes no justification to her. Relieved of any strong justificatory burden, Andy enjoys an "asymmetrical" privileged position, which results in a right to put a "veto" on Bea's demands without giving an adequate justification. In the eyes of critical theory, this justificatory asymmetry is prima facie suspicious. Public reason has a powerful emancipative potential, in that it demands that laws and institutional arrangements undergo public scrutiny – that they become acceptable to an enlightened public thanks to encompassing relations of justification. But the critical theorist is bound to ask: Are we sure that someone who rejects a coercive law is free from any strong justificatory burden? Couldn't this asymmetry between freedom and coercive interference unduly favor some social classes over other, perhaps socially underprivileged, groups of citizens? While questions of this kind are crucial to critical theorists such as Forst, and may partly motivate his criticism of the presumption in favor of liberty, Wall starts from a completely different assumption. As a liberal perfectionist, Wall takes it for granted that freedom is just a cherished value among others. Should coercion be necessary to promote some other objectively valuable goal, failure to coerce would call for justification.

378 See chapter 1, §1.3.1.

bly asymmetrical, convergence models do offer a more "asymmetrical" rendition of that presumption than consensus models. Let me clarify this point.

3.6.2 The Strong Burden Thesis and the Weak Burden Thesis

Once Bea has rebutted the presumption in favor of liberty by providing some convincing arguments in favor of a law *L* regulating ϕ-ing, Andy is committed to justifying ~*L* if he wants to preserve his freedom to ϕ. But this opens up a crucial question: *to whom* must he justify ~*L*? There are at least two possible answers:

(1): If Bea has rebutted the presumption against *L*, Andy can argue for ~*L* (i.e., liberty, no law at all on this matter) if he explains why, all things considered, *L* is in fact unjustified to him.

(2) If Bea has rebutted the presumption against *L*, Andy can argue for ~*L* (i.e., liberty, no law at all on this matter) only if he justifies ~*L* to Bea.

These two views are substantially different. If (1) is true, then Andy can reject coercive proposals on the basis of his private reasons: since he owes no justification *to Bea*, he is not committed to giving her reasons *she* can accept. According to (2), however, Andy would not be permitted to do that. Once Bea has rebutted the presumption in favor of liberty, according to (2), Andy must justify ~*L* in the strong sense that he must provide Bea with reasons that *she* can find acceptable. Let us turn (1) and (2) into two independent theses:

Weak Burden Thesis: If Bea's arguments for *L* meet the presumption in favor of liberty, Andy can argue for ~*L* (i.e., liberty, no law at all on this matter) by appealing to his private reasons because he is not committed to justifying ~*L* to Bea.

Strong Burden Thesis: If Bea's arguments for *L* meet the presumption in favor of liberty, Andy cannot argue for ~*L* (i.e., liberty, no law at all on this matter) by appealing to his private reasons because ~*L* must be justified to Bea.

Note that both the Strong Burden Thesis and the Weak Burden Thesis are compatible with the Principle of Political Liberty, and with the presumption in favor of liberty in general, for both views presuppose that liberty is the status quo. Moreover, neither view is "asymmetrical" in the strict sense indicated by Wall and Forst, for both theses hold that even freedom may call for justification.

However, the Strong Burden Thesis is "less asymmetrical", as it were, than the Weak Burden Thesis; the latter is more asymmetrical because it holds that proponents of coercive legislation have to justify their liberty-constraining claims *to others* whereas opponents of coercion are not committed to justifying their liberty-preserving claims *to* those proposing them.

Now the important point is that consensus is compatible with the Strong Burden Thesis, while convergence is not. Since convergence allows citizens to reject coercive laws and proposals by appeal to their private reasons, it is at odds with the Strong Burden Thesis: Andy may reject *L* without giving Bea reasons she can reasonably accept. By contrast, on a consensus view Andy could not do that. It thus follows that if the Strong Burden Thesis is correct, we ought to favor consensus over convergence. Conversely, convergence is an acceptable conception of public reason only if the Weak Burden Thesis is correct. The objection to convergence I now want to consider holds that convergence should be resisted because the Weak Burden Thesis is in fact wrong. I shall call this the "argument from symmetry" because it holds that public reasoning is "more symmetrical", as it were, than convergence models and their underlying Weak Burden Thesis seem to imply.

Before analyzing the limits and merits of this objection, however, I must dispel a possible misunderstanding about the Weak Burden Thesis. Since I started from Wall's and Forst's claim that some non-coercive actions call for justification, it might seem that, *mutatis mutandis*, the Weak Burden Thesis applies to the justification of actions. But this would be a mistake. In fact, that thesis is concerned with the justification of laws, and not with the justification of specific actions dictated by a given law. To see the significance of this point, consider two different cases:

Case 1): One Monday, while Andy is minding his own business in his apartment, Bea knocks on his door. She just broke her leg and begs him to take her immediately to the nearest hospital. Andy agrees that he is under a justified legal obligation to help people in need (call it *L*). However, he explains to Bea that although he is truly sorry about her broken leg, his religious creed prevents him from fulfilling positive duties on Mondays. He shuts the door and wishes her best of luck.

Case 2) Bea thinks that a "minimally decent Samaritanism" (*L*) should be required by law:[379] if one can rescue another person from an extreme danger at a

379 I borrow the term "minimally decent Samaritanism" from J. J. Thompson 1971.

reasonably low cost or risk, one is under a legally enforceable duty to do so. However, Andy contends that *L* is defeated in his belief system: he thinks that *L* would violate Kant's maxim that people should not be treated merely as means for promoting the welfare of others. Andy concludes that *L* is publicly defeated because it is not justified to him.

In both cases, Andy rejects a Samaritan duty *L* to help people in need by appeal to some private reasons of his, and yet cases 1) and 2) are very different. In case 1), Andy agrees that *L* is justified but insists he is exempt from it: he accepts *L* but refuses to act as *L* prescribes in a given situation in which *L* applies to him. In case 2), by contrast, Andy contests the very justification of *L*; he does not simply state his intention to disobey *L* under circumstances in which *L* would actually require him to help somebody in need.

Now the Weak Burden Thesis, and convergence models in general, would not warrant Andy's claim in case 1). Since in case 1) a "justified moral duty is in play" (and a compelling one indeed),[380] Andy is committed to complying with it unless he can give Bea powerful reasons *she* can accept, such as "I don't have a car to take you to the hospital", "I have a broken arm myself" etc. Neither convergence nor the Weak Burden Thesis corresponds to the view that noncompliance with justified norms can be justified on comprehensive grounds. What convergence and the Weak Burden Thesis claim is rather that one can reject *laws* on comprehensive grounds. Thus, the Weak Burden Thesis justifies Andy's objection only in situations like case 2). Of course, one could find Andy's claim in case 2) intuitively objectionable. Why should Andy be allowed to reject a minimal requirement of justice such as a minimally decent Samaritan duty on comprehensive grounds? Wouldn't it be entirely appropriate for Bea to insist that he owes a justification *to her* if she is to live in a society in which failure to respect such a fundamental principle of justice is not punished by law? It is on this intuition that the argument from symmetry turns.

3.6.3 Freestanding rationales and general interests

Let me better illustrate the idea behind the argument from symmetry. Suppose that *U* (i.e., the set of freestanding considerations arrived at via Ω) comprises *R*, a reason supporting a minimal Samaritan duty (cast in the form of a law *L*). Imagine further that *U* comprises no defeaters for *L*. In this case, *L* will be backed

380 G. Gaus 2010b: 191.

by what I have called a "freestanding rationale". According to the definition I gave in chapter 2 (§2.8.4), a freestanding rationale is not a freestanding reason taken in isolation. A freestanding rationale is rather the outcome of freestanding reasoning, whereby all single freestanding reasons are accounted for and factored in. If all participants in justificatory discourses, weighing and balancing all freestanding reasons available, conclude that *L* is justified, then *L* is backed by a freestanding rationale. Now whenever *L* is supported by a freestanding rationale, *L* is publicly justified on a consensus view, since by stipulation all freestanding reasons against *L* have been accounted for. Convergence theorists, by contrast, would insist that *L* could be defeated on comprehensive grounds.

But this might seem overly permissive. However we may wish to interpret Ω and the substantive content of *U*, the procedure of abstraction is meant to identify reasons that all could affirm from an impartial standpoint. Thus, if $R \rightarrow L$ is part of *U*, *R* expresses some freestanding value or general interest,[381] which all would/should reasonably care about as citizens with common fundamental needs, regardless of the comprehensive doctrines they happen to affirm. Surely it is hard to deny that one's interest in being rescued from situations of extreme danger is general in this sense. It is also hard to deny that a Samaritan duty protecting this interest such as *L* would be supported by a freestanding rationale. Regardless of our interpretation of Ω and *U*, we will most probably concur that, on the balance, all freestanding reasons related to this issue lead to *L*. In other words, the existence of a freestanding rationale would confirm that *L* does indeed protect a relevant interest of all, an interest which is not overridden by any conflicting values or interests accounted for by *U*.

But if this is the case, then it seems that if Andy rejects *L*, he should provide others with reasons they can accept. He has to justify *to them* why they should accept a state of "naked liberty" in which the relevant interests expressed by the freestanding rationale is not protected by law. Andy should not be allowed to get away with a comprehensive justification, as the Weak Burden Thesis would imply. Rather, he should be subjected to the requirement expressed by the Strong Burden Thesis. But since *ex hypotesi* all freestanding reasons have been already factored in, Andy is left with no generally acceptable reasons against *L*. The upshot is that given the Strong Burden Thesis, Andy should endorse any law *L* for which there are no freestanding defeaters, which is precisely what consensus models claim.

381 I talk about "general" interests in a loose sense, and not about morally "generalizable interests" in a Habermasian sense, since my purpose here is not to defend any specific version of Ω, but only to stress that, however we may interpret it, Ω will in some way identify values that all could care about if they reasoned from a detached perspective.

We can carry the issue to a higher level of abstraction by considering how private reasons could impact the justification of basic rights under convergence. I take it for granted that the members of the public have a number of shareable reasons for endorsing a comprehensive system of rights. To use Habermas's terminology, such a comprehensive system would safeguard both "private" and "public autonomy", in that it would encompass both personal rights such as freedom of speech, privacy, personal integrity etc. and political rights to democratic participation.[382] Yet if we held the Weak Burden Thesis we should allow private reasons to defeat the freestanding rationales that provide a case for basic rights. Again, though, this is too permissive according to the argument from symmetry. If Bea gives Andy a shareable rationale for accepting – say – a duty to respect other people's privacy, he must recognize that "privacy" is something worth caring about. It is a relevant interest, which he would neglect by rejecting that right. Arguably, we could encounter the same problem with respect to any "pro tanto" justifiable right.

Whenever the would-be coercer can reasonably claim that her proposal *L* is supported by a freestanding rationale, the prospective coercee cannot simply insist that *L* is in fact unjustified *to him*. Rather, if the argument from symmetry is sound we should endorse the Strong Burden Thesis and demand that Andy refrain from rejecting coercive proposal on account of reasons that others cannot reasonably accept. Of course, in cases of this kind Andy could embark on a complicated argument "from conjecture" or "convergence argument",[383] arguing that all comprehensive doctrines provide their adherents with reasons for converging against *L*. But this is obviously a pretty unlikely scenario. While in some cases some comprehensive doctrines might reject "pro tanto" justified laws, it is hard to imagine cases in which all comprehensive doctrines unanimously reject what Ω describes as a freestanding rationale. Consequently, it follows that Andy is committed to endorsing *L* whenever *L* is backed by a freestanding rationale. And, again, this is exactly what consensus theorists claim: private reasons should not be allowed to defeat "pro tanto" justified norms.

The immediate upshot of the argument from symmetry (assuming of course that it is sound) is that Rawls's "overlapping consensus" should have very little impact on public justification. Recall that, in Rawls's view, justification conducted on the basis of shareable reasons is only pro "pro tanto". As such, it should be supplemented with a further twofold justificatory stage ("full justification" and "public justification by political society") aiming at the achievement of an "overlapping consensus" of comprehensive doctrines. Although Rawls is ra-

382 See J. Habermas 1996, chapter 3.
383 See §3.2.2 above.

ther unclear about the exact normative weight of this further justificatory stage,[384] his basic intuition is easy to grasp. The Shareability Requirement imposes an "objectionable" and intrinsically "illiberal" restriction on citizens' deliberation. As Gaus says, "a person's value system is fundamental in her deliberations about what moral requirements she has reason to endorse".[385] Yet "by preventing appeal in moral justification to so much of what a person understands as basic to her evaluative outlook, she can only see these laws as rationally self-legislated in an extremely attenuated sense".[386] Rawls sees this, arguing that the outcome of "pro tanto" justification can be "overridden" by citizen's comprehensive doctrines. If the argument from symmetry is correct, however, the Rawls-Gaus view should be resisted because proponents and opponents of "pro tanto" justified principles are symmetrically placed.

3.6.4 Why the argument from symmetry seems appealing

The argument from symmetry is clearly appropriateness-based. Andy may be openly justified in believing that his comprehensive doctrine commits him to rejecting *L*, and yet the Shareability Requirement would commit him to eschewing any appeal to his private reasons. At best, then, he can endorse the Shareability Requirement on the grounds that it would not be appropriate to use his private reasons as defeaters.

Perhaps, though, one could contend that the argument from symmetry is in fact strength-based. Given symmetry, Andy is committed to the view that only shareable defeaters can rebut *L*. Now the verb "can" here might be taken to have a specific epistemic nuance, according to which private reasons cannot be strong enough to outweigh freestanding rationales supporting *L*. After all, the strength of a reason depends, among other things, on whether or not the addressee of justification is committed to accepting that reason in the light of her openly justified belief system. Recall the example of Fermat's last theorem.[387] Do the latest sophisticated proofs of that theorem count as reasons for actually believing that Fermat was right all along? Well, it depends on whom they are supposed to be reasons for. They are compelling reasons for an experienced mathematician, but they may have much less justificatory strength for a moral philosopher, and they certainly were no reasons at all for Aristotle. For pretty much the same reason,

384 See chapter 1,§1.4.2.
385 G. Gaus 2009: 119.
386 Ibid.
387 See chapter 2,§2.3.2.

one could argue, Andy's reasons defeating *L* can be more or less weighty depending on who is supposed to accept them as a justificatory. But given symmetry, the addressee of justification is the public at large. Hence, a reason R^* is stronger than another reason *R* only if *all* members of the public are committed to believing so. But if R^* is a private reason of Andy's this cannot be the case, since some other citizens will not even recognize $R^* \rightarrow \sim L$ as a sound inference in the first place. It seems, then, that the symmetrical character of public reason renders *R* stronger than R^* after all.

The problem, however, is that none of this entails that Andy should revise his own belief system. Reasoning from his private perspective, he can certainly maintain that R^* is indeed stronger than *R*. Consensus requires soaring into a more "detached" common perspective, from which the strength of publicly relevant reasons ought to be judged. If a reason has no epistemic weight for some of us, it has no public weight for any of us, since it is not a reason that can justify the law (or rejection of it) to all of us. But this is a roundabout way of saying that Andy should ignore his justified beliefs and reason from a perspective from which *his* beliefs do not matter. *L* might be epistemically justified to all if all reasoned in freestanding terms, but the argument explaining why people ought to embrace such a "detached" freestanding perspective is appropriateness-based. The argument from symmetry, then, does not exclude private reasons on epistemic grounds, but rather on the grounds that it would be inappropriate for Andy to use reasons that do not justify $\sim L$ to Bea – though those reasons might well justify $\sim L$ *to* him.

Now because the argument from symmetry is appropriateness-based, it must be pretty strong in order to rebut the twofold presumption in favor of convergence. I repeatedly emphasized that the claim that citizens should ignore potentially decisive reasons on grounds of inappropriateness is prima facie unappealing. Appropriateness-based consensus models insist that we should ignore the potential objections of some citizens on the grounds that these citizens should not be given a say, without however showing that freestanding reasons are conclusive and shareable from their perspectives. This is the fundamental problem vexing appropriateness-based consensus models. However, I also granted that this problem could be a tolerable price to pay should an appropriateness-based argument for consensus be sufficiently compelling. Now I take it that, if sound, the argument from symmetry would definitely provide such a compelling case. If the Strong Burden Thesis is true, convergence would violate the fundamental maxim underpinning the ideal of public reason: whenever you owe a justification to others, respect them by giving them reasons they could accept. I trust we would not evoke much dissent if we said that the paramount importance of this maxim would outweigh the twofold presumption in favor of convergence, should the argument from symmetry be sound. As we are about to see, however, the argument from symmetry is in fact misguided.

3.6.5 Why the argument from symmetry is misguided

Despite its intuitive appeal, the argument from symmetry incurs serious problems. Notice, first, that both the Strong Burden Thesis and the Weak Burden Thesis assume, quite rightly, that Andy is committed to justifying *~L* only if Bea has already rebutted the presumption in favor of liberty. In the absence of such a rebutting case in favor of *L*, no deviation from liberty understood as the fundamental normative baseline is justified, which means that Andy is not committed to justifying *~L* in the first place. Therefore, the argument from symmetry presupposes that whenever *L* is backed by a freestanding rationale, the original presumption in favor of liberty is rebutted. Otherwise, the claim that in any such case Andy should justify *~L* to Bea would not be warranted, for *~L* would not even stand in need of justification.

But in pointing out that a private reason of his (call it *R**) defeats the freestanding rationale for *L* (call it *FR*), Andy may argue precisely that *FR* does *not* rebut the presumption in favor of liberty. It will be recalled from chapter 1 (§1.5) that a private defeater *R** may be undermining, rebutting or suspending. Now if *FR* is undermined by *R** from Andy's perspective, *FR* cannot possibly rebut the presumption in favor of liberty, since *R** would show that within Andy's belief system there is actually no sound deliberative route leading from *FR* to *L*. But *FR* would fail to rebut the presumption in favor of liberty even if *R** were a suspending defeater. In fact, a suspending defeater shows that the (suspended) reason leading to a given belief (in this case: *L* is legitimate) falls short of the minimal threshold needed to warrant that belief. Thus, if *FR* is suspended by *R**, Andy has reason to presumptively assume that *~L* is justified over *L* because the presumption against *L* has not been met, just as a judge is committed to considering defendant innocent when the public prosecutor's case fails to meet the presumption of innocence.

To be sure, things would look differently should *R** rebut (as opposed to undermine or suspend) *FR*. In this case, Andy might agree that *FR* provides a rebutting case against the presumption in favor of liberty, since there may be a sound deliberative route from *FR* to *L*, which would not fall short of the minimal threshold required to endorse *L*. Once presented with *FR*, Andy may therefore be committed to justifying *~L*. And of course, the question must be raised as to whether or not he should do that in accordance with the Strong Burden Thesis. However, the fact that undermined and suspended freestanding rationales do not trigger any demand for justification significantly restricts the scope of the argument from symmetry.

Moreover, the argument from symmetry is ambiguous because it makes no distinction between general principles underpinning general laws on the one hand, and interpretations of general laws and principles on the other hand. In fact, the argument from symmetry draws much of its intuitive appeal from cases in which private reasons defeat fundamental principles of cooperation altogether. In sections §2.8.4 and §3.5.2, however, I pointed out that private defeaters will typically cross off the list of eligible proposals specific interpretations of general principles arrived at via Ω; they will rarely defeat those general principles altogether. If this is the case, then even under convergence basic rights and duties would be publicly justified.

Of course, above (§3.5.2) we saw that to avoid potentially "anarchical" or radically libertarian implications of convergence we need to assume that anarchists and arch-libertarians are not part of our constituency of public reason. But if these people are excluded, it is not implausible to assume that many pro tanto justified laws will gain an overlapping consensus, though of course many proposals (especially, again, interpretations of general laws and principles) may not. At the very least, it is by no means implausible to maintain that under these conditions convergence would safeguard the core tenets of a liberal conception of justice. For instance, and to come back to our example, we may well agree with Gaus that a "minimally decent" Samaritan duty would be publicly justified under convergence, though of course people may have private defeaters for some interpretations of it.[388]

To be sure, convergence would be obviously more prone than consensus to defeat many freestanding rationales. Indeed, this is unavoidable. If we shape the member of the public in a way that their private doctrines will always and necessarily confirm the outcome of "pro tanto" justification, then the second "convergence stage" becomes pointless. To consistently defend convergence as a true alternative to consensus, we need to assume that in some cases private reasons might defeat freestanding rationales. We can hope, to be sure, that most "pro tanto" justified norms will gain an overlapping consensus; what we cannot consistently do is assume a priori that if *L* is backed by a freestanding rationale, then *L* will be necessarily justified under convergence.

But rejecting such a priori assumption seems entirely consistent with (and indeed, required by) the fundamental commitment to publicly justify. As public reason liberals, we have to work out a theory of public reason which respects all

388 See G. Gaus 2011b: 365-67.

as free and equal by showing that all have reason to endorse the laws they are subjected to. But how is this commitment consistent with consensus models which insist on stopping at the "pro tanto" stage of public justification? How can Bea treat Andy as a free and equal fellow citizen if she is entitled to assume a priori that he will never have private defeaters for freestanding rationales? What if Andy is in fact openly justified in believing that some pro tanto justified law *L* is, all things considered, unjustified to him? Defenders of the Strong Burden Thesis would insist that in any such case Andy should justify his rejection of *L* to the public at large. But the problem is that if the Strong Burden Thesis is correct, then Andy may on occasion be subjected to laws which, being unjustified to him, violate his status as a free and equal, self-legislating agent. If *L* is not justified to some, why not opt for ~*L* (liberty, no law at all on this matter), which would respect all as free and equal?

One could insist that since the argument from symmetry is appropriateness-based, it is not concerned with *all* citizens, but only with citizens who are actually willing to endorse relevant appropriateness requirement. And because it is inappropriate to reject freestanding rationales by appeal to private reasons, those who are openly justified in assigning paramount weight to those reasons should be of no concern for the public reason liberal. Now of course this line of reasoning seems unavoidable when it comes to radically libertarian objections. But we already assumed that arch-libertarians should be ruled out. Here we are talking about citizens who do not deny authority to principles of social cooperation altogether, but simply contest the legitimacy of some coercive laws.[389] The Strong Burden Thesis entails that laws backed by freestanding rationales are necessarily consistent with the ideal of public reason, despite the fact that some (good-willed, decent, non-libertarian) reasoners may have defeaters for those rationales. This cannot be right. As I said above (§3.6.4), the fundamental maxim underpinning the ideal of public reason is that we should respect others by justifying our demands to them when these call for justification. Now the ruling idea behind the whole project of public reason is that *coercion must be justified to others.* Yet for all this, the Strong Burden Thesis entails that Bea can coerce Andy by giving him reasons which, all things considered, do not justify her demands to him. Again, this cannot be right. The Strong Burden Thesis skews, instead of doing justice do, the fundamental maxim underpinning the ideal of public reason. To say, as the Strong Burden Thesis implies, that Andy owes Bea a justification

389 Recalled that in §II.c and §3.5.2 we excluded radical libertarians and anarchists from the constituency of public reason, on the grounds that they are not sufficiently committed to social cooperation.

when he rejects her coercive proposals is to undermine the whole project of public justification.

Let me summarize this long argument. I started from Forst's and Wall's claim that even opponents of coercion may have to justify their liberty. I then argued that although such a view is not inconsistent with the presumption in favor of liberty, it can be turned into an objection against convergence models. Essentially, the idea is that convergence models are "too asymmetrical", so to speak, because they allow the (prospective) coercee to reject coercion on comprehensive grounds, while consensus models do not. To clarify this point, I introduced two distinct theses, namely the Strong Burden Thesis and the Weak Burden Thesis. If the Strong Burden Thesis is true, then (would-be) coercer and (prospective) coercee are symmetrically placed, in a way that makes convergence models problematic. I argued, however, that the Strong Burden Thesis is not only inapplicable when freestanding rationales are undermined or suspended by private reasons, but also implausible on its own merits, in that it distorts the fundamental commitment to publicly justify coercion.

3.7 From convergence to symmetrical convergence

3.7.1 The Non-Coercive Rejection Thesis

In the previous section I rejected the argument from symmetry and its underlying Strong Burden Thesis. However, we should explore further the idea that public reasoning could be symmetrical. As we are about to see, there is in fact a peculiar sense in which convergence is open to the charge of relying on an overly "asymmetrical" understanding of public justification. This does not mean that we should jettison the whole idea of convergent justification, nor that we should endorse anything close to the Consensus View of Public Justification. Still, the particular "asymmetry" objection to convergence that I propose to raise suggests amending Gaus's convergence view to a slightly different convergence conception, which I shall call the Symmetrical Convergence View of Public Reason.

Thus far, I have taken for granted that if Andy rejects Bea's coercive proposal *L*, he does not thereby coerce her. In other words, while *L* is coercive, *~L* is not, since *~L* is a stand in for freedom, or liberty, or no law at all on this matter. Let us call this the Non-Coercive Rejection Thesis:

Non-Coercive Rejection Thesis: Rejection of coercive laws or proposals is not itself coercive.

On the face of it, the Non-Coercive Rejection Thesis seems trivially true. We will see, however, that this is not the case. While as a general rule the Non-Coercive Rejection Thesis is correct, sometimes it is not only possible, but also inevitable that by rejecting a coercive proposal the (prospective) coercee will end up laying coercive counter-claims on the (would-be) coercer. In any such case, public reasoning will be symmetrical in a very straightforward sense: those who reject *L* assume the role of (would-be) coercers, just as those proposing *L* do. The next two sections (§3.7.2 – 3.7.3) explain under which circumstances the Non-Coercive Rejection Thesis is most likely to be false. Sections §3.7.4 and §3.7.5 explain what sets apart my argument from the Strong Burden Thesis, and why my argument leads to the Symmetrical Convergence View of Public Reason.

3.7.2 Contested property rights

One could challenge the Non-Coercive Rejection Thesis by arguing that sometimes liberty-preserving demands are themselves coercive, in the sense that they often invoke some further coercive rights. Suppose Bea proposes a discriminatory law *L* against homosexuals, which Andy rejects by advocating his right to privacy. He argues that policies such as *L* are publicly defeated because Bea has a duty not to interfere with others' sexual conduct. Andy would thus reject Bea's coercive proposal by imposing a legally enforceable duty on her. As a result, Bea and Andy would be engaged in a symmetrical justificatory discourse.

Now put in these terms, the objection is not particularly worrisome. Clearly defenders of the Non-Coercive Rejection Thesis could reply that rights can be appealed to only if they have been already (and asymmetrically) publicly justified. In other words, Andy can use the right to privacy to defeat *L* only if in a previous discussion he has been able to show that that right is justified to Bea in the light of her own evaluative standards. Alternatively, he could simply reject *L* by appeal to the presumption in favor of liberty, which could easily do the justificatory job. Sexual conduct, he could argue, should not be legally regulated. But by defending his liberty to act as he sees fit, he would not thereby restrict Bea's. Now although this twofold reply can work well as a general rule, a problem seems to arise in issues of distributive justice, when property rights are typically used as defeaters.

Suppose Bea supports a given law *L*, which in her view would improve the public health care system. Bea ranks *L* over no law at all. *L* would require gathering more funds for public health care; specifically, *L* would require raising the overall tax-rate by 1%. Andy, however, rejects *L*, insisting that it is an unnecessary piece of coercive legislation. Andy thus ranks ~*L* over *L*. Now it might be thought that here ~*L* is a stand in for liberty, or no law at all on this matter. But this is not quite right. In fact, in rejecting *L* Andy claims a right to property over his own income. To put it bluntly, Andy is not simply saying: "I claim a liberty not to pay that 1%"; he is rather saying: "Your demand is not justified to me, so get off my property!" Like any other legal rights, property rights are coercive. As Gaus says following Jeremy Waldron and A. M. Honoré, "ownership establishes the authority of the owner over other persons in respect of what is owned."[390] To say that Andy has a right to possess a thing is to say that he has a claim that Bea not interfere with his property. Therefore, in our case ~*L* is coercive because in rejecting *L* Andy claims a coercive right to property.

Now because they are coercive, Andy's property rights must be justified to Bea. Yet she thinks that part of his property should be utilized to support *L*, and hence that he has a publicly justifiable duty to devolve part of his pretax income. Thus if *L* is justified to her, she cannot believe that Andy's right to property is broad enough to justify his refusal to pay another 1%. But for pretty much the same reason, Andy will believe to have no duty to support *L* because that piece of taxation is not justified to him. He will probably take it for granted that since he earned his income through labor, there is at least a prima facie presumption in favor of his right to property. Maybe he could even agree with Liam Murphy and Thomas Nagel when they say that it is "*logically impossible* that people should have *any* kind of entitlement to all their pretax income. *All* that they can be entitled to is what they would be left with after taxes under a legitimate system".[391] Andy could agree, that is, that he has no conclusive right to property prior to taxation. Still, the prima facie presumption of ownership could still be in place. Unless Bea can rebut that presumption by showing that the tax rate needed to implement *L* is justified to Andy, his prima facie right to his pretax income ought to be turned into a conclusive right to property. And because Andy thinks that Bea has failed to provide an adequate rebutting case, Andy is committed to thinking that rejection of *L* provides a final case for his right to property.

Maybe one could insist that, like in the privacy case, one could argue that Andy's right to property might have been already justified to Bea at a previous justificatory stage. Yet this move would strike many as question-begging. What is at stake in debates over distributive justice is precisely whether the better off have a legitimate entitlement to what they claim is their property, as Rousseau and Marx insightfully noted. Once again, Bea could contend precisely that Andy

390 G. Gaus 2011b: 375; see also A. M. Honoré 1961 and J. Waldron 1988.
391 T. Nagel / L. Murphy 2002: 33.

does *not* have the right to property he advocates – a right, that is, to withdraw his financial support to *L*.

All this seems to undermine the Non-Coercive Rejection Thesis, at least when this is applied to issues of distributive justice. Contrary to what the Non-Coercive Rejection Thesis implies, in our case Andy and Bea are *symmetrically* defending two conflicting coercive proposals, none of which could have been previously justified. As a result, both *L* and *~L* stand in need of justification.

3.7.3 When liberty is not an available default

At this point, defenders of the Non-Coercive Rejection Thesis could reply that coercive proposals such as *L* can be rejected without thereby coercing the would-be coercer. Recall the example of Bea's discriminatory proposal against homosexuals. Andy could reject that proposal by invoking his previously justified right to privacy, but this is not the only option, since he could appeal to the presumption in favor of liberty. Similarly, one could insist that rejection of redistributive policies need not latch onto controversial rights to property. To see why, let us begin by considering the following case:

Case 1): Bea gets carjacked by Andy while she is driving her car.

In this case, Andy is manifestly coercing Bea. Although Andy may not be, strictly speaking, physically forcing her to hand him over the keys, he is coercing Bea by closing off any other options. By threatening her – say, with a gun – Andy makes her otherwise favorite option (keeping her car) highly ineligible. Surely the main reason why such a coercive act would be very difficult to justify is the fact that Bea owns the car. Bea could legitimately protest that Andy is wronging her *because* the car is hers. However, she might reasonably demand a justification from Andy even in the absence of such a right. For consider:

Case 2): After picking up an abandoned car, Bea gets carjacked by Andy.

In case 2), Andy does not take possession of Bea's recognized property. Even in this case, however, Bea could both claim that Andy's taking possession of the car is coercive and that his coercive act is not justified to her. What makes Andy's action coercive is not Bea's legal right to possess the car, but rather the bare fact that Bea *has* the car. Although the car is not, strictly speaking, hers, Bea is nonetheless in a relation of *de facto* ownership with that object: she has control over it, she uses it, she prevents others from driving it, and so on. Regardless of whether or not Bea is entitled to possess the car, Andy coerces her whenever he closes off the possibility of keeping the car. But this means that Andy is under a duty to justify his action to her. And it would seem entirely appropriate for Bea to protest that Andy has failed to provide her with such a justification. But obviously she could not invoke her property rights, since she simply happens to possess someone else's car. Yet she could simply insist that, no matter whether or not she has a right to own that car, Andy's coercive interference is not justified to her.

We can extend a similar line of reasoning to the case of taxation: taxation is coercive because it involves taking away part of one's income, regardless of whether or not one has a right to it.[392] Suppose Bea is a radical collectivist. She believes that because property rights are artificial boundaries between mine and thine sanctioned by centuries of momentous social exploitation, Andy has no prima facie right to private ownership – let alone a conclusive one. But Andy could concede this, at least for the sake of the argument. Still, when presented with Bea's demand that he contribute to child health care he could nonetheless maintain that *L* is coercive. As a matter of fact, Andy has some kind of *de facto* ownership of that money, even before taxation. Thus, although he is not, we take it, legally entitled to his income, taking away part of his money through taxation is plainly a form of coercion. So just as in case 2) the carjacker is not justified in coercing Bea, the state may not be justified in implementing coercive norms such as *L* even in the absence of fully-fledged rights to pretax income. This move would apparently warrant the claim the "Non-coercive rejection thesis" is correct even in cases of distributive justice. For if taxation can be rejected without appealing to property rights, rejection of coercion is not itself coercive.

To see where the problem with this reply lies, notice, first, that there is a major difference between Bea's status as a right-holder and her mere de facto possession of an object such as an abandoned car. As Kant aptly noticed, rightfully owning a thing involves more than merely having possession of it, however stable or secure such a de facto possession may be. To rightfully own a thing is rather to enter into a juridical relation such that "any hindrance of my use of it would constitute an injury to me, even when I am not in my possession of it (that is, when I am not a holder of the object)".[393] Without property rights, Andy only

392 Of course, cases 1) and 2) are about coercive actions, while the issue of taxation is about coercive laws regulating citizens' rights to pretax income. Above (§3.6.2) I stressed that the level of actions dictated or prohibited by laws should not be confused with the level of laws. However, I trust that for explanatory purposes we can safely extend our arguments about cases 1) and 2) to the issue of taxation without blurring the conceptual boundary between actions and laws.

393 I. Kant 1996: 312.

injuries Bea by taking her possession if he uses physical force or coercive threats against her narrowly construed natural person. If, on the other hand, the car is her property, injury is done not simply by reason of physical possession, but first and foremost by the expansion of her legal personhood through property rights, which extend her person to include her relation with that object.

Thus, if Bea should leave the abandoned car unattended and walk away, it would be no injury to her for Andy to make use of his Hohfeldian liberty and take the car. Because she has no right to own the car, her case against Andy's coercive acts is entirely dependent on her actually being in her physical possession of it, or, as Kant put in, on her actually being "a holder of the object". By the same token, if Andy had no right to own all his pretax income, Bea would injury him only if she took his income by means of physical force or direct threats against his physical person. Since Andy's juridical personhood is not broad enough to encompass his lawful relation with his property, he would have no right to complain if – say – Bea raided his bank account without resorting to any coercive threats. To be sure, Bea's sneaking into Andy's bank account might be constrained by other justified rights, such as his right to privacy. So it might seem that an encompassing set of personal rights has been publicly justified, there remains little legal room for Bea to interfere with Andy's de facto property. Again, though, Andy would not thereby claim that Bea has a legally enforceable duty to respect his property as such. But this reply incurs two major problems.

First, it would be bizarre, to say the least, to claim that by taking away Andy's belongings (though perhaps within the bounds of other rights), Bea would not wrong Andy. It would seem entirely appropriate for Andy would to Bea's action as a violation of his juridical person, which is extended and safeguarded, in Kant's sense, by a fundamental right to property. As Kant argued, the distinction between "mine" and "thine" can only occur "in a rightful condition," that is, "under an authority giving Laws publicly," that is, "in a civil condition," a state.[394] It is the "exit from the state of nature" (*exeundum e statu naturali*) that makes the setting of the boundaries between mine and thine possible, enabling individuals to move from a provisional claim to property to a settled and certain claim. Like Hobbes, Kant was thus well aware of the fact that property rights are purely conventional. Still, he maintained that private property is a major institution in modern bourgeois society, and that the primary authority of the state stems from its role in securing property rights, which are a fundamental requisite of any effective social order. For pretty much the same reason, Gaus stresses that property rights have a "fundamental place" in a liberal "free and social order".[395]

394 Ibid: 255.
395 G. Gaus 2011b: 509.

Second, and much more important, citizens in modern societies *are* as a matter of fact understood as juridical persons in the Kantian sense, to wit, as natural persons endowed with property rights. If I steal your bowl of salad as you nibble along, I am not coercing you. Nor am I violating any relevant personal rights of yours, except your alleged right to property. Maybe you could believe that my duty not to take your property was unjustified to me all along; consequently, you could believe that reporting my stealing to the police would be an unjustified course of action. But this would be an idle claim. The crucial point is that you *could* call the police if you wanted to. You would be legally entitled to demand that the authority punish me, and your actually refraining from doing so is as irrelevant as my beliefs about justified property rights. Insofar as the state treats you as a juridical person, the state treats you as the holder of property rights, which, as Kant stressed, are crucial to the very definition of juridical personhood. To put the point differently, ownership of income is the legal baseline in legal systems as we know them. As the analogy with the example of the carjacker suggests, there is nothing contradictory in the claim "I reject taxation but I do not thereby claim a right to property". But this presupposes that liberty is an available default position: "I have no claim to my income, you have no claim to my income, so feel free to consider my income as a dollar bill lying on the sidewalk". Clearly this is a mere philosophical fancy. Legal systems in modern societies uphold what I called the prima facie presumption of ownership. One's income, if obtained through legal means such as wages, salaries or rewards, becomes part of one's legally recognized and protected property until a rebutting case is provided. But to reject taxation simply *is* to claim that such a rebutting case has not been provided.

3.7.4 The narrow symmetry objection

The upshot concerning our case about public health care is straightforward. Because rights are inherently coercive, both *L* (public health care should be reformed) and *~L* (no increase in tax rate to support reforms of the public health care system) stand in need of justification. While Bea contends that Andy has a duty to financially support the piece of legislation she proposes, Andy claims that taxation is not justified to him. And in doing so, he ends up advocating some property right, which Bea necessarily contests. When it comes to issues of distributive justice and property rights, then, the Non-Coercive Rejection Thesis is false.

To be sure, apart from cases in which issues of this kind are at stake, the Non-Coercive Rejection Thesis seems valid. I cannot think of any other relevant cases in which the only way for Andy to reject Bea's coercive proposals is to appeal to rights that Bea will most likely contest. In any event, our discussion shows that there are cases in which the Non-Coercive Rejection Thesis does not apply. In any such case, public reasoning is clearly symmetrical, since both proponents and opponents of a given law *L* would make coercive demands on others. This seems a major problem for convergence models. Insofar as convergence allows citizens to reject coercive laws on comprehensive grounds, it cannot prevent them from imposing coercive counter-proposals on others whenever the Non-Coercive Rejection Thesis does not apply. Call this the "narrow symmetry objection" to convergence.

Before seeing how convergence theorists could and should reply to this objection, it is important to note that its underlying critique of the Non-Coercive Rejection Thesis differs in three crucial respects from the argument from symmetry based on the Strong Burden Thesis. Firstly, and most obviously, it rejects the view that Andy may have to justify *~L* to Bea even if *~L* is not itself coercive. In fact, in rejecting the Strong Burden Thesis I argued that in any such case Bea and Andy are indeed asymmetrically placed. The objection I sketched only applies to cases of narrow symmetry, that is to say, to cases in which both *L* and *~L* are coercive. Second, the narrow symmetry objection does not state that Andy has to justify *~L* to Bea only if there is some freestanding rationale *FR* in support of *L*, without which the presumption in favor of liberty would not be rebutted. Insofar as *~L* is a stand in for coercion and not for liberty, *~L* calls for justification regardless of the reasons Bea may or may not have given in support of *L*.

Thirdly, although the narrow symmetry objection is an objection against convergence, it does *not* justify the Consensus View of Public Reason. Consider again our case: Bea supports *L*, while Andy rejects it *L*; however both *L* and *~L* are coercive; yet while Bea ranks *~L* below no law at all, Andy ranks *L* below no law at all. But now let us add that *L* is backed by a freestanding rationale *FR*, which Bea deems conclusive, while Andy is openly justified in believing that *FR* is defeated by *R**, a private defeater of his. Now consensus models would give an inadequate answer to the question "What, if anything, is publicly justified in this case?" On the consensus view, Bea could legitimately insist on supporting *L* despite Andy's objection, which, being private, should not be taken into account. But if anything should be clear by now, it is that view is unacceptable. For Bea to simply foist upon Andy laws which he has reason to reject is inconsistent with her commitment to treat him as a free and equal, self-legislating fellow citizen.

Yet convergence looks equally problematic. It seems that on a convergence view Andy's objection would be allowed to defeat *L*, which would publicly justify *~L*. But this cannot be right, for the same reason why *L* cannot be the publicly justified option: since *~L* is coercive, and since Bea has reason to reject *~L*, Bea would not be treated as a free and equal, self-legislating moral person if she were subjected to ~*L*. Thus, apparently, neither consensus nor convergence deals with cases of narrow symmetry in an appropriate way.

3.7.5 The Symmetrical Convergence View of Public Reason

On closer inspection, however, convergence would not really justify ~*L* in our case. Rather, it would justify neither *L* nor ~*L*. Recall what the Convergence View of Public Reason claims:

Convergence View of Public Reason: (A) Liberty should be the norm; coercion stands in need of justification. (B) Coercive law *L* is publicly justified if, and only if, every reasonable citizen, taking all good reasons into account, would endorse *L*. (C) Both public and private reasons are good reasons.

Now because private reasons are good reasons (C) and because Andy can take those reasons into account in assessing the legitimacy of *L* (B), it might seem that ~*L* is publicly justified. But defenders of the Convergence View of Public Reason could reply that this would be the case only if ~*L* were not itself coercive. But because ~*L* is in fact coercive, and because ~*L* does not meet condition (B), ~*L* is as unjustified as *L*. As a result, neither could be legitimately imposed upon the public on the Convergence View of Public Reason.

This reply rescues convergence from the charge of upholding coercive (counter-)proposals that some reasonable citizens could rank below liberty, thus ultimately refuting the narrow symmetry objection. Still, we should not neglect two important conclusions we reached above. The first is that cases of narrow symmetry between coercive proposal and coercive counter-proposal typically occur when it comes to issues of distributive justice and property rights. The second is that in any such case liberty is not a viable default position. As our example suggests, *L* and ~*L* are the only options available: either Andy is required by law to pay the tax-rate indicated by *L*, or he is not, in which case he will claim a coercive right to his income. But to say that, if properly understood, convergence would cross both *L* and ~*L* off the list of legitimate proposals is to say that, in some way, no law at all (liberty) would be justified in this case. Yet liberty is *not* an available option. Unless we content ourselves with the unattractive conclusion that in any such case legitimacy is impossible to achieve, we should allow that at least one of the two (coercive) options on the table should qualify as legitimate.

It seems that we have ended up in a dead end. Consensus would justify *L*, while convergence would justify neither *L* nor ~*L*. None of these solutions, however, seems attractive. The good news is that there is a way out of this impasse. The doctrine of public reason requires identifying an "eligible set" of proposals. By "eligible set" of proposals I mean the battery of coercive laws which all citizens have reason to rank over no law at all. I introduced this concept in chapter 1 (§1.4.6), where I argued that political authority can only uphold proposals that fall within the eligible set. Now in our case the eligible set is empty: combining their openly justified preferences, Andy and Bea conclude that neither *L* nor *~L* is publicly ranked over no law at all. Still, they have to face up to the fact that *one* of the two options will be implemented. Given the peculiarity of this situation, it would seem reasonable for them assume that *both L and ~L can be legitimate even if none is publicly ranked over coercion*. That is, it would seem reasonable for Andy and Bea to accept that both options are reasonable, permissible proposals, though of course none is fully justified.

To better illustrate this point, let us introduce the idea of a "reasonable set" of proposals. Like the "eligible set", the "reasonable set" includes only proposals that may be legitimately chosen through democratic procedures. Unlike the eligible set, however, the reasonable set may include proposals that some reasonable citizens rank below liberty, should the eligible set be empty. In our case, it seems reasonable to assume that *L* and *~L* should figure in the reasonable set, while the eligible set would remain empty. Instead of insisting that, whatever option democratic procedures of adjudication happen to pick out, legitimacy cannot be achieved, Andy and Bea should concede that both options are sufficiently reasonable in the light of the circumstances, and sufficiently legitimate for that reason.

To be sure, in a publicly justified polity situations of this kind should not eventuate too often, since the key idea behind the doctrine of public reason is that legitimate laws must be preferred by all to liberty. In other words, the "reasonable set" should generally be identical with the "eligible set". The more we loosen this idea of legitimacy as to include proposals that some reasonable citizens rank below liberty, the more we undermine the ideal of public reason. Still, in a reasonably limited amount of cases, loosening the idea of legitimacy seems unavoidable for the reasons I have indicated. These considerations suggest amending the Convergence View of Public Reason to

Symmetrical Convergence View of Public Reason (in short: "symmetrical convergence"): (A) Liberty should be the norm; coercion stands in need of justification. (B) Coercive law *L* is publicly justified if, and only if, every reasonable citizen, taking all good reasons into account, would endorse *L*. (C) Both public and private reasons are good reasons. (D) If d1) a private reason *R** defeats a freestanding rationale supporting *L*, d2) both *~L* and *L* are coercive, d3) no third option is available and d4) the eligible set of coercive proposals is empty, then d5) both *L* and ~*L* should be part of the reasonable set of coercive proposals.

Symmetrical convergence is strikingly similar to the convergence view defended by Gaus, but has two important advantages. First, it makes it explicit that private reasons cannot be used to impose coercive counter-proposal upon others, should *L* and ~*L* be symmetrically coercive. Second, it holds that in some peculiar cases the reasonable set can comprise proposals that some reasonable citizens will inevitably rank below no law at all.

3.8 The dominant view of public reason rejected

3.8.1 Against public reason's Shareability Requirement

Three conclusions can be drawn from what I have said in this last chapter. The first conclusion is that convergence can hardly be rejected on grounds of moral inappropriateness, since appropriateness-based arguments for consensus are far from persuasive. The second conclusion is that the Convergence View of Public Reason should be refined and turned into the Symmetrical Convergence View of Public Reason.

The third, crucial conclusion is that the twofold presumption in favor of (symmetrical) convergence is still fully in place. As I argued in chapter 1 (§1.5.6), such a presumption has two elements. First, public justification must be conclusive, as stated by the Conclusiveness Thesis (CT). But because the Shareability Requirement endorsed by consensus models excludes potentially decisive (private) defeaters, freestanding reasoning may not cater to conclusively justified results. Second, consensus models rely on what I have called the Freestandingness Thesis (FT), according to which *R* is a public/shareable reason if and only if it is freestanding – where a freestanding reason is a reason identified through the correct and suitably conducted procedure of abstraction Ω, which leads to the full set of freestanding considerations *U*. But because freestanding reasons may in principle be defeated by private reasons, *R* may not be shared by all (as a justificatory reason) even if *R* is part of *U*.

To rebut this twofold presumption, consensus theorists should show that public reasons are in fact immune against private defeaters, either because private reasons lack epistemic strength or because they are morally inappropriate. Yet in the previous chapter we saw that strength-based arguments for consensus fail, while in this chapter we ruled out the possibility of defending consensus on appropriateness-based grounds. As a result, freestanding reasoning may be unable to meet the Conclusiveness Thesis, whereas the Freestandingness Thesis is false and should be amended to the following thesis:

Shareability as Common Open Justification (SCOJ): *R* is a public reason for endorsing law *L* if, and only if, *R* is a reason according to the Expanded View of Reasons[396] (or a reason that all reasonable citizens could regard as justificatory in the sense indicated by the Weakly Externalist Justificatory View of Shareability).[397]

SCOJ is similar to the Undefeated Public Reasons Thesis, which I introduced in chapter 1 (§1.5.5), but stresses that justificatory reasons must be openly justified to all reasonable citizens in the sense indicated in chapter 2 (§2.7.2). Because freestanding reasons, being in principle vulnerable to private defeaters, may indeed be non-justificatory in the sense indicated by SCOJ, it follows, again, that Ω may identify reasons that are neither conclusive nor shareable. Once the Freestandingness Thesis is rejected, the consensus view turns out to be paradoxical and self-defeating: the Shareability Requirement eschews all appeals to private reasons despite the fact that private reasons are necessary to determine what counts as a shared reason in the first place. This establishes a strong and, I take it, conclusive case against the Consensus View of Public Reason.

3.8.2 A further problem

Let me close with a last critical remark about the Consensus View of Public Reason. Consider a case in which a given law *L* is supported by a freestanding rationale, which, however, is unable to provide a complete ordering of the interpretations of *L*:

396 See chapter 1, §1.5.4.
397 See chapter 2, §2.7.2.

Comprehen-sive doctrine A (Σa)	Comprehen-sive doctrine B (Σb)	Comprehen-sive doctrine C (Σc)	Comprehen-sive doctrine D (Σd)	Freestanding rationale (ΣF)
L_2	L_2	L_2	L_2	L_1, L_2, L_3, L_4
L_4	L_1	L_1	L_3	L_5
L_3	L_4	L_3	L_1	No law at all
L_5	L_3	L_5	No law at all	
No law at all	No law at all	L_4	L_4	
L_1	L_5	No law at all	L_5	

Display 3

Here all private doctrines are fundamentally consistent with the freestanding rationale, in the sense that neither party has private reasons for rejecting all eligible interpretations of *L*. However, ΣF is unable to provide any internal ranking of the members of the set, though it justifies the set as a whole over L_5 and no law at all. This is by no means an unlikely scenario, for three main reasons.

First a), given reasonable pluralism we should expect the pool of freestanding reasons to come down to relatively few, abstract values. Second, b) and for pretty much the same reason, *U* will often contain few if any "strength-affecting" or "reason-weighing" reasons.[398] And in the absence of "reasons-weighing reasons", public discourse conducted in freestanding terms will be forced to "zoom out", as it were, and focus on abstract laws or general principles. Any such law or principle will be abstract because the freestanding rationale supporting it will comprise different freestanding reasons, without however assessing their relative degrees of weight. Different ways of weighing and balancing the reasons comprised by a freestanding rationale will result in different interpretations of the abstract law justified by that rationale. Finally, and more generally c), abstract reasoning leads to abstract results. But if this is so, then any abstract law justified by *U* will be open to a number of equally permissible interpretations of it, none of which is conclusively justified over the others. To use Habermas's terminology, *U* is most likely to encompass "moral" principles, which, however, will typically be abstract and open to different interpretations.[399]

398 See chapter 1, §1.3.2.

399 Discourse theory is by no means insensitive to this major problem. To solve it, Klaus Günther has introduced the notion of "discourses of application", which Habermas has

In sum, display 3 depicts a pretty likely scenario, as far as a "freestanding ranking" based on a freestanding rationale is concerned. But if this is so, private reasons can help narrow down the list of permissible interpretations of principles justified by a freestanding rationale. This is manifestly clear in the situation represented in display 3: all parties converge on L_2, which all have reason to regard as the best alternative in the light of their private evaluative standards. Here it seems really appropriate to say that L_2 is publicly justified, despite the fact that no public reasons justify it over the other options. Why shouldn't this be the case if all have reason to see L_2 as the best option? Still, defenders of consensus would be committed to the view that L_2 is as justified as L_1, L_3 and L_4, since the Shareability Requirement bars all appeals to private reasons. Surely, though, this is counterintuitive. But now consider another situation:

explicitly taken up (K. Günther 2008; J. Habermas 1994; 1996). In discourses of application the question is no longer: "Which norm is of equal interest to all those affected" but rather: "Which valid norm is appropriate given the specific circumstances?". In fact, "in appropriateness argumentation the moral validity of norms is simply presupposed and recognized as given" (K. Günther 2008: 244; it goes without saying that Günther's notion of "appropriateness" has nothing to do with my account of "appropriateness", which I have contrasted with that of "strength"). In order to correctly interpret and apply general norms, we have to put aside the actual interest of the moral agents involved and focus on the features that we believe to be relevant in our specific situation. Hitherto inexperienced application situations compel us to pay regard to the constellations of historical, social and political features that will help us decide (in terms that all can accept) which norm is appropriate under given circumstances. Günther's theory tries to steer a middle way between Kant's abstract universalism, which tends to disregard the problem of context-sensitive application, and traditional hermeneutical approaches, which tend to rely entirely on the situation-dependent discovery of legal norms. While Kant-like discourses of justification are of little help when it comes to making decisions on specific *hard cases*, the problem of the indeterminacy of abstract norms cannot be overcome solely by the applicator's hermeneutical pre-understanding constituted within a specific form of life. Rather, we have to make a clear distinction between universal context-free validity (which is verified by "discourses of justification") and context-sensitive appropriateness (which is verified by "discourses of application"). Both stages are necessary in moral argumentation. When we deliberate about hard cases, we can do justice to the ideal of impartiality (as opposed to hermeneutical contextualism) only if our moral judgement is already equipped with a battery of abstract prima facie valid norms, whose appropriateness is to be assessed (by means of rational "discourses of application") in the light of the contingent features we are presented with. Now the important point is that for Günther and Habermas discourses of application should be able to single out the better or "more coherent" interpretation of any given abstract moral norms. I cannot even attempt to discuss Günther's overall theory here, but I think it suffices to stress that, given a) and especially b), even discourses of application seem very likely to yield indeterminate results at the political level (though not necessarily at the level of judicial review).

Comprehensive doctrine A (Σa)	Comprehensive doctrine B (Σb)	Comprehensive doctrine C (Σc)	Comprehensive doctrine D (Σd)	Freestanding rationale (ΣF)
L_4	L_2	L_3	L_2	L_1, L_2, L_3, L_4
L_5	L_4	L_4	L_4	L_5
No law at all	L_5	L_2	L_3	No law at all
L_3	L_3	No law at all	L_5	
L_2	L_1	L_5	No law at all	
L_1	No law at all	L_1	L_1	

Display 4

Here the parties do not converge on any proposal. Note, however, that according to consensus models proposals defeated by freestanding rationales should be crossed off the list. Given the transitivity of their orderings, the parties would therefore be left with the following rankings:

Comprehensive doctrine A (Σa)	Comprehensive doctrine B (Σb)	Comprehensive doctrine C (Σc)	Comprehesive doctrine D (Σd)	Freestanding rationale (ΣF)
L_4	L_2	L_3	L_2	L_1,L_2, L_3, L_4
L_3	L_4	L_4	L_4	L_5
L_2	L_3	L_2	L_3	No law at all
L_1	L_1	L_1	L_1	

Display 5

It might seem that here public justification has run its course. Neither freestanding nor private reasons can help identify the best alternative, so the parties should stop discussing and take a vote. Public reason has already done its job, it might appear, by excluding "no law at all" and L_5; but it has nothing to say about any of the other four options. Yet if we look at display 5 more closely we can notice that public reason does have something more to say. As a matter of fact, there is a "reverse" overlapping consensus, so to speak, on L_1. While the freestanding evaluative standard ΣF does not provide the parties with reasons for excluding exclude L_1, all private evaluative standards converge in eliminating it from the optimal set. All parties would in fact unanimously agree that since it is strictly dominated by all other options, L_1 should be eliminated from the eligible set.

Clearly, though, the Shareability Requirement would not allow the parties to filter L_1 out, as to do so they would employ non-shareable reasons, which are always "bad reason" on the standard consensus view. Hence, consensus conceptions seem committed to the counterintuitive view that – say – a public official who supported L_1 would not thereby defy the ideal of public reason, despite the fact that all have reason to eliminate L_1 from the eligible set. It might be objected that a moral duty or commitment not to support L_1 would amount to little, since neither party has an interest in supporting what *all* regard as a suboptimal option. But this would be a mistake. The rankings in displays 3 to 5 are based on the parties evaluative standards; they represent what the parties have reason to regard as the better options in the light of their openly justified beliefs about right and wrong. But the fact that – say – a politician who affirms comprehensive doctrine C is committed by his own beliefs to seeing L_1 as a bad option by no means entails that he also has a strategic interest in not supporting it. Politics is complicated, and there are innumerable strategic reasons why a party could choose to withdraw their favored proposals or to support bad laws.

The same is true of the situation shown in display 3. Although L_2 gains an "overlapping consensus" of private doctrines, some party might oppose it out of sheer strategic reasons. Even in this case, however, the standard consensus view would give citizens no opportunity to complain. To avoid these counterintuitive results, defenders of the Shareability requirement should at the very least amend the Consensus View of Public Reason to a more permissive consensus conception:

Permissive Consensus View of Public Reason: (A) Liberty should be the norm; coercion stands in need of justification. (B) Coercive law *L* is publicly justified if, and only if, every reasonable citizen, taking all good reasons into account, would endorse *L*. (C) Public reasons are good reasons. Private reasons are good reasons if and only if they overlap in support of (or against) some interpretation(s) of a given law supported by a freestanding rationale.

Displays 3 to 5 suggest that the Permissive Consensus View of Public Reason is preferable to the standard consensus view: insofar as private reasons do not defeat public rationales, they can be used to narrow down the list of eligible proposals. The Consensus View of Public Reason is not only unable to rebut the twofold presumption in favor of convergence. It is also open to the charge of not excluding from the eligible set coercive proposals which all members of the public have reason to reject, even when doing so would not threaten any freestanding rationale.

3.9 Summary

In chapter 1 I made a distinction between two broad families of arguments for consensus: strength-based arguments on the one hand, and appropriateness-based arguments on the other hand. In chapter 2 I criticized four major strength-based arguments for consensus: the "top-down" argument, the argument "from universalization", the "discourse-theoretical" argument and the "social" argument. I argued that since arguments of this kind are inherently flawed, only appropriateness-based based arguments for consensus can rebut the twofold presumption in favor of convergence. These arguments do not suppose that freestanding reasons are "objective" considerations which have greater epistemic weight than private reasons. Rather, they insist that private reasons are inappropriate justificatory grounds, and hence that the constituency of public reason should only comprise members that are willing to put them aside in public political debate. In this last chapter I considered five such arguments, which I called the "argument from sincerity", the "argument from publicity", the "argument from normative stability", the "argument from reasonable compliance" and the "argument from symmetry". Yet even these arguments fail to convince.

In defending public reason's principle of sincerity, Quong rightly stresses that convergence permits (or even requires) citizens to be insincere with one another (§3.2.1 – 3.2.3). However, his overall argument is both unable to rank consensus over negative convergence (§3.2.4) and open to the charge of leading to a "populist" conception of public reason (§3.3.1 – 3.3.3) – a charge to which "political" liberalism in general is vulnerable (§3.3.4). The argument from publicity (§3.4.1) is ambiguous because it may be taken to imply either that publicity should be achieved truth open discussions within the public sphere (§3.4.2) or that publicity is a justificatory device and thus part of public reason (§3.4.3). Either way, though, that argument fails. The "argument from normative stability" overestimates the worry that private reasons could defeat most if not all pro tanto justified principles of social cooperation (§3.5.1). The "argument from reasonable compliance" wrongly equates reliance on private reasons with sheer instrumental rationality (§3.5.2). The argument from symmetry (§3.6.1 – 3.6.3), albeit intuitively appealing (§3.6.4), should be resisted because it rests on the Strong Burden Thesis, which seriously risks skewing the fundamental commitment to publicly justify coercion (§3.6.5). My critique of the Non-Coercive Rejection Thesis, instead, points to a real problem with the use of private defeaters (§3.7.1 – 3.7.4). This does not mean, however, that we should endorse consensus, but only that the convergence view defended by Gaus should be turned into a slightly different, "symmetrical" convergence model. In conclusion, consensus models are unjustified – in addition to being less plausible than "permissive" consensus models (§3.8.2).

I should like to stress that the arguments for consensus I reviewed in this book so far are not peripheral contributions to the debate over public reason. On the contrary, they reflect widespread views about the alleged inappropriateness of private reasons. This is true especially of the argument from universalization and of the argument from reasonable compliance. The former upholds a very powerful intuition: if the law must be justified to all, it must be justified by appeal to reasons that all can accept; in other words, impartiality demands that the law be justified on the basis of impartial reasons. The latter rehearses an intuitive worry about convergence: how can people concerned exclusively with furthering their own private interests reason themselves into "reasonable" persons that resist the temptation to cheat? The other arguments, though perhaps less prominent in the literature, complete the picture. To my knowledge, no further arguments for consensus have been advanced by public reason liberals. Therefore, although consensus is almost orthodoxy in the literature on public reason, the twofold presumption in favor of (symmetrical) convergence is still entirely in place (§3.8.1). This is bad news for advocates of consensus.

Conclusion

In this book I tackled one of the thorniest issues in political philosophy, and one which typically defies satisfactory solution: *the justification of political authority*. If political authority is to be seen as having "a license to issue certain rules and a title to enforce them coercively",[400] it must meet certain criteria of legitimacy, which, in turn, must be tied to some publicly recognizable standards of justifiability. In short, collectively binding and legally enforced norms are legitimate only if they can be reasonably and sufficiently justified to those subjected to them. This fundamental link between legitimacy and justifiability takes us back to the pressing philosophical question toward which much philosophical debate gravitates: What constitutes a proper justification of the exercise of political power?

The vast majority of justificatory liberals take it for granted that the answer to this question is simple: in justifying their political proposals to one another, citizens committed to the ideal of public reason should advocate only public or shareable reasons. Rainer Forst subscribes to this view: "Since the norms that have to be justified by reasons will turn into *reciprocally* and *generally* binding and legally enforced norms, the reasons that confer legitimacy upon them must themselves be reciprocally and generally justifiable".[401] In a similar vein, Charles Larmore claims that we honor public reason when we justify our proposals on the basis of reasons that "all citizens" could "affirm together"[402], while Gerald J. Postema argues that all participants in deliberation ought to "present evidence, arguments and interpretations that they can fully endorse".[403] S. Macedo, J. Quong, S. Freeman, J. Habermas, K. Korsgaard, M. Schwartzman and many others concur.

In this book I argued, however, that this widespread view is misguided and should be replaced with an alternative view, which I termed "symmetrical convergence". Symmetrical convergence has several distinctive features. First, it is a *broad* (as opposed to narrow) view of public reason because it holds that all exercise of political power (and not only a subset of laws) should be publicly justified. However, as I stressed from the outset, symmetrical convergence only ap-

400 R. Martin 1993: 7.
401 R. Forst 2001: 362.
402 C. Larmore 2003: 385.
403 G. J. Postema 1995b: 369

plies to the exercise of political power within the *national* state. Moreover, symmetrical convergence is a *pluralist* conception, in two senses. Firstly, and most obviously, it is pluralist because it allows for a plurality of *non-public reasons* being brought to bear in public reasoning. Secondly, it is pluralist in the sense that it relies on a *pluralist epistemology*. Furthermore, symmetrical convergence accepts and defends a *two-step approach* to public justification. I repeatedly stressed that the correct freestanding procedure Ω (whatever it is) plays an important role in identifying potentially justified principles of social cooperation. However, this is only a first step, which should be supplemented with a second, convergence stage, in which citizens verify whether the "pro tanto" justified freestanding principles are justified to them all things considered. Moreover, symmetrical convergence is a *procedural* model of public reason: it simply serves as a framework for public justification, without purporting to determine in advance which substantive principles and laws are publicly justified. Finally, I argued that two elements set apart symmetrical convergence from the standard convergence view. First, symmetrical convergence makes it explicit that private reasons cannot be used to impose coercive counter-proposal upon others, should *L* and *~L* be *symmetrically coercive*. Second, it holds that in some peculiar cases the *reasonable set of coercive proposals* can comprise proposals that some reasonable citizens will inevitably rank below no law at all.

I defended symmetrical convergence in three steps. In chapter one I laid the basis for my argument by describing the general Concept of Public Reason as a combination of two fundamental principles (§1.1). The first principle, which I called the Principle of Political Liberty, holds that liberty should be the norm, while all exercise of political power backed by the threat of legal sanctions stands in need of justification (§1.2.1). In defending this first principle, I tried to identify and dispel some misunderstandings about the "liberal" presumption against coercion and its underlying conception of liberty (§1.2.2). First, I stressed that the Principle of Political Liberty it is not concerned only with actual interference, but more generally with legal rights that entitle citizens to interfere with others. Moreover, the Principle of Political Liberty does not view a state of formal liberties tainted by material inequalities as the status quo. Quite the contrary, I explained that the Principle of Political Liberty is entirely consistent with the view that material inequalities stand in need of justification. Furthermore, the Principle of Political Liberty and its underlying presumption in favor of liberty do not imply that only coercion stands in need of justification. I took up this important point in chapter 3 (§3.6.3), when I rejected the argument from symmetry.

In discussing the Principle of Political Liberty I also stressed that all coercive laws need to be justified. This led me to reject the "narrow view" of public reason, which limits the site of public reason to fundamental issues of justice and constitutional essentials (§1.2.3). Moreover, I rejected the Derivative Justification Thesis, arguing that public justification may not be achieved derivatively or indirectly, to wit, by means of publicly justified democratic procedures which in some way "transfer" justification (as opposed to some weaker degree of political legitimacy) to their outcomes (§1.2.4). Next I introduced the second principle comprised by the general concept of public justification, which I called the Principle of Public Justification. According to this second principle, a coercive law is publicly justified if and only if all reasonable citizens, taking all good reasons into account, would endorse it (§1.2.5).

Then I defined consensus and convergence as two conflicting interpretations of the general Concept of Public Reason (§1.3.1). The dominant consensus view insists that only public or shareable reasons are good reasons – though I stressed that consensus theorists need not endorse strong consensus, according to which citizens must accept the law for the very same reasons (§1.3.2). The alternative convergence conception, instead, holds that even private reasons qualify as good reasons. After defining the concepts of "public reasons" (§1.3.3) and "publicness" (§1.3.4), I tried to show that despite its minority status, convergence is prima facie preferable to consensus, for two related reasons.

To begin with, convergence expunges from the domain of public reason a number of reasons (especially religious reasons) to which some citizens might assign primary importance (§1.4.1). Starting from Rawls's suggestions about the need for an "overlapping consensus" (§1.4.2 – 1.4.3), I argued that the exclusion of private reasons is problematic because reasons justifying coercion should be conclusive (§1.4.6), which means that they should not be defeated (§1.4.4 – 1.4.5). But since consensus fails to take private defeaters into account, consensus is open to the charge of falling foul of the conclusiveness requirement. I argued that this establishes a first presumption in favor of convergence (§1.4.7). Then I introduced a core thesis against which I have argued at length in this book, namely the Freestandingness Thesis or FT (§1.5.1), according to which a reason *R* is public/shareable if and only if is part of *U*, or, which is the same, arrived at through a correct (and suitably conducted) procedure of abstraction Ω. Although both consensus and convergence theorists endorse it (§1.5.2), FT is false. As a result, the Shareability Requirement advocated by consensus models is paradoxical and self-defeating. Since freestanding reasons might be undermined (§1.5.3), rebutted (§1.5.4) or suspended (§1.5.5) (in short: defeated) by private reasons, and since defeated reasons do not qualify as shareable (justificatory) reasons, the Shareability Requirement would make it impossible to determine which reasons are public (§1.5.6).

I thus argued (§1.5.7) that that there is a strong, twofold presumption in favor of convergence. To rebut it, consensus theorists should come up with an argument that can substantiate the claim that private reasons are "bad reasons". In this case, it would make little sense to claim that freestanding reasons might be neither conclusive nor shareable (§1.6.1). Specifically, one could still defend consensus if one managed to show that private reasons are either epistemically weak (§1.6.2) or morally inappropriate (§1.6.3 – 1.6.4).

In the second chapter I examined the first strategy that could be (and sometimes has been) adopted by consensus theorists. On a strength-based consensus view, it is an error to believe that private reasons can defeat freestanding reasons because the former lack epistemic strength, and are therefore unable to tip the balance of justificatory reasons (§2.2.1). As a result, freestanding reasons are necessarily shareable (as the Freestandingness Thesis (FT) states) and conclusive (as the Conclusiveness Thesis (CT) demands). In chapter 2 I reviewed four major strength-based arguments for consensus: the top-down argument for consensus, the argument from universalization, the discourse theoretical argument for consensus and the social argument for consensus seek to show that only freestanding reasons can contribute, epistemically speaking, to the full justification of coercive laws.

I tried to show that all such arguments fail. In criticizing the attempt to defend consensus on epistemic (strength-based) grounds, I stressed that strength-based arguments for consensus rest on two core premises. The first premise is that freestanding reasons are objective reasons – though of course the arguments I reviewed rely on quite different conceptions of objectivity (§2.2.2). The second premise is that objective reasons are by definition either defeated by freestanding reasons (as moderate strength-based arguments claim) or defeated by the very fact that they are private (as radical strength-based arguments claim). Rather than rejecting the first premise, I argued that strength-based arguments fail because the second premise is unwarranted. In fact, no strength-based argument for consensus (be it radical or moderate) manages to show that private reasons are necessarily defeated.

To begin with, the top-down argument for consensus assumes that because *there are* some objective reasons, every rational agent *has* conclusive reason to act and believe as those objective reasons instruct them to act and believe – which means, again, that private reasons are necessarily defeated (§2.3.1). This claim, however, is warranted only if we endorse either a strongly externalist (§2.3.2) or a moderately externalist (§2.3.3) conception of reasons. Following Gaus, I argued that both views should in fact be resisted, whereas weak externalism (§2.4.1 – 2.4.2), as opposed to sheer internalism (§2.3.4), is the correct conception of reasons. As a result, the top-down argument for consensus fails (§2.4.3). In fact, the "pluralistic" epistemic account of justified beliefs I defended lends plausibility to the opposite view: as citizens may be justified in holding diverse views, convergence is better able than consensus to identify conclusively justified proposals.

Then I turned my attention to the radical discourse-theoretical argument for consensus, which understands Ω as a procedure for identifying provisionally objective reasons by means of discursive procedures (§2.5.1). While I granted that freestandingness may well be interpreted in this way (§2.5.2 – 2.5.3), I also argued that there is little reason to believe that private reasons are by definition defeated (§2.5.4 – 2.6.1). Essentially, the problem is that publicly relevant rightness claims (i.e. prospective or existing coercive laws seeking discursive validation) are not truth-analogous and can therefore be justified by "overlapping" private reasons (§2.6.3 – 2.6.3). I therefore argued that the radical discourse theoretical argument fails (§2.6.5). Building on my critique of the radical discourse-theoretical argument, I argued that even the argument from universalization (§2.6.4) and the social argument for consensus (§2.7.1) should be resisted: the former wrongly assumes that since laws must be justified to all, they must be justified to all with the same reasons; the latter errs by assuming that because ought-claims must have some social linguistically mediated backing, they must be affirmed by all members of a given society. Finally, I added that even moderate strength-based arguments for consensus (especially in a discourse-theoretical fashion) are far from convincing (§2.7.2 – 2.8.4). I concluded chapter 2 by arguing that the twofold presumption in favor of convergence cannot be rebutted on epistemic grounds. Epistemically speaking, freestanding reasons may be neither conclusive nor shareable, as private reasons might on occasion defeat them. As a result, FT is false and consensus may not live up to the public reason's conclusiveness requirement.

In chapter 3 I considered the second strategy to which consensus theorists can resort to defend the Shareability Requirement. Many justificatory liberals (especially political liberals) claim that although private reasons are "good reasons" epistemically speaking, they are morally inappropriate justificatory grounds. I started with the sincerity objection to convergence, which has been recently raised by Quong. In defending public reason's principle of sincerity, Quong rightly stresses that convergence permits (or even requires) citizens to be insincere with one another (§3.2.1 – 3.2.3). However, his overall argument is both unable to rank consensus over negative convergence (§3.2.4) and open to the charge of leading to a "populist" conception of public reason (§3.3.1 – 3.3.3) – a charge to which "political" liberalism in general is vulnerable (§3.3.4). Then I turned to the argument from publicity, focusing especially on Macedo's version of it. I argued that Macedo's argument (§3.4.1) is ambiguous because it may be taken to imply either that publicity should be achieved truth open discussion within the public sphere (§3.4.2) or that publicity is a justificatory device and thus part of public reason (§3.4.3). Then I considered the "argument from normative stability", which holds that under convergence private reasons could defeat most if not all pro tanto justified principles of social cooperation (§3.5.1). I argued that this worry is overstated. Next I rejected the "argument from reasonable compliance" arguing that it mistakenly equates reliance on private reasons with sheer instrumental rationality (§3.5.2). The argument from reasonable compliance attacks some versions of convergence such as Gauthier's, but not convergence in general.

Finally, I critically reviewed the "argument from symmetry". Building on Forst's and Wall's objections to the presumption in favor liberty (§3.6.1), the argument from symmetry claims that convergence should be resisted because those rejecting freestanding rationales owe a justification to the public at large (§3.6.2 – 3.6.3). But despite its intuitive appeal (§3.6.4), the argument from symmetry has unacceptable implications, which seriously risk skewing the fundamental commitment to publicly justify coercion (§3.6.5). I argued, however, that public reasoning is indeed symmetrical whenever proposal and counter-proposal are coercive (§3.7.1). This kind of symmetry is particularity likely to occur in issues of distributive justice and property rights (§3.7.2 – 3.7.3). This does not mean, however, that we should endorse consensus. Rather, the potential symmetry between proposals and counterproposals suggests amending the convergence view defended by Gaus to a slightly different convergence model, which I called the Symmetrical Convergence View of Public Reason. I concluded that since the arguments for consensus fail and have inacceptable implications (§3.8.2), the twofold presumption in favor of (symmetrical) convergence remains unaltered (§3.8.1).

The alternative convergence conception I defended in book is interesting because it can open up a number of fruitful research projects, as it invites us to rethink many important themes in contemporary political philosophy. In particular, three such themes stand out. The first concerns the role of religious beliefs in a publicly justified policy, an issue which has sparked heated controversies in the last decades. My argument against consensus models suggests that much current debate about the role of religious reasons is misguided. To begin with, even theorists of public reason who are open to religious contributions are normally held captive by the dominant consensus view, in that they insist that private reasons are permissible only if they can be in some way supported by (forthcoming) public reasons offered in due course. But this view is too restrictive. We should rather pursue J. Stout's attempt to work out a convergence conception which gives a say to all (epistemically plausible) religious reasons, including non-translatable ones. Moreover, it is often unclear whether consensus theorists understand the ban on religious reasons as applying to the public sphere or rather to the domain of public justification. As I argued in chapter 3 (§3.4.1), these are two distinct concepts, and it is important not to conflate them. Since convergence is a theory of public reason, and not a view about the public sphere and its scope, my arguments suggest rethinking the role of religious reasons as reasons able to justify or defeat coercive laws.

Secondly, switching from the standard consensus view to the conception I develop involves rethinking much current understanding about the role of political deliberation. Currently, deliberative democracy is a dominant paradigm in political theory. Indeed, deliberative democracy seems to have become a mandatory label for any acceptable theory of democracy. If you are not a deliberative democrat, you may as well quit calling yourself a democrat. Yet on a (symmetrical) convergence view political deliberation looks less crucial to the achievement public justification than most public reason liberals and democrats appear (bound to) to imply. Deliberation seems a promising justificatory tool for overcoming disagreement insofar as we assume that citizens reason essentially in the same way, as consensus models ultimately claim. But this simplifying assumption is naïve and epistemically unwarranted. Because our personal value systems, trade-off rates and ways of assessing relevant evidence differ in all sorts of subtle ways, only convergence reasoning can do fully justice to the fact of reasonable pluralism. Convergence reasoning, however, may reach extraordinary levels of complexity. Indeed, it is hard to see how even the most sophisticated reasoner could fully grasp and critically evaluate from a second-person perspective all of other people's private beliefs. Thus, actual political deliberation cannot be realistically expected to yield anything more than highly fallible, tentative and reasonably contestable results. To be sure, deliberative democrats in the Habermasian tradition have largely recognized this. However, insofar as they insist that deliberation should, at least ideally, aim at consensus, deliberative democrats end up underestimating the depth of reasonable disagreement lurking beneath political discussion. We can hardly appreciate the diversity of reasons and worldviews thriving under liberal institutions if we do not abandon the hope that, ultimately, good-willed and fully-informed citizens will reason in the same way.

Finally, my argument about consensus and convergence models of public reason points to the intimate connection between public justification and epistemology, a connection that would be worth exploring at greater length in future research. While some justificatory liberals (especially "political" liberals) insist that the doctrine of public reason should not presuppose any epistemic theory, one of the core claims of this book is that without a moral epistemology the project of public reason cannot get off the ground in the first place. Apart from Gaus, few justificatory liberals (if any) have tried to develop an epistemology suitable for the doctrine of public reason. I believe this is unfortunate. Our understanding of public reason would immensely benefit from some fresh research devoted to studying the epistemic presuppositions of public justification.

Bibliography

Ackerman, Bruce A. (1980): *Social Justice in The Liberal State*, New York: Yale University Press.

Anderson, Scott (2006): "Coercion", Stanford Encyclopedia of Philosophy: http://plato.stanford.edu/entries/coercion/

Apel, Karl-Otto (1981): *C. S. Peirce: From Pragmatism to Pragmaticism,* translated by J. M. Krois, Amherst: University of Massachusetts Press.

Audi, Robert (1991): "Religious commitment and secular reason: a reply to Professor Weithman", *Philosophy & Public Affairs* 20: 66–76.

--- (2000): *Religious Commitment and Secular Reason*, Cambridge: Cambridge University Press.

--- (2001): *The Architecture of Reason: The Structure and Substance of Rationality*, New York: Oxford University Press.

Baier, Kurt (1995): *The Rational and the Moral Order – The Social Roots of Reason and Morality*, Peru, IL: Open Court.

Barry, Brian (1995a): "John Rawls and the Search for Stability", *Ethics* 105: 874-915.

--- (1995b): *Justice as Impartiality*, Oxford: Oxford University Press.

Baynes, Kenneth (2010): "Deliberative Democracy and Public Reason", *Veritas* 55(1): 135-163.

Benn, Stanley (1988): *A Theory of Freedom*, Cambridge: Cambridge University Press.

Berlin, Isaiah (1969): *Four Essays on Liberty*, Oxford: Clarendon Press.

--- (1990): "Alleged Relativism in Eighteenth-Century European Thought", in H. Hardy (ed.), *The Crooked Timber of Humanity: Chapters in the History of ideas*, Princeton: Princeton University Press.

Besson, Samantha / Martì, Josè Luis (2006): *Deliberative Democracy and its Discontents*, Aldershot: Ashgate Publishing, Ltd.

Black, Duncan (1958): *The Theory of Committees and Elections*, Cambridge: Cambridge University Press.

Bobbio, Norberto (1993): *Thomas Hobbes and The Natural Law Tradition*, translated by D. Gobetti, Chicago: Chicago University Press.

Bohman, James (1997): *Public Deliberation: Pluralism, Complexity and Democracy*, Cambridge: MIT Press.

Bond, Edward Jarvis (1983): *Reason and Value*, Cambridge: Cambridge University Press.

Calhoun, Craig (ed.) (1992): *Habermas and The Public Sphere*, Cambridge, MA: MIT press.

Ceppa, Leonardo (2008): "La sfida di Habermas tra Kant e Darwin", *Micromega* 6/2008: 63-79.

Cohen, Joshua (1989): "Moral Pluralism and Political Consensus", in D. Copp / J. Hampton / J. E. Roemer (eds.), *The Idea of Democracy*, New York, Cambridge University Press: 270-291.

--- (1998): "Democracy and Liberty", in J. Elster (ed.), *Deliberative Democracy*, Cambridge: Cambridge University Press.

--- (1997a): "Deliberation and Democratic Legitimacy", in J. Bohman / W. Rehg (eds.), *Deliberative Democracy: Essays on Reason and Politics*, Boston, MIT Press: 67-92.

--- (1997b): "Procedure and Substance in Deliberative Democracy", in J. Bohman / W. Rehg (eds.), *Deliberative Democracy: Essays on Reason and Politics*, Boston, MIT Press: 407-37.

--- (2010): *The Arc of the Moral Universe and Other Essays*, Harvard: Harvard University Press.

Condorcet, Jean-Antoine-Nicolas de Caritat, Marquis de, [1785] (1972): *Essai sur l'application de l'analyse à la probabilité des décisions rendues à la pluralité des 30 voix*, New York: Chelsea Publishing Company.

Connoly, William E. (1993): *The Terms of Political Discourses* (1974), Princeton: Blackwell.

D'Agostino, Fred (1995): "Value Pluralism, Public Justification, and Post-modernism: The Conventional Status of Political Critique", *The Journal of Value Inquiry* 29: 351-366.

--- (1996): *Free Public Reason – Making It Up As We Go*, Oxford: Oxford University Pres.

Dryzek, John (2000): *Deliberative Democracy and Beyond: Liberals, Critics, Contestations*, Oxford: Oxford University Press.

Dworkin, Ronald (1978): *Taking Rights Seriously*, Harvard: Harvard University Press,.

Eberle, Christopher, (2002): *Religious Conviction in Liberal Politics*, New York: Cambridge University Press.

--- (2010): "Religion, Conscientious Engagement and Respect" (unpublished).

Ellis, Elisabeth, (2004): "Provisionalism in the Study of Politics", in I. Shapiro / R. M. Smith / T. E. Masoud (eds.), *Problems and Methods in the Study of Politics*, Cambridge: Cambridge University Press: 350-76.

--- 2008: *Provisional Politics: Kantian Arguments in Policy Context*, New Haven, NJ: Yale University Press.

Ely, James W. Jr (1992): *The Guardian of Every Other Right: A Constitutional History of Property Rights*, New York: Oxford University Press.

Estlund, David (1993): "Making Truth Safe for Democracy", in D. Copp / J. Hampton / J. E. Roemer (eds.), *The Idea of Democracy*, New York: Cambridge University Press: 71-100.

--- (1997): "Beyond Fairness and Deliberation: The Epistemic Dimension of Democratic Authority", in J. Bohman / W. Rehg (eds.), *Deliberative Democracy: Essays on Reason and Politics,* Cambridge, MA: MIT Press: 173-204.

--- (2008): *Democratic Authority*, Princeton: Princeton University Press.

Feinberg, Joel (1984): *Harm to Others* (*Moral Limits for Criminal Law*, Vol 1), New York: Oxford University Press.

Fish, Stanley (1996): "Why We Can't All Get Along", *First Things* 60: 18-26.

Flores D'Arcais, Paolo (2007): "Le tentazioni della fede (undici tesi contro Habermas)", *Micromega* Nov. 2007: 3-13.

--- (2008): "L'insostenibile distinzione di Habermas", *Micromega* 6/2008: 42-62.

Foley, Richard (1987): *The Theory of Epistemic Rationality*, Harvard: Harvard University Press.

Freeden, Michael (1978): *The New Liberalism: An Ideology of Social Reform*, Oxford: Clarendon Press.

--- (1991): *Rights*, Minneapolis: University of Minnesota Press.

Freeman, Samuel (2003): "Introduction" to *The Cambridge Companion to Rawls*, in S. Freeman (ed.) *The Cambridge Companion to Rawls*, Cambridge: Cambridge University Press.

--- (2007): *Rawls*, New York: Routledge.

Forst, Rainer (2001): "The Rule of Reasons – Three Models of Deliberative Democracy", *Ratio Juris* 14(4): 345-378.

--- (2002): *Contexts of Justice – Political Philosophy Beyond Liberalism and Communitarianism*, translated by J. Farrel, Berkeley, CA: University of California Press.

--- (2005): "Political Liberty. Integrating Five Conceptions of Autonomy", in J. Christman / J. Anderson (eds.), *Autonomy and the Challenges to Liberalism*, Cambridge, MA: Cambridge University Press: 226-244.

--- (2011): *Kritik der Rechtfertigunsverhältnisse*, Frankfurt am Main: Suhrkamp.

--- (2012): *The Right to Justification: Elements of a Constructivist Theory of Justice*, translated by J. Flynn, New York: Columbia University Press.

Galston, William (1991): *Liberal Purposes: Goods, Virtues, and Diversity in the Liberal State*, Cambridge: Cambridge University Press.

Garsten, Bryan (2006): *Saving Persuasion: A Defence of Rhetoric and Judgment*, Cambridge, MA: Cambridge University Press.

Gaus, Gerald (1996): *Justificatory Liberalism – An Essay on Epistemology and Political Theory*, New York: Oxford University Press.

--- (2000): *Political Concepts and Political Theories*, Boulder, CO: Westview Press.

--- (2003): *Contemporary Theories of Liberalism*, London: SAGE.

--- (2005): "The Place of Autonomy within Liberalism", in J. Christman / J. Anderson (eds.), *Autonomy and the Challenges to Liberalism*, Cambridge, MA: Cambridge University Press: 272-306.

--- (2008): "The (Severe) Limits of Deliberative Democracy as the Basis for Political Choice", *Theoria: A Journal of Social and Political Theory* 117: 26-53.

--- (2009a) "Recognized Rights as Devices of Public Reason", *Philosophical Perspectives: Ethics* 23: 111-136.

--- (2009b): "The Place of Religious Belief in Public Reason Liberalism", in M. Dimovia-Cookson / P.M.R. Stirk, *Multiculturalism and Moral Conflict*, London: Routledge: 19-37.

--- (2010a): "Coercion, Ownership, and the Redistributive State: Justificatory Liberalism's Classical Tilt", *Social Philosophy & Policy* 27: 233-275.

--- (2010b): "On two critics of justificatory liberalism: A response to Wall and Lister", *Politics, Philosophy & Economics* 9(2): 177-212.

--- (2011a): "A Tale of Two Sets: Public Reason in Equilibrium", *Public Affairs Quarterly* 25(4): 305-25.

--- (2011b) *The Order of Public Reason – A Theory of Freedom and Morality in a Diverse and Bounded World*, New York: Cambridge University Press.

Gaus, Gerald / Vallier, Kevin (2009): "The roles of religious conviction in a publicly justified polity: The implications of convergence, asymmetry and political institutions", *Philosophy & Social Criticism* 35: 51-76.

Gauthier, David (1986): *Morals by Agreement*, Oxford: Clarendon Press.

--- (1995): "Public Reason", *Social Philosophy & Policy* 12: 19-45.

Gert, Joshua (2004): *Brute Rationality*, Cambridge: Cambridge University Press.

Gewirth, Alan (1978): *Reason and Morality*, Chicago: The University of Chicago Press.

Gilovich, Thomas / Griffin, Dale / Kahneman, Daniel (eds.) (2002): *Heuristics and Biases: The Psychology of Intuitive Judgment*, Cambridge, MA: Cambridge University Press.

Gosepath, Stephan (ed.) (1999): *Motive, Gründe, Zwecke. Theorien praktischer Rationalität*, Frankfurt am Main: Fischer Verlag.

Gray, John (1977): "On the contestability of Social and Political Concepts", *Political Theory* 5: 331-348.

--- (2000): *Two Faces of Liberalism*, Cambridge, MA: Polity Press.

Greenawalt, Kent (1988): *Religious Convictions and Political Choice*, Oxford: Oxford University Press.

--- (1995): *Private Consciences and Public Reasons*, New York: Oxford University Press.

Günther, Klaus (2008): *The Sense of Appropriateness. Application Discourses in Morality and Law*, translated by J. Farrel, New York: SUNY.

Gutmann, Amy / Thompson, Dennis F. (1996): *Democracy and Disagreement*, Cambridge, MA: Harvard College.

Habermas, Jürgen (1973): *Theory and Practice*, translated by J. Viertel, Boston, MA: Beacon Press.

--- (1984): *The Theory of Communicative Action*, vol. I: *Reason and the Rationalization of Society*, translated by T. McCarthy, Boston, MA: Beacon Press.

--- (1988): "Law and Morality", translated by K. Baynes, *The Tanner Lectures on Human Values* 8: 219-279.

--- (1989): *The Structural Transformation of The Public Sphere*, translated by T. Burger, Boston, MA: MIT Press.

--- (1990): *Moral Consciousness and Communicative Action*, translated by C. Lenhardt and S. W. Nicholsen, Boston, MA: MIT Press.

--- (1992): *Postmetaphysical Thinking – Philosophical Essays*, translated by W. M. Hohengarten, Boston, MA: MIT Press.

--- (1994): *Justification and Application. Remarks on Discourse Ethics*, translated by C. Cronin, Boston, MA: MIT Press.

--- (1995): "Reconciliation through the Public Use of Reason: Remarks on John Rawls's Political Liberalism", *Journal of Philosophy* 92/3: 109-131.

--- (1996): *Between Facts and Norms – Contributions to a Discourse Theory of Law and Democracy*, translated by W. Rehg, Boston, MA: MIT Press.

--- (1998): *The Inclusion of the Other: Studies in Political Theory*, edited by C. Cronin and P. DeGreiff, Cambridge, MA: MIT Press.

--- (2001): *On the Pragmatics of Social Interaction*, translated by B. Fultner, Cambridge, MA: MIT Press: 1–103.

--- (2003): *The Future of Human Nature*, translated by W. Rehg, M. Pensky, and H. Beister, Cambridge, MA: Polity.

--- (2006): "Dankesrede anlässlich der Verleihung des Staatspreises 2006", Petersberg bei Bonn.

--- (2008a): *Between Naturalism and Religion*, translated by C. Cronin, Cambridge, MA: Polity.

--- (2008b): "A «Post-Secular» Society – What Does It Mean?", *Istanbul Seminars – Reset Dialogues on Civilizations*, available at: http://www.resetdoc.org/EN/Habermas-Istanbul.php

--- (2008c): "Repetita iuvant: una risposta a Paolo Flores d'Arcais", translated by L. Ceppa, *Micromega* 6/2008: 35-41.

Hayek, Friedrich August (1960): *The Constitution of Liberty*, London: Routledge.

Hohfeld, Wesley (1913): "Some Fundamental Legal Concepts as Applied in Judicial Reasoning", *Yale Law Review* 23: 16-59.

Honoré, M. A. (1961): "Ownership", in A. G. Guest (ed.), *Oxford Essays on Jurisprudence*, Oxford: Clarendon Press: 107-47.

Horkheimer, Max (1982): *Critical Theory*, New York: Seabury Press.

Hume, David [1739] (1975): *A Treatise of Human Nature*, edited by L. A. Selby-Bigge, Oxford: Clarendon Press.

Hurley, Susan (1989): *Natural Reasons*, New York: Oxford University Press.

Hurka, Thomas (1990): *Perfectionism*, Oxford: Oxford University Press.

Kagan, Shelley (1989): *The Limits of Morality*, Oxford: Clarendon Press.

Kant, Immanuel (1996) *Gesammelte Schriften* edited by P. Natorp for the Königlich Preussischen Akademie der Wissenschaften, Berlin and Leipzig: de Gruyter, 1900–), translated by M. Gregor, Cambridge: Cambridge University Press.

Kornhauser, Lewis A. / Sager, Lawrence (1986): "Unpacking the Court", *Yale Law Journal* 96: 82-117.

Korsgaard, Christine (1996a): *Creating the Kingdom of Ends*, Cambridge: Cambridge University Press.

--- (1996b): *The Sources of Normativity*, Cambridge: Cambridge University Press.

Kuhn, Thomas (1962): *The Structure of Scientific Revolutions*, Chicago: Chicago University Press.

Larmore, Charles (1990): "Political Liberalism", *Political Theory* 18: 339-60.

--- (2001):"Der Zwang des besseren Arguments", in L. Wingert / K. Günther (eds.), *Die Öffentlichkeit der Vernunft und die Vernunft der Öffentlichkeit. Festschrift für Jürgen Habermas* Frankfurt am Main: Suhrkamp: 106-125.

--- (2003): "Public Reason", in by S. Freeman (ed.), *The Cambridge Companion to Rawls*, Cambridge: Cambridge University Press: 369-393.

--- (2008): *The Autonomy of Morality*, New York: Cambridge University Press.

List, Christian / Goodin, Robert E. (2001): "Epistemic Democracy: Generalizing The Condorcet Jury Theorem", *Journal of Political Philosophy* 9: 277-306.

Lister, Andrew (2010): "Public justification and the limits of state action", *Politics, Philosophy & Economics* 9(2): 151-176.

Locke, John [1689] (1960): *Two Treatises of Government*, in Peter Laslett (ed.), Cambridge: Cambridge University Press: 283-446.

Long, Graham (2004): *Relativism and the Foundation of Liberalism*, Oxford: Imprint.

Macedo, Stephen (1990): “The Politics of Justification”, *Political Theory* 18(2): 280-304.

--- (1991): *Liberal Virtues: Citizenship, Virtue and Community in Liberal Constitutionalism*, Oxford: Clarendon Press.

--- (2000): “In Defense of Liberal Public Reason: Are Slavery and Abortion Hard Cases?” in . P. George / C. Wolfe (eds.), *Natural Law and Public Reason*, Washington, DC: Georgetown University Press: 11-49.

--- (2010): “A Republic of Reasons: Public Reason and the Constitution of the Public Sphere”, Paper presented at the annual meeting of the APSA 2008 Annual Meeting Hynes Convention Center, Boston, MA. Available at http://www.allacademic.com/meta/p278027_index.html.

--- with Gillian K. Hatfield (2011), “Rational Reasonableness: Toward a Positive Theory of Public Reason”, *Law and Ethics of Human Rights*, forthcoming.

de Marneffe, Peter (1990): “Liberalism, Liberty, and Neutrality” *Philosophy & Public Affairs* 19: 253-274.

Martin, Rex (1993): *A System of Rights*, Oxford: Oxford University Press.

McCarthy, Thomas A. / Hoy, David C. (1994): *Critical Theory*, Cambridge, MA: Blackwell.

McCarthy, Thomas A. (1996): “Legitimacy and Diversity: Dialectical Reflections on Analytical Distinctions”, *Cardozo Law Review* 17/4-5: 1083-125.

Mill, John Stuart (1979): *Collected Works of John Stuart Mill*, edited by J. M. Robson, Toronto: University of Toronto Press.

Mulhall, Stephen / Swift, Adam (1996): *Liberals and Communitarians: Second Edition*, Oxford: Blackwell.

Nagel, Thomas (1986): *The View from Nowhere*, Oxford: Oxford University Press.

--- (2003): “Rawls and Liberalism”, in S. Freeman (ed.), *The Cambridge Companion to Rawls*, Cambridge: Cambridge University Press.

Nagel, Thomas / Murphy, Liam (2002): *The Myth of Ownership: Taxes and Justice*, New York: Oxford University Press.

Neal, Patrick (2009): "Is Political Liberalism Hostile to Religion?”, in S. P. Young (ed.), *Reflections on Rawls: An Assessment of His Legacy*, Burlington, VT: Ashgate: 153-176.

Newey, Glenn (1998): “Value Pluralism in Contemporary Liberalism”, *Dialogue* 37: 493-522.

Niesen, Peter (2002): “Legitimität ohne Moralität. Habermas und Maus über das Verhältnis zwischen Recht und Moral”, in R. von Schomberg / P. Niesen (eds.), *Zwischen Recht und Moral*, Münster: LIT Verlag.

Nozick, Robert (1969). “Coercion”, in S. Morgenbesser / P. Suppes, / M. White, *Philosophy, Science, and Method: Essays in Honor of Ernest Nagel*, New York: St. Martin's Press: 440-472.

--- (1974): *Anarchy, State and Utopia*, New York: Basic Books.

O’Neill, Onora (2003): “Constructivism in Rawls and Kant”, in S. Freeman (ed.): *The Cambridge Companion to Rawls*, Cambridge, MA: Cambridge University Press: 347-67.

Paul, Ellen Frankel / Miller, Fred D. / Paul, Jeffrey (eds.) (2007): *Liberalism: Old and New*, New York: Cambridge University Press.

Perry, Michael (1988): *Morality, Politics and Law*, New York: Oxford University Press.

--- (1991): *Love and Power: The Role of Religion and Morality in American Politics*, New York: Oxford University Press.

Pollock, John L. / Cruz, Joseph (1999): *Contemporary Theories of Knowledge*, Lanham: Rowman & Littlefield.

Postema, Gerald J. (1995a): “Public Practical Reason: An Archeology”, *Social Philosophy & Policy* 12: 43-86.

--- (1995b): ‘Public Practical Reason: Political Practice’, in I. Shapiro and J. W. De Crew

(eds.), *Nomos XXXVI: Theory and Practice*, New York: New York University Press: 345 85.

Quine, Willard v. O. (1951): “Two Dogmas of Empiricism”, *The Philosophical Review* 60: 20-43.

Quinn, Philip (1997): "Political Liberalisms and Their Exclusions of the Religious," in P. Weithman (ed.), *Religion and Contemporary Liberalism*, Notre Dame, IN: University of Notre Dame Press: 138-161.

Quong, Jonathan (2011): *Liberalism Without Perfection*, New York: Oxford University Press.

Rawls, John (1955): *A Study on the Grounds of Ethical Knowledge: Considered with Reference to Judgments on the Moral Worth of Character*, Ph.D Dissertation, Princeton University, *Dissertation Abstracts* 15.

--- (1958): “Justice as Fairness”, in *Collected Papers*, edited by S. Freeman, Cambridge, MA: Harvard University Press, 1999: 47-72.

--- (1971): *A Theory of Justice*, Cambridge, MA: Harvard University Press.

--- (1980): “Kantian Constructivism in Moral Theory”, in *Collected Papers*, edited by S. Freeman, Cambridge, MA: Harvard University Press, 1999: 303-358.

--- (1982): “Social Unit and Primary Goods”, in *Collected Papers*, edited by S. Freeman, Cambridge, MA: Harvard University Press, 1999: 359-397.

--- (1985): “Justice as Fairness: Political and not Metaphysical”, in *Collected Papers*, edited by S. Freeman, Cambridge, MA: Harvard University Press, 1999: 388-414.

--- (1987): “The Idea of an Overlapping Consensus”, in *Collected Papers*, edited by S. Freeman, Cambridge, MA: Harvard University Press, 1999: 421-448.

--- (1988): “The Priority of Right and Ideas of the Good”, in *Collected Papers*, edited by S. Freeman, Cambridge, MA: Harvard University Press, 1999: 449-472.

--- (1989): “Themes in Kant’s Moral Philosophy”, in *Collected Papers*, edited by S. Freeman,

Cambridge, MA: Harvard University Press, 1999: 497-528.

--- (1993): *Political Liberalism* (expanded edition 2005), New York: Columbia University Press.

--- (1995): “Political Liberalism. Reply to Habermas”, *The Journal of Philosophy* 92(3): 132-180.

--- (1997): “The idea of Public Reason Revisited”, in *Collected Papers*, edited by S. Freeman,

Cambridge, MA: Harvard University Press, 1999: 573-615.

--- (1998): “*Commonweal* interview with John Rawls” (conducted by B. Prusak), in *Collected*

Papers, edited by S. Freeman, Cambridge, MA: Harvard University Press, 1999: 616-622.

Raz, Joseph (1975), *Practical Reason and Norms*, Oxford: Oxford University Press.

--- (1999), *Engaging Reason*, Oxford: Oxford University Press.

Reidy, David A. (2000): “Rawls’s Wide View of Public Reason: Not Wide Enough”, *Res Publica* 6: 49-72.

Rescher, Nicholas (1993): *Pluralism. Against the Demand for Consensus*, Oxford: Oxford University Press.

Rousseau, Jean-Jaques (1987): *On The Social Contract*, Indianapolis: Hacket.

Ryan, Cheyney C. (1980): "The Normative Concept of Coercion", *Mind* 89: 481-498.

Sandel, Michael (1982): *Liberalism and The Limits of Justice*, Cambridge, MA: Cambridge University Press.

Scanlon, Thomas (1982): "Contractualism and Utilitarianism", in A. Sen / B. Williams (eds.), *Utilitarianism and Beyond*, 8th edition 1999: 103-128.

--- (1998): *What We Owe to Each Other*, Cambridge, MA: Harvard University Press.

--- (2003): "Rawls on Justification", in Samuel Freeman (ed.), *The Cambridge Companion to Rawls*, Cambridge: Cambridge University Press: 139-167.

Scheffler, Samuel (1992): *Human Morality*, New York: Oxford University Press.

--- (1994): "The Appeal of Political Liberalism", *Ethics* 105: 4-22.

Schwartzman, Micah (2004): "The Completeness of Public Reason", *Politics, Philosophy & Economics* 3: 191-220.

--- (2008): "Judicial Sincerity", *Virginia Law Review* 94: 987-1027.

--- (2011): "The Sincerity of Public Reason", *Journal of Political Philosophy* 19(4): 375–398.

Stout, Jeffrey (2004): *Democracy and Tradition*, Princeton: Princeton University Press.

--- (2009): "Religious Reasons in Political Argument", in C. J. Stanton (ed.), *The Ethics of Citizenship: Liberal Democracy and Religious Convictions*, Waco: Baylor University Press: 261-292.

Strawson, P. F. (1961): "Social Morality and Individual Ideal", *Philosophy* 36: 1-17.

Thomson, Judith Jarvis (1971): "A Defense of Abortion", *Philosophy and Public Affairs* 1(1): 47-66.

Waldron, Jeremy (1988): *The Right to Private Property*, Oxford: Clarendon Press.

Wall, Steven (1998): *Liberalism, Perfectionism, and Restraint*, Cambridge, MA: Cambridge University Press.

--- (2002): "Is Public Justification Self-Defeating?", *American Philosophical Quarterly* 39(4): 385-394.

--- (2010): "On Justificatory Liberalism", *Politics, Philosophy & Economics* 9(2): 123-150.

Weithman, Paul (1997) (eds.): *Religion and Contemporary Liberalism*, Notre Dame: University of Notre Dame Press.

--- (2002): *Religion and the Obligations of Citizenship*, Cambridge, MA: Cambridge University Press.

--- (2010): *Why Political Liberalism? On John Rawls's Political Turn*, New York: Oxford University Press.

Wertheimer, Alan (1987): *Coercion*, Princeton: Princeton University Press.

Williams, Andrew (2000): "The Alleged Incompleteness of Public Reason", *Res Publica* 6: 199-211.

Williams, Bernard (1973): *Problems of the Self*, Cambridge: Cambridge University Press.

--- (1981): *Moral Luck*, Cambridge: Cambridge University Press.

--- (1995): *Making Sense of Humanity*, Cambridge: Cambridge University Press.

Wittgenstein, Ludwig [1953] (2001): *Philosophical Investigations*, London: Blackwell.

Wolterstorff, Nicholas (1997): "The Role of Religion in Decision and Discussion of Political Issues", in N. Wolterstorff / R. Audi, *Religion in the Public Square: The Place of Religious Convictions in Political Debate*, Lanham: Rowman & Littlefield: 67-120.

Zoffoli, Enrico (2012): "The Place of Comprehensive Doctrines in Political Liberalism. On Some Common Misgivings About the Subject and Function of the Overlapping Consensus", *Res Publica* 18(4): 351-366.